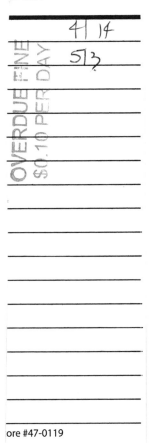

Clueless
about
WINE

Clueless about WINE

Richard Kitowski & Jocelyn Klemm

FIREFLY BOOKS

A Firefly Book

Published by Firefly Books Ltd. 2007

First printing

Publisher Cataloging-in-Publication Data (U.S.)

Kitowski, Richard.
   Clueless about wine / Richard Kitowski and Jocelyn Klemm.

[216] p. : photos. ;   cm.

Includes index.

ISBN-13: 978-1-55407-249-1 (pbk.)
ISBN-10: 1-55407-249-2 (pbk.)

1. Wine and wine making. I. Klemm, Jocelyn. II. Title.

641.22 dc22   TP548.K586   2007

First published in Canada by Key Porter Books Limited

Published in the United States by
Firefly Books (U.S.) Inc.
P.O. Box 1338, Ellicott Station
Buffalo, New York 14205

Electronic formatting: Jean Lightfoot Peters
Illustrations: John Lightfoot

Printed and bound in Canada

Contents

The Opening   7

What Is Wine, Anyway?   9

Vine to Wine   28

A Wine Is a Wine Is a Wine   38

Where in the World Does Wine Come From?   52

The Art of Tasting Wine   114

Wine Has Style   140

Would You Like Wine with That?   158

Buy, Buy Wine   177

Mine, All Mine   197

Index   212

Dedication

We would like to dedicate this book to our families, for your love, patience and support as we continue our journey with wine. We're sure we drive you crazy when we go on and on about wine, but you never show it. Thank you for allowing us to indulge our passions.

Acknowledgements

For your help with the successful first vintage of our book, we acknowledge Clare McKeon, Monica Meehan, Laurie Coulter, Teresa Ross, Raymond Kitowski, Valerie Toth, and the staff at Key Porter Books. Your support, enthusiasm, advice, and thoughtful comments helped craft and refine our words before they were bottled. We want to especially acknowledge Lyn Cadence for getting us all the excellent media attention and Cuisine Canada for the Culinary Book Award.

As we prepare our second vintage, we thank Jordan Fenn and Jonathan Schmidt for believing in our approach.

And thanks to the many people we've talked to about our book that encouraged us along the way.

To all of you we raise a glass of wine.

The Opening
Ready to Pop the Cork?

"Let's see—is it white wine with white meat, red wine with red meat? My boss is having salmon, our important new client is a vegetarian and I'm ordering pork! And I'm expected to pick the wine! What am I supposed to do?"

Like the stressed-out person in this situation, you too may have come to the realization that you are clueless about wine. Relax, you are not alone. Everyone starts out clueless. Even the great wine experts were clueless about wine at one time—whether they like to admit it or not.

Most wine books and magazines seem to be written for people with some wine knowledge, or assume the reader is already a professional wine taster. That's where we come in. We wrote *Clueless about Wine* to take the mystery out of wine and replace the intimidation factor with knowledge and enjoyment. Wine store clerks and sommeliers don't have the monopoly on wine knowledge; everyone can learn about wine.

This book is packed with practical information. From the basics about how wine is made, to where it's made and what it should taste like, to which wine goes with which food. We'll also talk about what and how to buy, how to entertain with wine, how to keep wine, and even how to give it away. We've even included an easy-to-use four-step process to help you learn how to taste wine like a professional. So turn the page, maybe pour yourself a glass of whatever wine you have, and prepare to be clued in about wine.

What Is Wine Anyway?
A Basic Survival Kit

Chances are you don't give much thought to the wine you drink. As long as you like how it tastes, what it costs, and how well it goes with what you're eating, what more do you need to know? After all, do you need to know how an engine works to drive a car?

With wine, reputation and quality and many other factors affect the price you pay. It's worth your while to know a little more about what goes into the bottle, in the same way that knowing a little about mechanics may save you money when you're having your car repaired.

But talking about winemaking and grapes can be pretty boring. It's what you can do with the information that's interesting. So in the following pages we'll give you only the absolute basics of what goes into making a bottle of wine. Sort of like the little survival kit your parents may have given you when you got your first car or apartment.

Is It Only Fermented Grape Juice?

Well, mostly. Wine can be made from hundreds of different fruits and plants (ever had dandelion wine?), but the type we are going to focus on is made from grapes. Check any dictionary and you'll find wine defined as "a beverage made from fermented grape juice." But there's more. Fermentation is how grape juice is converted into wine. We aren't talking about the kind of juice you find on your grocer's shelf (although one of us did make wine from Welch's grape juice in high school biology), but juice from grapes grown specifically to make wine.

Typically the winemaker adds yeast to the juice, which reacts with the natural sugars in the grapes to produce alcohol. There are a couple of other by-products—heat and carbon dioxide—one of which (carbon dioxide) is important in the production of sparkling wines.

The ripeness of grapes determines their sugar content, which in turn determines the potential alcohol content of the finished wine. Generally speaking, the riper the grapes, the higher the alcohol content. There is a limit, however, as most yeasts die off when the alcohol level reaches about 16%. This is why you will never see a table wine stronger than 16%.

Chemistry 101

Sugar (in the grape juice) + Yeast ➜ Alcohol + CO_2 + Heat

If the grapes don't ripen enough, some countries or regions allow sugar to be added to the grape juice to boost alcohol levels in the finished wine. If you want to impress your friends, this is called *chaptalization*. This practice is the exception, however, not the rule.

No sugar is added to the finished wine itself to make it sweeter. Sometimes if the natural grape sugars aren't totally consumed by fermentation, some sugar—called *residual sugar*—remains in the finished wine, making it taste sweet. Even so-called dry wines have residual sugar, but the levels are low and almost undetectable.

A typical bottle of table wine is made up of 84% water, 12% alcohol and 4% natural compounds—some 500 by last count. These natural compounds include vitamins, minerals, sugars, and acids that are very important to the taste, smell, and texture of the wine.

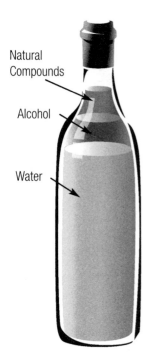

Natural Compounds

Alcohol

Water

Why Doesn't Wine Smell Like Grapes?

When we teach our wine classes, often one of the first questions we're asked is, "If wine is made from grapes, then why does it smell like raspberries or vanilla or green peppers and not grapes?" followed by, "What makes one wine smell and taste different to another?" So let's talk about smell and taste for a moment.

Things smell because of the odorous compounds they emit. Wine has about 200 known odorous compounds. They trigger a memory of something else—maybe something fruity, spicy, earthy, or something you can't quite put your finger on. Some wines will remind you of raspberries, others pineapples. One wine (Sauvignon Blanc) is even said to remind people of cat's pee! These compounds tend to be set for each type of wine and give each one a signature aroma. Once you get to know the signature aroma of a grape variety, you have a good chance of being able to remember it again.

Taste is a bit different. We can taste only four things: sweetness, sourness, bitterness, and saltiness. Since there shouldn't be any dis-

WineSpeak

Acidity—a vital component in wine that gives it freshness and longevity

Aroma—the smells of a wine derived from the grapes themselves

Aromatic—highly scented or fragrant

Balanced—when the key components of fruit, acidity, and tannins are in harmony

Big—full of flavor

Body—the weight or feel of a wine in your mouth—light, medium, or full

Bouquet—the smells of a wine derived from the fermentation or maturation in the bottle

Chewy—a full-bodied wine with noticeable tannins

Classic—"textbook" example of a wine, a benchmark

Clean—no unusual smells

Complex—a multi-dimensional wine with many layers of aromas and flavors

Corked—a defect in the wine that smells like damp cardboard or a musty basement

Crisp—refreshing levels of acidity, usually referring to a white wine

Earthy—rustic aromas or flavors in a wine, suggesting soil or minerals

Elegant—refined or delicate aromas or flavors

Extracted—an abundance of natural compounds (namely pigments, tannins, sugars, and minerals) evident in the wine

Finish—end flavor or aftertaste of a wine once it has been swallowed or spit out; described in terms of length

Flabby—lacking in balancing acidity

Flavor—perception of smell and taste of a wine

Gamey—pungent musky, meaty aromas

Green—unripe aromas and flavors

Herbaceous—pleasant aromas of grass, leaves, and green vegetables

Intense—powerful aromas and flavors

Jammy—aromas and flavors of cooked or overripe fruits, usually associated with wines from warmer climates

Length—amount of time the wine's flavor lingers in your mouth (short, medium, or long)

Neutral—not distinctive

Oaky—the smell or taste of barrels in the wine; associated with vanilla, spicy, or buttery aromas and flavors.

Petrol—pungent smell, reminiscent of diesel, common in good quality, mature Riesling wines

Round—balanced and complete, nice mouth feel—nothing out of place

Rustic—simple, unrefined qualities in a wine

Silky—smooth mouth feel

Simple—a wine lacking in depth or complexity

Soft—a red wine low in tannins or a white wine low in acidity

Spicy—exotic aromas and flavors of spices in the wine (e.g., cinnamon, clove, nutmeg, ginger, or black pepper)

Steely—crisp, with minerally aromas and pure fruit flavors, usually referring to a white wine

Tart—bracing acidity

Terroir—describes the unique expression of the vineyard's soil, site, and microclimate in the wine

Varietal—a wine named after the dominant grape variety from which it is made, or the characteristics of that grape variety

Vintage—the year of the harvest

Zippy or Zingy—refreshing acidity

cernible taste of salt in wine, that leaves three. Without our sense of smell we can only determine if one wine is more or less acidic, sweeter or bitter than another wine. When we put smell and taste together we have *flavor*—the true taste of a wine.

So if wine is mostly water why does it taste and smell the way it does? Because of three factors: the grape itself, where it's grown, and how it is made into wine.

What's in a Grape?

Think of the different varieties of apples that are available at any given time at your local grocery store: Macs from Nova Scotia, Red Delicious from Washington, or Granny Smiths from New Zealand. Each has its own specific color, smell, and taste. Some are good for eating and others are better for cooking.

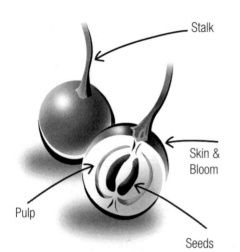

Stalk

Skin & Bloom

Pulp

Seeds

Grapes are just like that too, and grapes grown specifically for making wine have characteristics that make them stand out from the rest. There are literally thousands of different grape varieties, from almost every corner of the world, but only a few are used to make most of the wine we drink.

You've probably not thought much about grapes before. You just buy a bunch at the store, wash them, and eat them. Now, we don't know what kinds of table grapes you buy, but we do know that they aren't white or red. Wine grapes aren't white or red either. For the most part, white wines are made from light-skinned greenish grapes and red wines are made from darker skinned purplish grapes.

- **Stalk:** contains tannins and may or may not be used in winemaking.
- **Skin:** contains color, tannins and some flavor compounds.
- **Bloom:** the waxy stuff on the skin, contains wild yeasts and bacteria.
- **Pulp:** contains water, sugar, acids, and minerals.
- **Seeds:** or pips, contain bitter oils.

In winemaking, the most important parts of the grape are the skin and the pulp. They contain the key building blocks of wine—sugar, acids, and tannins.

- **Sugar** is converted into alcohol through fermentation. If grapes are picked at perfect ripeness, the desired level of alcohol can be reached.
- **Acids** present in the grapes are transferred to the wine. Acidity keeps a wine fresh as it ages, brings out its fruit flavors, and balances the sugar and the alcohol. A lack of acidity leaves the wine tasting lifeless and "flabby," the way a piece of fruit tastes when it's past it's prime.
- **Tannins** from the grape skins, and from the stalks and seeds, contribute to the wine's color, taste (bitterness), and body (fullness). They also help red wines age. Grape variety and winemaking technique affect the amount of tannins in the wine.

The flavor compounds in the skin and pulp are unique to each grape variety and are primarily responsible for the aromatic qualities of the wine.

Do I Need to Know Grape Names?

Not so long ago, wine knowledge meant knowing about a few French regions and maybe port and sherry. If you knew where Bordeaux and Burgundy were, and that they produced fine wine from Cabernet Sauvignon and Pinot Noir grapes respectively, you were well on your way to being an expert.

Times have changed. France is still a leading wine region but many others are nipping at its heels. And quality wine is now made from hundreds of different grape varieties. Today, if you want to know the difference between Beaujolais and Barolo, it helps to know something about the grapes behind the wines.

All grapes grow on vines but there is only one type or genus of vine that is important for winemaking: the genus *Vitis* (VEE-tis). Of the 60 or so species of *Vitis*, classic winemaking grapes come from *Vitis Vinifera* (VEE-tis vin-IF-uh-ra). Chardonnay, Cabernet Sauvignon, and Pinot Noir are examples of vinifera grapes.

There are several thousand vinifera grapes and each one brings its own aromas and flavors to the bottle. You don't need to learn about all of these grapes, so let's just look at a few of them. Be forewarned, though, as not all grape names will appear on the wine label. If the wine is from Europe, more often than not the regional name will have top billing on the label.

A wine is considered in balance when these componants are in harmony.

> **Did You Know?**
> There are six times more tannins in red wine than in white wine.

The Top Seven

The first seven grape varieties we're going to talk about—three white and four red wine grapes—are the key wine grape varieties. Know these grapes and you know about 75% of the wine made in the world.

The Top Seven can produce simple, inexpensive wines as well as the most expensive. Some are best when enjoyed with food; others are just fine on their own. And they're all good fallbacks in case you forget everything else you read in this book.

> **Did You Know?**
> Vitis vinifera grapes were first cultivated in Asia Minor in an area between and south of the Black and Caspian Seas—the Caucasus and Mesopotamia (now known as Syria).

Chardonnay (shar-duh-NAY)
The chameleon grape

This is the white wine you are guaranteed to see in every wine shop and restaurant wine list. It has taken a lot of criticism from some wine critics, and while some of it might be deserved, it is unfair to paint all wines with the same brush.

The grape itself doesn't have much character but is highly adaptable to manipulation in the vineyard and in the winery. Chardonnay often receives some kind of oak treatment by the winemaker, sometimes so excessively that you'd think it was actually made from oak, not grapes.

Thankfully, Chardonnay can also be made into a nicely balanced, rich, and intense wine. Wines from cool-climate wine regions, or when the use of oak is restrained, tend to be the best examples.

Tasting Note:
Where does Chardonnay come from?

Region on the label	Burgundy (France)
Grape name on the label	United States, Australia, Chile, Languedoc (France), Canada
Which are the very best?	Chablis, Meursault, Le Montrachet (all in Burgundy)

Signature aromas:

Cool climate (e.g., Chablis)	Citrus, apple, and minerals
Warm climate (e.g., Australia)	Ripe peach, pineapple, and mango

Sauvignon Blanc (SO-veen-YON BLON)
Zippy and fresh

When made into wine, this grape is unrestrained, even nervy. It can be aggressively aromatic but it's not for everyone: it appeals to those who like zingy white wines.

Sauvignon Blanc's greatest feature is its high acidity. This makes it a great apéritif wine—much better than Chardonnay, in fact. Winemakers rarely give Sauvignon Blanc any oak treatment. Instead, they highlight its naturally aromatic characteristics. In California, Sauvignon Blanc may be sold under the name Fumé Blanc.

Tasting Note:

Where does Sauvignon Blanc come from?

Region on the label	Loire and Bordeaux (France)
Grape name on the label	New Zealand, South Africa, Chile, United States, Italy (Friuli), Canada
Which are the very best?	Sancerre (Loire), Bordeaux, and New Zealand (Marlborough)

Signature aromas:

Cool climate (e.g., Loire)	Gooseberry, citrus (lime), and cut grass
Warm climate (e.g., South Africa)	Citrus (grapefruit), melon, and asparagus

Riesling (REECE-ling)
Racy and aromatic

While a versatile and food-friendly grape, Riesling isn't as popular as it deserves to be. This is too bad because Riesling is one the world's greatest white wines. Try a good version and you'll be convinced.

Riesling can produce crisp, dry, austere wines as well as rich, luscious sweet dessert ones. In all versions, Riesling tends to be lower in alcohol than most white wines and has very good acidity. And if you're patient, some sweeter-style Riesling wines can age for decades.

Liebfraumilch

Liebfraumilch (LEEB-frow-meelsh) was probably responsible for introducing most baby boomers to wine. Medium-sweet Liebfraumilch is actually a blend, primarily of Müller-Thurgau and not Riesling grapes.

Tasting note:

Where does Riesling come from?

Grape name on the label	Germany, Alsace (France), Canada, Austria, United States, Australia
Which are the very best?	Mosel-Saar-Ruwer, Nahe, Pfalz, Rheingau (Germany), Alsace, Canada (Niagara), Clare Valley (Australia)

Signature aromas:

Cool climate (e.g., Germany)	Crisp green apple, citrus (lemon), floral, and mineral
Warm climate (e.g., Australia)	Rich citrus (lime), tropical fruit, peach, and passion fruit

Cabernet Sauvignon (CAB-err-nay So-vee-NYON)
Deep, dark, and aristocratic

Cabernet Sauvignon (sometimes just called Cabernet) is probably the most famous red wine grape in the world. Although sometimes blended with other grapes, Cabernet Sauvignon can produce wines that can age for decades; its top versions are highly prized by wine collectors.

Although Cabernet Sauvignon's wine characteristics are recognizable wherever it's grown, it also has the distinction of being able to reflect the unique character of the location in which it was grown. The French call this *terroir*.

Never the lightest wine in the glass, when young, Cabernet Sauvignon wines can be big and tannic—they need time to come around. Be patient and you will get your reward.

Tasting note:

Where does Cabernet come from?

Region on the label	Bordeaux (France)
Grape name on the label	United States, Australia, Canada, South Africa, Languedoc (France), Chile, Eastern Europe
Which are the very best?	Pauillac (Bordeaux), Napa Valley (California), Coonawara (Australia)

Signature aromas:

Cool climate (e.g., Bordeaux)	Blackcurrant (cassis), plum, cedar, and tobacco (cigar-box)
Warm climate (e.g., Napa)	Ripe (jammy) blackcurrant, mint, and eucalyptus

Merlot (mare-LOW)
Soft and plummy

Like Chardonnay, Merlot is pretty well made everywhere, and is subject to a bit more criticism than other red wines. (If you've seen the hit movie *Sideways* you'll see what we mean). On the other hand, it can make a nice soft, and round, easy-drinking wine.

Merlot is often a blending grape, adding softness and flavor to its big brother Cabernet Sauvignon in Bordeaux reds. On its own, Merlot, when handled well in the winery, it can produce plump, juicy, almost sweet red wines. One of the world's most expensive wines—Château Petrus from Pomerol—is made from Merlot.

Tasting note:
Where does Merlot come from?

Region on the label	Bordeaux (France)
Grape name on the label	Languedoc (France), United States, Chile, Canada, New Zealand, Italy (Piave), Eastern Europe
Which are the very best?	Pomerol (Bordeaux)

Signature aromas:

Cool climate (e.g., Pomerol)	Plum, cocoa powder, and mint
Warm climate (e.g., Napa Valley)	Baked cherries, plum compote, chocolate, and mint

Pinot Noir (PEE-no-NWAHR)
Silky and seductive

While Riesling is the most food-friendly white wine, Pinot Noir (sometimes just called Pinot) holds that distinction for reds. Pinot Noir is also a match for many meats—which Riesling isn't.

Quality Pinot Noir isn't always easy wine to find, however, as there are a lot of insipid versions out there. "Stick with the best and avoid the rest" is our recommendation. At its best, Pinot Noir is silky and elegant, with good acidity and understated tannins and alcohol. Pinot Noir is often referred to as the "heartbreak grape" because it is very difficult to grow well.

Tasting note:
Where does Pinot Noir come from?

Region on the label	Burgundy (France)
Grape name on the label	California and Oregon (United States), Canada, New Zealand, Australia, Germany (called Spätburgunder)
Which are the very best?	Burgundy, Sonoma, California, Oregon, Martinborough (New Zealand)

Signature aromas:

Cool Climate (e.g., New Zealand)	Raspberry, (sour) cherry, cranberry, and earthy
Warm Climate (e.g., Sonoma)	Ripe Bing cherry, raspberry, and smoky

Syrah (see-RAH)
Bold and spicy

Are there in fact two names for this grape? While we can blame the Australians for the dual identity—they prefer to use the name **Shiraz** (she-RAHZ) for this noble French grape—you also have to give them credit for bringing the grape back from relative obscurity in the 1980s. Whatever it is called, Syrah is one of the hottest red-wine grapes on the market today.

Heady and aromatic, Syrah is drinkable young (especially the Aussie versions), but its ample acidity and firm tannins help it age for decades. Syrah can also reflect the *terroir* of the region. This is as true in the Rhône—Syrah's ancestral home—as it is in Australia. The choice of name forms the dividing line between the styles: Syrah is deep, austere, earthy, and spicy, while Shiraz is richer, fruitier, and more intense. Like Cabernet Sauvignon, this is not the lightest wine in the glass—the bigger versions need time to come around.

Tasting note:

Where does Syrah/Shiraz come from?

Region on the Label	Rhône (France)
Grape Name on the Label	Australia, South Africa, Languedoc (France), United States
Which are the very best?	Cornas, Hermitage, Côte Rôtie (all Rhône), Barossa Valley (Australia)

Signature aromas:

Cool climate (e.g., Rhône)	Blueberries, prunes, bacon, coffee, black pepper, violets, leather, smoke, and herbs
Warm climate (e.g., Barossa Valley)	Ripe raspberries, blackberries, plum, cherry, chocolate, sweet spices, black pepper, and eucalyptus

Quick Identification Chart

Think of the following chart as a cheat sheet for remembering the key words for describing the Top Seven grapes and where to look for good versions to try.

Grape	Key Words	Locations
Chardonnay	Creamy, peach, citrus	Burgundy and Sonoma, California
Sauvignon Blanc	Grassy, gooseberry	Loire and Marlborough, New Zealand
Riesling	Zingy, citrus	Germany and Niagara, Canada
Cabernet Sauvignon	Blackcurrant and cedar	Bordeaux and Napa, California
Merlot	Plum and leather	Bordeaux and Washington State
Pinot Noir	Silky, cherry	Burgundy and Sonoma, California
Syrah/Shiraz	Spicy, blackberry	Rhône and Barossa Valley, Australia

The Contenders

The following grape varieties are less well known internationally. On their home turf, however, they're made into some interesting and sometimes spectacular wines. Since they make up about 20% of the world's wine production, they're worth knowing, just not in so much detail. If you see any of them in a wine shop or on a restaurant wine list give them a try. We promise you won't be disappointed.

First the white wine grapes:

Albariño (ahl-bar-REE-nyoh) is grown in the Galicia region of Spain and is found in the better versions of Portuguese Vinho Verde. (In Portugal, it is called Alvarinho [ahl-va-REE-nyoh]). It produces light, refreshing, and very aromatic (peaches and apricots) wines that are at their best when consumed young.

Chenin Blanc (SHEH-nin BLON) produces some of the most long-lived white wines in Loire Valley (France). It's the most-planted grape in South Africa, where it is also known as Steen. Chenin Blanc has searing acidity and aromas of apple, honey, and almonds.

Garganega (gar-GAN-ega) is the dominant grape in Soave—Italy's leading white wine export. It can produce delicate dry white wines with aromas of lemon and almonds, as well as luscious dessert wines (Recioto di Soave) with aromas of honey, nuts, and caramel.

Gewürztraminer (geh-VURTS-trah-MEEN-er) produces highly aromatic wines—reminiscent of rose petals and lychees—that run the range from full-bodied, dry wines to elegant dessert wines. The

No Wine before Its Time

As a general rule, regardless of the grape, the best wines in the best vintages will improve with age. They gain complexity and just become more interesting to drink.

Most wines (95%) are meant for early consumption, though, and shouldn't be kept longer than a few months after purchase.

main growing areas are Alsace (France), Alto Adige (Italy), and Germany.

Grüner Veltliner (GROO-ner felt-LEE-ner) is the most important grape in Austria, and one that is becoming increasingly popular with the more adventurous wine crowd. It produces food-friendly wines with good acidity, and citrus and peppery aromas.

Muscadet (mu-scuh-DAY) is mainly grown in the Loire (France), where it produces dry, crisp, light-bodied neutral wines.

Muscat (MUSS-kat) is one of the most ancient grape varieties. The four principal versions of the grape produce a number of different styles of wine, from the frothy (Asti) to the dry (Alsace), the sweet (Australian "stickies"), and the fortified (Rhône). The main growing areas are Alsace and Rhône (France), Piedmont (Italy), Greece, South Africa, and Australia.

Pinot Blanc (PEE-no BLON) does well in cooler climates, like Alsace (France) and British Columbia (Canada), where it produces soft wines with aromas of apple, apricot, and honey. Also called Pinot Bianco in Italy, Klevner in Alsace, and Weissburgunder in Germany.

Pinot Gris (PEE-no GREE) comes in a range of styles and under a host of aliases—most notably Pinot Grigio (PEE-no GREE-jee-oh) in Italy, Tokay-Pinot Gris in the Alsace (France), and Rülander (ROO-lan-DER) in Germany. Styles range from the crisp and fresh (Italy) to the spicy, exotic, and full-bodied (Alsace), with aromas of citrus, apples, nuts, and honey. Good Pinot Gris is also produced Oregon, and British Columbia.

Prosecco (pro-SEK-oh), an Italian grape, primarily grown in the Veneto region, famous for the production of a range of very good yet inexpensive sparkling wines of the same name.

Sémillon (say-mee-YOHN) in Bordeaux is blended with Sauvignon Blanc to make very good dry white wines as well as the world-famous sweet wine, Sauternes. It also stands on its own as Australia's famous Hunter Valley Semillon (the Australians drop the accent and pronounce it sem-ill-on). A good substitute for Chardonnay, Sémillon has aromas reminiscent of pineapples, peaches, nuts, and honey. It's also grown in California and Washington State.

Trebbiano (treb-ee-AH-no), a prolific but ordinary Italian blending grape used in white wine production, including Orvieto and Soave. Under its French synonym, Ugni Blanc (oo-nee BLON), it is the base wine used to make Cognac and Armagnac.

Verdicchio (vur-DEE-kee-oh), an Italian grape grown in the Marches region, is famous for its production of excellent lemony crisp dry wines of the same name.

Verdelho (vur-DELL-oh), a Portuguese grape variety used in the production of Madeira, and now a popular Australian table wine. The best Australian examples come from cooler-climate regions and have fresh, lime and tropical fruit aromas, are medium- to full-bodied, with very good acidity.

Vidal (VEE-dall), a French hybrid well-suited to cool climate regions. It flourishes in Canada's Niagara Peninsula, where it is primarily used to produce wonderfully rich icewine, with flavors of apricots and honey. In the right hands it can produce food-friendly table wines. Vidal is also grown in New York State.

> ## Who's #1
> By the way, Chardonnay isn't the most-planted grape in the world. It doesn't even make the top ten. Airén is #1 and it's all grown in Spain. It is mainly used to make wine that is then distilled to make Brandy. And Grenache is #2.

Viognier (VEE-ohn-YAY), a traditional Rhône varietal, is gaining popularity around the world, especially in California. It is exotically aromatic, featuring white peaches, spice, and honeysuckle. Viognier's relatively high alcohol levels make it seem sweeter than it really is. The main growing areas are in the south of France (Rhône and Languedoc-Roussillon), California and Australia.

And now the red wine grapes:

Baco Noir (BAH-ko Nwahr), a French hybrid widely planted in Canada's Niagara Peninsula. It is used to produce deep, brooding wines with smoky, fruity flavors.

Barbera (bar-BEAR-ah), the second most-planted grape in Italy (Piedmont), doesn't have the prestige accorded its loftier cousin Nebbiolo. Barbera produces incredibly mouth-watering red wines that simply cry out for food. They are low in tannins and high in acidity, with aromas of sour cherries, plums, and herbs.

Cabernet Franc (CAB-err-nay FRAHNK) is actually one of the parents of Cabernet Sauvignon (the other is Sauvignon Blanc). Like a parent, it often doesn't get the respect it deserves. This early ripening grape produces outstanding wines in the Loire (France) and in Canada's Niagara Peninsula, but most of the time it adds acidity and aromatics to the famous blended wines of Bordeaux. On its own, it can exhibit more herbaceous (bell pepper) aromas as well as raspberries and blackberries.

Dolcetto (doll-CHET-oh)—meaning "the little sweet one"—makes light, dry, uncomplicated, food-friendly wines for everyday drinking. These rustic and earthy wines are low in tannins with aromas of tart cherry, licorice, and almonds. Grown mainly in Piedmont (Italy), the name of the grape appears on the label alongside the town or area where it is grown.

Beaujolais Nouveau

Every year on the third Thursday in November, with wines barely six weeks old, producers in the Beaujolais region of France release their new vintage of *Beaujolais Nouveau*. At one time these easy-to-drink wines were released to considerable fanfare and ceremony, but nowadays much of the fizzle has come out of the event. Other regions, including Italy with its Novello, try to get in on the festivities but there is only one true Beaujolais Nouveau.

Gamay (ga-MAY) is best known under its more famous name Beaujolais. This is the name of a region in southern Burgundy and one of the places in the world where the grape grows very well (although it is grown elsewhere). It generally produces light and lively, low tannin wines with tutti frutti flavors of cherry (think cherry-cola), strawberry, and raspberry. Only the best Gamay wines age well, so it's best to drink it when you buy it, preferably slightly chilled.

Grenache (gre-NASH) loves the hot temperatures of Spain (where it's called Garnacha) and of the south of France—who wouldn't? It's blended with the Tempranillo grape in Spain to make Rioja and with other grapes in France to make the famous Châteauneuf-du-Pape. In Italy, Grenache is called Cannonau. Australia produces bold wines from this grape but unfortunately a lot of the older vines were torn up years ago. Grenache can also be made into excellent dry rosé wine (France and Spain). Often part of a blend, it has sweet and spicy aromas of raspberry and strawberry, and because it is low in tannin it generally doesn't age well.

Malbec (mal-BECK) is traditionally used in Bordeaux blends for its color and tannin. It also is grown in Cahors (France) where it is called Auxerrois. In fact, Malbec possibly has more synonyms than any other grape. Argentina's best red wines are made from Malbec, and are less tannic and more berry-fruit flavored than their French counterparts.

Nebbiolo (neh-bee-OH-low) is the grape behind the famous Barolo and Barbaresco wines. These are not beginner's wines; they pack a powerful punch and it can take years for the grip of the tannins to ease up. When they do, however, they can be amongst the most surreal wines you have ever tasted. In the best examples, you'll discover layer upon layer of sweet dark cherries, chocolate, truffles, violets, licorice, prunes, tar, roses, and cinnamon.

Petite Sirah (peh-TEET see-RAH)—grown in California and South America—produces dark, tannic, savory wines. While it name may suggest otherwise, Petite Sirah isn't related to Syrah.

Pinotage (pee-no-TAJ) is a crossing of Pinot Noir and the French grape called Cinsaut and is grown extensively, although decreasingly so, in South Africa. Pinotage produces sweet-smelling, plummy wines but they can come across a little bit gamey or rustic.

Sangiovese (SAN-joh-VAY-zay) is the most-planted grape in Italy. You probably know it better as Chianti, the famous red wine of Tuscany. It offers lovely aromas of sour cherries and herbs tied together with tea-like bitterness and an earthy spiciness. Sangiovese also appears in more heavyweight versions as Brunello di Montalcino and Vino Nobile di Montepulciano, also from Tuscany.

Tempranillo (tem-pruh-NEE-yo) is the workhorse grape behind Spain's Rioja and Ribera del Duero red wines. Tempranillo produces lushly textured wines, with aromas of strawberries and blackberries and a spicy, earthy edge.

Zinfandel (zin-fan-DELL) was generally thought to be California's "native" grape; however in 2001 experts determined its origins were actually Croatian. Scientists from the University of California at Davis found that while Zinfandel's roots may be European, the wines it produces are definitely Californian all the way. Adaptable, it is used to produce sweet "blush" wines (White Zin), fruity, easy-drinking wines, and even classic, full-bodied wines. The aromas range from bright, juicy cherry and raspberry to deep, lush blackberry, blueberry and figs.

> ## Did You Know?
> Zinfandel was genetically identical to Crjenak Kaštelanski (sirl-yen-knock kas-tel-an-ski) and the Italian grape Primitivo (preem-i-TEE-vo) from Apulia.

The contender grapes might be a little harder to locate on store shelves or wine lists. Some of them come from emerging wine regions, are blended with other grapes, or appear under different names on the label. Ask the wine clerk or your server to help you find one of these if the description appeals to you. They just might surprise you with something special at a really great price.

Where in the World Do Grapes Come From?

Next to the grape itself, climate is probably the most important factor to influence the smell and taste of wine. After all, it's climate that determines which grapes can grow where and how the grapes develop and ripen.

Do They Grow Grapes in Botswana?

Grapes actually grow in two bands around the Earth between latitudes 30° and 50°. There are a few exceptions (e.g., parts of Brazil, Peru, Kenya, and Germany), but generally the locations within these bands have the ideal growing and ripening conditions for wine grapes.

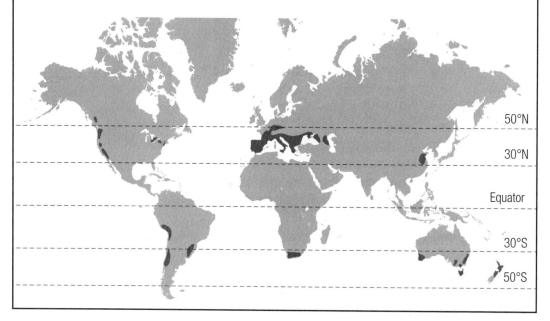

Cool Climate—Warm Climate

Countries farthest from the equator are said to be *cool-climate* wine-growing regions and those closer to the equator are *warm-climate.*

Germany is considered a *cool-climate* region, as is New Zealand and British Columbia. While each of these regions receives enough sunshine to ripen the grapes, cooler temperatures keep acid levels in the grapes up. As a result the wines are lighter bodied, crisper, and less intense than warmer climates. Growers prefer to plant early ripening grape varieties in these regions.

The south of France and Barossa Valley in Australia are examples of *warm-climate* regions. Higher temperatures mean riper grapes, but by the time the flavors are at their peak, acid levels in the grapes may have dropped too low, resulting in higher alcohol, sometimes "flabby," wines. Later-ripening grape varieties do better in warmer climates and, on the whole, they produce bolder, fuller-bodied wine with higher alcohol content.

Even within a country or region the climate isn't homogenous. In the Burgundy region of France, the climate of the Côte d'Or is different than that of Chablis, only about 140 km further north. While visiting Ghislaine Barthod in Chambolle-Musigny, we learned that adjoining vineyards in the area and even rows within each vineyard have slightly different microclimates. Grapes develop and ripen at different rates according to their specific location within the vineyard. For certain wines—those from Burgundy, for example—the microclimate determines the quality and price of the wine in a given year.

Time To Pick

Wine grapes are quite small, green, and tart, right up until a few weeks before they are harvested. While buds emerge on grape vines early in the Spring, this is what happens in the final six to eight weeks before the grapes are fully mature in the Fall.

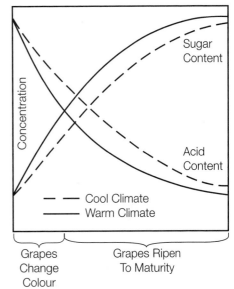

Raising Healthy Grapes

Four main climatic factors influence how grapes develop: sunshine, heat, rainfall, and wind.

Sunshine. To ripen properly, grapes need a minimum of 1,500 hours of sunshine over the growing season. Red wine grapes need more sun than white wine grapes. That's why you more often see quality white wines, than red wines, from cool-climate regions. This is true in Germany, for example.

Heat. If the mean growing season temperature isn't around 60°F (15°C), the vines won't produce. If the temperatures get too high, vines will shut down, and if it's too cold in the winter, the vines will be killed off. Nearby bodies of water—oceans, lakes, or rivers—can moderate temperatures and help grapes ripen in otherwise marginal areas. For example, Canada's Niagara Peninsula grape-growing region might actually be too cold to grow grapes if it weren't for the moderating influence of Lake Ontario. You will notice on our map (on page 24) that almost all the major wine-growing regions are close to large bodies of water.

> ### Grapes in High Places
> For every 330 feet (100 meters) above sea level the temperature drops 1.8°F (1°C) and adds a couple more weeks onto the ripening period for grapes. This can be a real asset in warm locations like Argentina.

Frost is particularly bad. If it hits after the buds have appeared in the spring, it can ruin a harvest. There are ways to reduce the impact of frost, but they are expensive and often not enough to save the whole vineyard.

Rainfall. Vines need a minimum of 26–27 inches (70 cm) of rainfall during the growing season. Rain early in the spring is much better than in the fall during harvest. If rain hits at the wrong time, it can burst the berries and create an environment for unwanted diseases. If there is little natural rainfall, some regions allow irrigation.

Wind. Some air movement is beneficial for vines. It can help keep vines dry and free of disease. It can also moderate temperature in warm-climate regions.

Bad Soil Is Actually Good

Soil is important for raising healthy vines. It gives the roots a place to grow and also supplies the minerals necessary for proper development of the grapes. But grapes actually grow best in "bad" soils. The more the vines have to struggle to find water and nutrients, the stronger the vine and the better the grapes. Overly fertile soils encourage too much vegetative growth that can shade the grapes during the key ripening period.

The best soils for vines are porous and drain well (vines don't like wet feet), are moderately acidic, and are good at retaining heat or reflecting sunlight.

There are many different soil types, even within wine growing regions, and certain grapes do better in certain soils. The Chardonnay grape, for example, is at its best in the chalky soils of Champagne, Chablis, and other parts of the Burgundy region of

France. Finding the right soil type for each type of grape is a science. Prices can be astronomical for the right piece of land. Some wineries go to great lengths—even employing expensive satellite technology—to find the perfect spot for a vineyard. And yes, you can taste—and pay for—the difference a well-chosen vineyard location makes.

Vine to Wine

Getting the Grapes into the Bottle

Not so long ago, winemakers were pretty well stuck with what was available to them at harvest. Their local wine regulations usually determined what grapes they could grow, and how they should grow them, and they were totally at the mercy of the weather.

Nowadays, with less rigid controls on grape selection, coupled with modern technological advances, it is possible to consistently produce better wine. On the other hand, it is also possible to make Chilean and Australian Chardonnay pretty well smell and taste the same—so much that you'd think there was only three or four wine-makers in the whole world. In fact, some of the larger wineries can produce their wines to match any style the market desires.

The skill of the winemaker should not be taken lightly. Two wineries, located adjacent to each other, can make wines of different quality from the same fruit grown under the same conditions. Like chefs, some winemakers use their skill and knowledge to create elegant masterpieces while others can only make simple "cookbook" wine.

Whether it is art, skill, science or the result of deep pockets, let's see how different wines are made and the effect human factors have on the aromas, taste, and quality of a wine.

Our Three-minute History Lesson

While the history of wine and winemaking is fascinating, we promise not to bore you with countless details and facts. So here's our three-minute history lesson—the microwave version of 9,000 years of winemaking!

- Millions of years ago, grapes played an important role in the lives of ancient tribes. This little fruit was eaten fresh or dried and could be crushed and drunk as a liquid, though not as wine at this point. Grapes had medicinal qualities and were used for flavoring, tenderizing, and preserving food.

- Early humans discovered that grape juice left in containers fermented naturally, and the result had different flavors and "power." Winemaking was born. The timing is open to discussion but there is evidence that primitive winemaking was practiced in Asia Minor, south of the Black and Caspian Seas. The oldest known pips (seeds)—carbon-dated to between 7000 BC and 5000 BC—of cultivated vines were discovered on Mount Ararat. Further excavations along the southern slopes of the Caucasus Mountains in Armenia, Georgia, and Northern Iran unearthed large clay jars used to make and store wine.

- As early as 3500 BC, Sumerians developed efficient irrigation systems in the barren lands known as Mesopotamia (between the Tigris and Euphrates rivers). Successive civilizations—the Assyrians and Babylonians—showed equal interest in making and trading wine.

- The Egyptians (2800–550 BC) generally drank beer but wine was consumed by the wealthy and in royal circles. The Pyramids in the Valley of Kings and Valley of Nobles are decorated with images depicting grape-harvesting and winemaking. Records show the Egyptians understood the negative effects of air on wine as they began to seal their wine vessels with pitch and grease. They were the first to mark these containers with details about origin of grapes, the date of harvest, and the name of the winemaker. The first labels!

- The Greeks (2000–350 BC) identified and catalogued grape varieties, invented the pruning knife, recorded winemaking techniques, and developed clay amphorae in which to store wine.

- The seafaring Phoenicians (1400–200 BC) are credited with spreading and propagating vines throughout the Mediterranean Basin.

- The Romans (750–450 BC) further developed grape growing and winemaking practices, including pruning, fertilization, and adding alkaline substances to reduce acidity in the wine. Pliny the Elder, probably the first known "wine writer," classified grapes as to color, time of ripening, and soil preferences. The Romans' most significant contribution, however, was to spread grape growing throughout the Empire: France, Germany, Switzerland, Austria, Hungary, Spain, Portugal, and even England.

- In the Middle Ages (500–1400 AD) the Christian Church, in need of a steady supply of wine for sacramental purposes, slowly started acquiring land needed for grape growing. By the end of the first millennium, it was the largest holder of European vineyards. The educated clergy continued to advance the art of making wine. While quantity was the foremost objective of the bacchanalian past, the Church began to be interested in quality. Monks meticulously recorded their results and started to classify wine by variety, vineyard, and vintage.

  For many, wine wasn't a luxury—it was a necessity. Water in most villages and cities was impure, while wine, because of its antiseptic properties, was a much safer alternative. People of all ages consumed it and production focused on getting the highest possible alcohol levels.

  Countries that could not grow grapes (Norway and Sweden) or where production was too small to satisfy local demand (England) began to import wine. Trade became lucrative and many wars were fought and alliances sought over it.

- During the Renaissance, wine became a more refined, cultured beverage. As trade in wine flourished, and demand for quality increased, vineyard acreage grew, and new vinification techniques were discovered. The use of bottles and corks, and the English invention of the corkscrew, made it more feasible to keep wine for more than a year and by the beginning of the eighteenth century speculative buying (now called wine futures) was established.

  Dom Perignon, a Benedictine monk in charge of his abbey's cellars, established some of the principles of blending sparkling wine now known as champagne. It was actually the English, a few decades earlier, who are credited with the actual discovery of sparkling wine.

- The Industrial Revolution, and the economic growth it brought about, developed a new demand for very cheap wine. The wine trade was in full force as were the wines—alcohol levels were considerably higher than they are today.

  Colonization brought vines to Africa, Australia, North and South America. In North America, European vines didn't take due to indigenous diseases but in other countries they flourished.

  Throughout Europe, wine regions were experimenting with grape varieties in order to find the right match to the climate and soil. In 1855, the region of Bordeaux developed its famous wine classification system, still in use today, to protect its wine trade.

- On of the most important historical events in recent wine history occurred in the mid to late 1800s. Native American grape vines were shipped to Europe for experimental purposes and they carried with them a tiny insect or louse called *Phylloxera vastatrix*. The North American vines had developed a resistance to the insect, but Europe's vines had no resistance whatsoever. First spotted in 1863, within 10 years the louse had spread throughout most of Europe, almost completely wiping out its vineyards.

  Early attempts to control the louse with pesticides were all unsuccessful. Finally, around 1880, it was thought that since the North American rootstocks were impervious to the insect, grafting European vines onto these rootstocks could solve the problem. This theory proved to be true, and grafting and cloning are now very much part of modern-day grape growing.

- As a result of the First World War, Europe's wine reserves were pretty much depleted. Faced with a renewed demand and low supply, opportunity knocked and some unscrupulous merchants began selling fake wine. Cheap wine labeled as Bordeaux and Burgundy was actually fermented raisins in water with dangerous chemicals added for color. The French were the first to fight back by passing laws and regulations guaranteeing authenticity. These policies formed the basis of the first wine production laws.

- In 1919, the Eighteenth Amendment was created prohibiting the sale of alcoholic beverages in the United States. Prohibition ended in 1933, but by that time the American wine industry had been decimated.

- In the past 50 years, fueled to a certain extent by the baby boom, and now the echo generation, world wine consumption has increased substantially. And since 1970, wine production has increased dramatically in Australia, Canada, Chile, New Zealand, and the United States of America. Ironically, in recent years, wine consumption has decreased in France, and other parts of Europe.

- Industry consolidation, combined with an emphasis on global marketing, has produced an unfortunate glut of bland yet fashionable, internationally branded wines—ones with cutesy names or pictures of little animals on the labels. The demand for quality wine is increasing, however, and as consumers learn more about wine they are willing to try new things and spend more money.

From Grapes to the Bottle

The skills to grow grapes properly and to make wine can be learned through university or college programs or, as is often the case, acquired on the job. The process itself is simple enough to be even done at home, either in your garage or basement, or, if allowed by local law, at a make-your-own type of store.

In the following pages, we will describe the process that takes place at most major wineries. If you ever have an opportunity to visit a winery, take it, as it is definitely the best way to understand and appreciate all that goes into making wine. Besides, most wineries offer free samples, and it is a great way to practice what you learn from this book.

In the Vineyard

Probably the two most important decisions a grower makes is how many grapes to harvest—called yield—and when to harvest them. Vines are prolific: left to their own devices they will produce literally tons of grapes. They aren't interested in making wine; they just want to produce as many offspring as possible. Grape growers have to control this growth if they want to produce good fruit for winemaking.

If the grape grower tries to grow lots of grapes per vine, the minerals and nutrients the vine produces are spread out over more grapes. The juice from these grapes will be more dilute and much less flavorful, as will the wine made from it.

The current trend is towards lower yields. This means cutting away bunches of grapes long before they have developed—called *green harvesting*—to ensure higher quality and more flavorful grapes. The winemaker pays more for these grapes because the grower has fewer of them to sell. In turn, the wine will be more costly to produce.

Grapes are harvested when the optimum amount of sugar has developed in the grape relative to the acid levels and the particular style of wine the winemaker wants to make. Each grape variety reaches its optimum level at a different time: for example, Pinot Noir ripens earlier than Cabernet Sauvignon.

Waiting until the sugar-acids balance is just right is no easy task. Pick too early and the grapes may be underripe and tart; too late and the grapes may become overripe and jammy, or have no

> ### Did You Know?
> In the northern hemisphere the harvest takes place in the fall, from about August to October. In the southern hemisphere grapes are harvested from February to April. Wines from the southern hemisphere have a six-month jump on the northern hemisphere.

varietal character at all. Rain during harvest, however, can dilute the wines or bring on unwanted fungal diseases.

When the grapes have ripened properly, or the grower can't wait any longer, the grapes are picked either by hand or by a mechanical harvester and brought to the winery.

In the Winery

The harvested grapes are put into a crusher/destemmer, where they are separated from their stems and leaves and crushed into a pulp called *must*. Before machines, workers merrily stomped the grapes with their bare feet to achieve essentially the same result. In some regions, winemakers still believe that the human foot is better suited for this process than a harsh machine.

The must is then pumped directly to a press, for white wine, or to a tank, for red wine. The juice in almost all grapes is clear, and the color of a wine comes entirely from the grape skins. White wine must is pressed immediately so no color is extracted from the skins. Red wine must is allowed to steep on the grape skins (*macerate)* for days, even weeks, to extract the amount of color and tannins the winemaker wants.

In the press, juice is squeezed from the must. Care is taken to make sure the must isn't pressed too much; otherwise the juice will become cloudy and astringent. The best juice—called "free-run" juice—runs off before the pressing begins and is often kept separate from the press juice.

The juice is then fermented. Fermentation can take place in any type of vat or vessel depending on the flavor desired. White wines are often fermented in stainless steel tanks; while red wines may be put into oak barrels. Sometimes a combination of both is used. The temperature of the fermenting juice is monitored and sometimes controlled. When the temperature is too low, yeast cells won't multiply sufficiently and fermentation is slow to start. On the other hand, if it is too warm, the fermentation may stop altogether and unwanted aromas may develop in the wine. Modern wineries have temperature-controlled tanks to make sure the desired temperature is maintained.

Brix

Brix is a unit of measurement used to determine sugar levels in grapes. For example, 22° Brix is considered an ideal measure for grapes that will be made into a dry table wine.

There are other units of measure used by growers including Oechsle, Baumé, and KMW.

Biodynamics

Based on the writings of Austrian philosopher Rudolf Steiner, biodynamics has evolved as a method of holistic, self-sustaining agriculture that actively works with the health-giving forces of nature and the cosmos. The oldest non-chemical agricultural movement, it predates organic agriculture by some 20 years. Biodynamic winemaking is practiced around the world, and by some leading wine producers including: Domaine Leroy, Zind-Humbrecht, and M. Chapoutier from France; Alvaro Palacios in Spain; and, Benzinger and Araujo Estates in the United States.

When fermentation stops, the wine—yes, it can be called wine now—is moved or *racked* to another vessel to mature. Racking removes the wine from as much of the grape solids and spent yeast cells (or *lees*) that collect on the bottom of the vessel as possible. Like fermentation, the wine can mature in a non-reactive or inert tank or in oak barrels.

Depending on the amount of time the wine needs to mature or age, further racking may be necessary to clarify the wine. More expensive wines may be racked several times over the two to three years the wine is in the barrel. Clarifying agents may be used to speed up the process but care must be taken not to strip the wine of its qualities. The use of egg whites (albumin) is considered to be a very gentle method. Some red wines receive no clarification at all; that's why you may find some sediment in the bottle.

Once the winemaker has decided the wine is ready to sell, it is blended with other wines or sent directly to the bottling line. Bottling may be done manually, in the case of small producers, or on computer-controlled bottling lines, for large commercial wineries.

Despite this oversimplification, making wine is a complex interaction of natural and human elements. It can be as much art as it is science. The result can be beautiful and surreal; or it can be simply a nice bottle of cheap plonk!

Costly Barrels

Contrary to the romantic image of wines aging in a cellar, not all wines are put into barrels. Since a new French oak barrel can easily cost $1,000, their use adds to the cost of the wine, which the winemaker must try to recover in the price.

Barrels allow the wine to develop unique flavors by providing contact with the air and the wood itself. By allowing some evaporation, they also concentrate the wine. The type of wood used (oak is common), and the age of the barrels, impart other aromatic compounds to the wine and change the wine's texture. The amount of time a wine is left in a barrel also adds to the complexity of the wine.

In the Bottle

Glassmaking has been around since the time of the Egyptians and the Phoenicians, but glass was too fragile and expensive until around the sixteenth century. Before that wine drinkers could only afford to buy and use clay containers (amphorae) for wine storage or leather bags (wine skins) to carry their wine. The corkscrew wasn't invented until the seventeenth century, so bottles as we know them weren't very practical until then.

Nowadays, wine bottles come in all shapes and sizes. Producers use the label and bottle to make their wine stand out on a store shelf and to make a statement about their wine.

Did You Know?

It takes the juice of about 200–300 grapes, (about 3 lbs of grapes), to make a 750 ml bottle of wine.

Bottle Shapes

While some wines are packaged in designer bottles, and some even in boxes or Tetra Pak® containers (like juice boxes), most of the wine we drink comes in standard glass bottles. The shape of the bottle can provide clues as to what's inside and where it's from. Local laws dictate some of the styles, while others are used by tradition. Châteauneuf-du-Pape wines (from France) always have the Pope's emblem on the bottle, while Italy's Gattinara bottle has a handmade look to it.

Standard wine bottles come in five major styles:

- The **bocksbeutel** may be the one you are least likely to see on the shelf and yet the most characteristic—that is, unless you're very familiar with Mateus Rosé from Portugal. This short squat, green bottle is also used in Franconia (Germany).

- The **flûte** is the tall, slim green or brown bottle that we all associate with German wines. By law in Alsace (France), producers must bottle their wines in the flûte-style bottle.
- The most common bottles you will come across are the **Bordeaux** style and the **Burgundy** style. The Bordeaux-style version has pronounced "shoulders" with parallel sides. The Burgundy-style version has sloping shoulders, tapering down to a broader base.

  Now if life were simple, you would find Bordeaux and Bordeaux-style wines (Sauvignon Blanc, Cabernet Sauvignon and Merlot) wines in Bordeaux-style bottles, and Burgundy and Burgundy-style wines (Chardonnay and Pinot Noir) in Burgundy-style bottles. But in reality this only holds true for wines from Bordeaux and Burgundy: by law, producers in the Bordeaux and Burgundy regions of France must use the regionally-approved style of packaging. So the red and white wines of Bordeaux, including sweet wines, are packaged in bottles with shoulders, while the red and white wines of Burgundy are packaged in the bottles with the sloping sides. Also in France, Loire and Rhône wines tend to be in the Burgundy-style bottles.

- The **champagne** bottle is a variation on the Burgundy style, but it's made with thicker glass, has an even broader base, and the famous punt in the bottom which allows the server to safely hold the bottle in a horizontal position while pouring.

Increasingly, traditionalists are bringing back the bottle shapes used by their ancestors. This could be a marketing ploy but it is also an indication of the intent of the producer to shun modern wine-making practices. And outside of the Old World, really any wine can be put in any bottle—it's up to the producer to decide. Always check the label to see what's really inside.

Wine-in-a-box

For convenience, wine is sold in "Bag-in-a-box" containers—essentially a plastic foil bag of wine inside of a cardboard box. These range in size from 3–15 litres and great for large parties or outdoor picnics. Since the bag is usually filled without air, and the spigot is airtight, the contents can last much longer than bottled wine when opened. The quality of the wine isn't always the highest but the price is usually right.

Bottle Sizes

Bottle capacities range from as little as 100 ml to 15 000 ml (equivalent to 20 standard bottles), but the standard bottle size is 750 ml. This is roughly comparable in size to the first wine bottles in the sixteenth and seventeenth centuries. The size of these early bottles was thought to be a function of the lung capacity of a typical glass-blower. The round shape has changed, however, to make it easier to store the bottle on its side.

Since the demand is low, only a small percentage of wines produced are packaged in alternatives to the standard 750 ml bottle. The most common option is the magnum (1500 ml), which is double the standard capacity, while half bottles—either 375 ml or 500 ml—are popular with restaurants. Here, to impress your friends and neighbours, are the other bottle sizes:

- Jeroboam   3000 ml (4 bottles)
- Rehoboam   4500 ml (6 bottles)
- Methuselah   6000 ml (8 bottles)
- Salmanazar   9000 ml (12 bottles)
- Balthazar   12 000 ml (16 bottles)
- Nebuchadnezzar   15 000 ml (20 bottles)

You may recognize some of these names as biblical; however, no one seems to know why this is.

Bottle Color

You may have noticed that nearly all wine is packaged in light green, dark green or dark brown bottles. The tint protects what's inside from one of its natural enemies—light.

Exposure to sunlight and fluorescent light is very bad for wine. When you see wine packaged in a clear bottle, usually it's to show off what's inside, say the color of a rosé wine. If the wine is expensive, like rosé champagne, it'll be wrapped in ultraviolet-resistant orange wrap. Not so for a still rosé wine. It's meant to be bought and consumed, and has little risk of seeing much light in its lifetime.

Some wine regions require bottles to be of a certain color. In Germany, for example, a green flûte bottle is used for wines from the Mosel, and a brown flûte for wines of the Rhine. Some producers also use color, design, and even the style of glass to make the wine package part of their marketing plan for the wine. For example, Vernaccia (from Italy) often comes in a green-tinted amphora-shaped bottle, and Black Tower (from Germany) comes in a distinctive ceramic bottle so you will always be able to identify these wines quickly on a shelf.

Did You Know?

The biggest bottle of wine ever made, the Maximus, was produced by Beringer Vineyards in 2004. It holds the equivalent of 173 bottles of Beringer's 2001 Private Reserve Napa Valley Cabernet Sauvignon, stands 4.5 ft (1.4 m) tall and weighs 340 lbs (154 kg).

A Wine Is a Wine Is a Wine

So What's on the Shelves?

Thousands of different wines are available on the market today. Some of the range and selection comes from the grape variety—for example, hundreds of different bottles of wine labelled *Pinot Noir*. But that's only part of the explanation. Pinot Noir is used to make red Burgundy, it's part of the blend in champagne, and is now even used to make icewine in British Columbia. Three different types of wines (still wine, sparkling wine, and a dessert wine) and the only thing they have in common is the grape!

It isn't necessary to memorize thousands of wines, but it helps to break them down into manageable categories. We've picked five that we are sure you're probably already familiar with: still (a.k.a table wine), sparkling, fortified, dessert, and aromatized.

Still Wine

This is the wine you most likely drink on a regular basis. Some people also call it *table* wine. Most wines in this category fall between 8% and 15% alcohol by volume, and much of it is close to the middle of that range, around 12.5%. German wine laws allow wine to be as low as 6.5% and some Italian wines can reach as high as 16%.

Still wines are produced all over the world and can be made in a *dry* and *off-dry* style. This refers to the amount of residual sugar present in the wine. If all the grape sugars have been converted into alcohol, then a wine is considered dry. If the sugars aren't fully converted, or the fermentation is stopped before this happens, the wine is considered off dry. These wines have a distinct impression of sweetness but aren't truly sweet wines.

Still wines come in three colors: red, white, and rosé. Certain grapes are usually associated with certain wine colors but there are exceptions. White wine grapes like Riesling can only be made into white wines, whereas red wines like Pinot Noir can be made into red, rosé, and even white wines like Champagne.

Red Wine

Made from dark-skinned grapes, red wine gets its color from an extended maceration on the skins. Typically maceration can last anywhere from six to 12 days, depending on the desired color (longer maceration usually results in deeper, darker wines).

In addition to color, *tannins* are also drawn out of the skins during maceration. Because tannins are a natural preservative and help wines age, winemakers try to get the maximum amount of tannins out of the grape skins (Cabernet Sauvignon, for example).

Red wines ferment at higher temperatures than white wines and winemakers may have to use temperature-controlled tanks to raise and maintain must temperature throughout the process.

Red wines usually receive some aging in barrels. These can vary in size from the huge Italian *botte* to the smaller French *barrique*. The type of barrel, the wood it is made from, and the length of time the wine stays in the barrel all affect the wine.

Examples of red wine grapes are Cabernet Sauvignon, Pinot Noir, Sangiovese, Merlot, and Zinfandel.

Punching Down the Cap

A fermenting vat of red wine quickly develops a thick layer of skins, pulp, and seeds. The juice below will develop very little color unless this layer is mixed or pushed down into the juice. This can be done manually or with a machine and has many fancy French names like *remontage*, *foulage*, or *pieage*.

White Wine

Made from light-skinned grapes, white wine has to be treated more carefully than red wine. The grapes are pressed on arrival at the winery to avoid the risk of oxidation and darkening. A few hours contact with the skins at cool temperatures is sometimes allowed to impart more flavor and fruit character. Since there is essentially no maceration time, white wine has far fewer tannins than red wine.

White wines ferment at cooler temperatures than red wines. Temperature-controlled tanks maintain the low temperature throughout the process to concentrate fruit flavors and to capture freshness in the wine. This is especially needed in warm-climate countries like Chile and Australia.

Barrel aging adds an extra dimension to the wine. Too much oak, however, often masks poor winemaking or poor quality fruit.

Softening Up Wines

Another type of fermentation (malolactic fermentation) occurs in most red wines and may be encouraged in some white wines like Chardonnay. This softens the harsher (malic) acids in the wine and changes them into lactic acids.

Examples of white wine grapes are Chardonnay, Pinot Gris, Riesling, Sauvignon Blanc, and Viognier.

Rosé Wine

This may be the most misunderstood style of still wine. Many people associate rosés with the sweet blush White Zins of California. However, rosés can also be refreshingly dry wines from the south of France and Spain and now increasingly from the United States and Canada.

Rosé wine is made from the same grape varieties used to make red wine. There are three ways to make it:

- Macerating red grape must for only a few days and fermenting the pale-colored juice. This is the traditional method;
- Fermenting the juice of quickly pressed red wine grapes, the same way white wine is made. Technically this is called a *vin gris;* or
- Fermenting siphoned-off juice from red wine production. Technically this was how the phenomenon called *White Zin* was discovered.

It is illegal in parts of Europe to make rosé wine by blending finished white and red white wines, but some wineries do it anyway. In fact this is sometimes how champagne rosé is made, by blending in up to 15% of Pinot Noir wine.

Rosé wines are low in tannins (about the same as white wine) and should be consumed right away—they lose their freshness over time.

Examples of rosé wine grapes are Grenache, Zinfandel, and Cabernet Franc. But most red wine grapes can be made into rosé.

Sparkling Wine

While still wine is the wine most people drink on a day-to-day basis, sparkling wine is the wine we suspect they would like to drink more often. And why not? It is fun to drink and is usually associated with happy events—weddings, promotions, and ship launchings. Sparkling wine, unfortunately, is rarely considered as a wine to be served with a meal.

Sparkling wines are produced all over the world and can be made in various styles and sweetness levels. Most sparkling wine has between 8% and 12% alcohol by volume. The most prestigious, and the most famous, sparkling wine is champagne.

What is the difference between sparkling wine and still wine? In a word, bubbles. Carbon dioxide is a by-product of fermentation, and instead of letting the carbon dioxide escape into the air, as it does with still wine, the gas is made to dissolve or be absorbed into the wine. This is done in one of three ways:

- Second fermentation in the bottle;
- Second fermentation in a tank; or
- Carbonation.

A second fermentation happens when more yeast and sugar are added to already fermented wine. For carbonation you hook up a CO_2 tank to some wine and presto, sparkling wine.

In the Bottle

The first method is usually associated with champagne, the wine. Since only sparkling wine made in the French wine region of Champagne can legally be called *champagne*, all other sparkling wines made this way must use the term *méthode traditionelle* or "traditional method" on the label. So if you see "champagne" on the label, you know you're drinking the "real thing."

All sparkling wines, including champagne, begin as still wine. By law, champagne can be made using only Chardonnay, Pinot Noir, Pinot Meunier, or a combination of these grapes. Other sparkling wines made using the méthode traditionelle may use different grapes and many of these are unique to the region or country. The Xarel-lo, Parellada and Macabeo grapes, for example, are used to make a pleasant Spanish sparkling wine called Cava.

Depending on the house style of the producer, different still wines are first blended together. This is called *assemblage*. A measured amount of yeast and sugar is added to the blend to start a second fermentation and the wine is bottled. The bottle used for champagne is much heavier than a usual wine bottle as a considerable amount of pressure builds up during the second fermentation. This is also the bottle you will see when you buy the wine, but the cap that is used at this point is temporary and looks like a beer cap.

Red Grapes Make White Wine?

Pinot Noir and Pinot Meunier are both dark-skinned grapes yet they are used to make a white wine—champagne. How so? In making the base wine, the grapes are almost immediately pressed in a special pie-shaped press, and the skins are not allowed to macerate with the rest of the wine at all.

The wine is stored (in vast underground chalk tunnels in Champagne) until the second fermentation has stopped and the wine has properly interacted with the lees (spent yeast cells) to acquire the characteristic fine bubbles and toasty aromas. This can take as little as a few months or as long as three years for vintage champagne. The more time, the more bubbles.

Lees are unsightly—sort of a cloudy blob—and have to be removed without losing all the fizz that has built up. Through a complicated and slow process of manipulation called *remuage*, the *riddler,* as he is called in Champagne, works with the bottles until the sediment collects at the neck of the bottle. The neck is then dipped in a cooling liquid to freeze the sediment and the cap is removed. The pressure that has built up in the bottle, forces out the frozen blob, leaving the wine clean and bubbly. Here's a word to impress your friends—this process is called *dégorgement* (disgorgement).

A little wine is added to the bottle to replace what may have been lost. The winemaker may add sweetened wine (*dosage*) if a sweeter style of sparkling wine is desired; otherwise champagne is dry. Finally, the bottle has to be corked—that big fat mushroom-cap shaped cork—and fitted with a protective cage. The pressure in the bottle is far too great for standard corks and sparkling wine producers don't want any of that sparkle to be lost until you open your bottle to toast your next celebration!

As a rule, sparkling wine—even champagne—should be consumed soon after purchase. The winery has stored it for you and determined when it is ready to drink. The very best vintage champagne can age and should be treated the same way you would a very good white wine—with respect.

Examples of other sparkling wines using this method include: *Cava* (in Spain) and *Cremant* (in France). You will also find good quality méthode traditionelle wines from Australia, New Zealand, United States (California), and Canada.

In the Tank

Lower-priced sparklers are made by allowing the second fermentation to occur in a large sealed tank instead of in the bottle. This is called the *Charmat, bulk,* or *tank* method. It is unlikely that you will see this listed on the label; however, if it doesn't say "champagne" or "méthode traditionelle", assume this method was used.

Essentially the whole process occurs in "bulk", in a tank instead of the bottle. The yeast and sugar necessary to start the second fermentation are added to the blended wine in a tank. The fermentation builds up carbon dioxide, and again this gas is absorbed into the wine. Once the fermentation is complete, the wine is filtered and bottled while still under pressure. The whole process can take only months instead of years; therefore, wineries can therefore adapt to market conditions much faster than the big champagne houses.

There are fewer restrictions on the grapes that can be used to make sparkling wines this way, and many of them are unique to a particular region or country where the wine is made. The Prosecco grape, for example, is used to make very nice sparkling wine in the Veneto region of Italy.

The bubbles produced using this method are generally larger and not as persistent as champagne. If you don't mind slightly larger bubbles or are planning to make cocktails with it, there are some excellent wines out there for you to try. Italian Asti and German Sekt (for example, Henkel Trocken), are two lower-priced alternatives that still offer up the fun of more expensive sparklers.

Win a Formula One Race Lately?

The *transfer method* is a variation on the traditional method and a way to make good sparkling wine faster, and at a lower price. Avoiding the slow *remuage* process, wineries empty the contents of the bottles into a pressurized tank then filter out the lees, but also lose a few bubbles and some complex aromas along the way. The wine is then re-bottled into new, less expensive, bottles and sold. If you've wondered, this is how producers make those huge bottles of champagne that are used to celebrate the end of a Formula One race.

All Gassed Up

The cheapest way to make sparkling wine is using carbonation. This is akin to making soda pop and the result is sometimes no better than cream soda. The bubbles are very large and often disappear before you have your first sip. The price difference between carbonated and tank method sparklers is very little, so spend the extra money—you're worth it.

Fortified wine

We are often get asked if fortified wine is in fact wine at all. The answer is yes. The only major difference between still and fortified wines is that alcohol has been added to the latter wine at some stage in the winemaking process.

There are two main types of fortified wines:

- Wines in which alcohol is used to stop fermentation *before* it is complete; and
- Wines in which alcohol is added *after* fermentation is finished

Wines in the first category (port for example) are generally sweeter than those in the second category (sherry for example). Fortified wines are usually stronger than still wines, having an alcohol content somewhere in the range of 18–20%.

Port

Port, like champagne, is the proprietary name given to fortified wine produced in the Douro region of northern Portugal. However, for simplicity, we will use the term port to describe wines fortified *before* fermentation is complete.

When you drink a glass of port you will notice three things. First, unless it is white port, it is a relatively deep, dark red color. Second, its alcohol content is somewhat high. Third, it's sweet. These three characteristics are a result of the unique way port is made.

The speedy extraction of color and tannins is important to port. Remember, tannins are a preservative, and port usually needs to be stored for years before it is drinkable. Winemakers must work quickly because they need to fortify the wine before fermentation is complete.

These Feet Were Made for Treading

The traditional method to extract color quickly was to tread the grapes, usually to music. The foot is perfectly designed to apply the right amount of pressure without bruising the grapes or breaking the pips. In about one day, a team of highly skilled treaders will extract the right amount of color and tannins from the grapes. Don't worry, everyone's feet are checked for cleanliness before they are allowed into the vat.

After about two or three days of maceration, the wine reaches the right sweetness level (about 6% to 8% alcohol) and is considered ready for fortification. The wine is added to a neutral spirit (77% alcohol called *aguardente*) to kill off the yeasts and stop the fermentation. The resulting wine contains about 20% alcohol with some residual sugar. The port is then placed in a wooden barrel called a *pipe* for aging.

Depending on the vineyard, the quality of the grapes, and the needs of the market, different types of port can be made from this wine. We describe the different types of port a bit later in our book.

Madeira

Just off the coast of Portugal is an island called Madeira. Here they make a unique fortified wine called—you guessed it—madeira. What makes madeira unique is that the wine is literally cooked (sometimes for years), either under the sun, in *estufas* (tanks warmed by heaters), or in steam lodges (rooms or buildings heated by steam). This caramelizes the sugars in the wine and promotes oxidation—usually undesirable in wine, but good for madeira. This rare process results in a very unique and long-lived wine. The best madeira is given 20 or more years of barrel aging.

For the sweeter styles of madeira (Bual and Malmsey) alcohol is added to stop fermentation (like port.) For the drier versions (Sercial), the alcohol is added after fermentation is complete (like sherry.) Verdelho is a medium-sweet style of madeira.

Cooked Wine

Madiera was an important trading stop for the British on their way to Africa and the New World. To make the trips bearable, the traders fortified the local wine in order for it to survive the long voyages. Apparently the wine actually improved with exposure to the intense sweltering heat as the ships crossed the equator and so madeira the wine was born.

For a number of years, British dealers continued to make madeira by shipping barrels to India to mature, but that process has now been replaced by more modern methods that reproduce the cooked effect of the seaward journey.

Sherry

Sherry is the generic name given to wines fortified *after* fermentation is complete. Real sherry—one of the world's greatest wine secrets—comes from the south of Spain and takes its name from the town of Jerez (pronounced hair-eth).

Much to the surprise of most people, sherry is usually dry, not sweet. Because the wine is allowed to fully ferment before the fortifying spirit is added, there is no residual sugar in it. There are some sweet sherries that have been sweetened (and probably colored) artificially or with sweet grape juice, but sherry is generally dry and consumed as an apéritif.

Unlike port, sherry is made from light-skinned wine grapes. And like a white wine, the juice is pressed off the skins and allowed to ferment. Winemakers conduct a sort of quality triage on the wine, and then it is fortified with grape spirit.

Wine made from the best grapes, usually Palomino, grown in the best soil, will be made in the *fino* style and fortified up to about

15.5% alcohol. This is the ideal level for *flor* to develop. Flor is yeast that forms on the surface of the wine and feeds off the alcohol in the wine and the oxygen in the barrel. In turn, it reduces the overall acidity of the wine and gives it a dry, clean, tangy taste.

If the wine isn't going to be a fino, then it will be made into an *oloroso* and fortified to about 18%. This prevents the flor from developing. Oloroso is also dry, but with raisiny, nutty, burnt toffee aromas and flavors.

Both fino and oloroso are then aged in a *solera*—a complex series of barrels—until ready for sale.

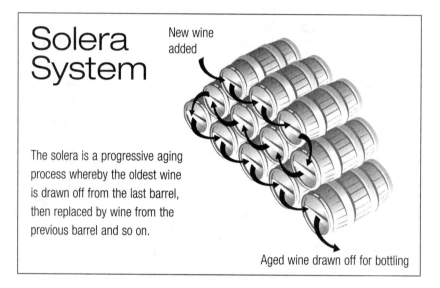

Solera System

New wine added

The solera is a progressive aging process whereby the oldest wine is drawn off from the last barrel, then replaced by wine from the previous barrel and so on.

Aged wine drawn off for bottling

Flor and the solera are unique to true sherry and are rarely reproduced elsewhere. Sherry-style wines made in Canada, Australia, or South Africa are usually sweeter and can't really be compared to the original.

Dessert Wine

These wines are much sweeter than regular still wines. Not regular off-dry sweet, like a White Zin or an off-dry Riesling. We're talking super sweet: from 20 grams to as much as 500 grams per litre of unfermented sugar (by comparison, dry wines can be as low as 2 grams per litre). Sometimes called sweeties, stickies, or even pudding wines, dessert wines are among some of the greatest wines in the world, yet they are a relatively obscure category for most people. Stick with us and we will help change your perspective.

To make luscious, rich sweet wines you need grapes that are so ripe that the yeasts simply cannot ferment all the sugar. When the yeasts stop working lots of sugar remains in the fermented wine. The key to greatness and longevity, however, isn't just sweetness but also the acidity in the grapes. When these elements are in balance the wines are sublime.

Dessert wines are usually made with light-skinned grapes. A few are made with dark-skinned grapes but these are the exception.

How do grapes get super-sweet? Here are three ways:

- The grapes are affected by "noble rot," a fungus (yum!);
- The grapes are air-dried or allowed to shrivel up (i.e. "raisining"); or
- The grapes freeze on the vine.

Whatever the method, the result is "dessert in a glass."

Noble Rot

No, we're not talking about cheap wine drunk at Buckingham Palace. This is the name of a fungus (*Botrytis cinerea*, pronounced BO-trite-is sin-er-eea) that is allowed to attack grapes and help them become sweet.

There are "good" fungi and "bad" fungi. If the "bad" type affects grapes, they will be ruined. On the other hand if you are lucky enough to have your grapes—particularly your white wine grapes—affected by the benevolent form then you are indeed blessed. "Noble rot"—or *pourriture noble*, if you prefer—consumes the water stored inside the grape, thereby concentrating the sugars. The resulting sugar levels are many times higher than those in regular grapes, so that a lot more residual sugar remains in the wine after fermentation has finished.

Grapes may also get sweeter if they hang on the vine long after the harvest is over, even if not affected by noble rot. Wines made from these grapes are less sweet than the noble-rot versions and are usually called *late-harvest* wines.

The most famous, and usually the most expensive, version of sweet wine made by grapes affected by noble rot is Sauternes from Bordeaux (France). The one that has been made the longest is Tokaji Aszú of Hungary, predating Sauternes by some 200 years. Botrytized wines are also made in other countries including Australia, Chile, United States, and Canada.

Dried Grapes

A number of different wines fall under this category—even to some extent late-harvest wines—but essentially these are wines made from dried, or raisined, grapes. Italian winemakers are famous for making *passito* wines by picking and drying the grape bunches (on trays or by hanging them from rafters) for many months. This shrivels up or "raisins" the grapes and concentrates the sugars. Vin Santo from Tuscany and Recioto from Veneto are perhaps the most famous passito wines.

Many other traditional air-dried wines are now fortified, but in France true *vin de paille*, as they are called, is still made in the Jura region. In Austria, some winemakers still dry their grapes on straw mats. Here, the wine is called *Strohwein*.

Icewine

Finally, there's one of our favorite dessert wines, icewine. While entrepreneurial winemakers use cryo-extraction (post-harvest freezing in a freezer), *real* icewine is made by allowing the grapes to freeze naturally on the vine. This is possible in only a few places, including Canada, northern United States, Germany (where it is called Eiswein), Austria, and parts of Eastern Europe.

The grapes are left on the vine until December or January when the temperature drops to –8° C (18°F) or colder for a few days. It is important to note that the grapes are picked *and* pressed at this temperature; if the must is allowed to warm above this temperature, by law the wine is no longer icewine and becomes essentially very expensive late-harvest wine.

When the frozen grapes are pressed, only the sticky sweet juice comes out. The water remains frozen with the rest of the grape, leaving the must very concentrated. As you can imagine, it takes a long time to extract sufficient juice to make icewine. This, to a certain extent, justifies the high prices these wines command. The resulting wine is pure nectar and, at times, worth every penny.

Icewine is usually made with light-skinned grapes, mainly Riesling and Vidal. A number of wineries in Canada are also experimenting with dark-skinned grapes but the supply is very limited. A few wineries also make sparkling icewine, or use icewine as the dosage in traditional sparkling wine. Whatever the style, please don't encourage counterfeits—purchase only authentic icewine, from reputable producers, to fully enjoy this style of wine.

Aromatized Wine

Vermouth is probably the best known example of "aromatized" or flavored wine. There are different, and sometimes ancient, recipes for making aromatized, or flavored, wines, but whatever the formula, it usually involves macerating spices, fruits or herbs in a base wine and sometimes adding sugar for sweetness and caramel for color. Some wines—especially French vermouth—are aged in barrels, but this isn't necessary.

In general, Italian vermouth is red and sweet, while French versions are gold and drier. While Vermouth is also fortified, *Retsina* from Greece is an example of an unfortified, flavored wine. Technically wine coolers also fall into this category.

Is Wine Good For You?

Are any of these wines—still, sparkling, or especially dessert—good for you? Only your doctor can really answer that question. Nonetheless you may have heard of the French Paradox—people in France with high-fat diets drinking red wine and enjoying some of the lowest rates of heart disease in the world. When this connection was publicized in the early 1990s, red wine consumption spiked. It's been on the increase ever since. It turns there's something in red wine—and in red grape juice—with medicinal properties.

Throughout history, wine was thought to have healing benefits. Until recently, there hasn't been much research to support this. Increasingly, medical research is finding links between the moderate consumption of wine and a range of health benefits. Guidelines suggest "moderate" means one to two standard glasses per day; however guidelines don't apply to individuals equally. How you metabolize alcohol and how it affects your health will depend on your age, gender, body type, state of health, any medications you are taking, and whether you are drinking on a full or empty stomach. Your predisposition will determine what amount of wine can be consumed without damage to your overall health.

The Good

Wine, in particular red wine, is full of antioxidant compounds or phenolics. The most famous of these is resveratrol. It helps improve the balance between the "good" HDL cholesterol and the "bad" LDL cholesterol, providing a protective effect against cardiovascular disease.

Wine Was Safer than Water

For centuries, wine wasn't a luxury—it was a necessity. The water in most Medieval towns and cities was so impure, and disease bearing, that wine, because of its antiseptic properties, was a much safer alternative. People of all ages consumed it and production focused on high potency (and not taste).

As a bonus for those who prefer cool-climate wines, red wines from regions like Burgundy and Canada contain higher concentrations of resveratrol.

There's a connection between moderate wine consumption and improved digestion. The polyphenols in wine seem to have antibacterial properties, wiping out certain bacteria connected to food poisoning and to inhibit a strain that causes ulcers.

Other beneficial effects associated with the consumption of red wine include reduced hypertension, improved bone density, and a strengthened immune system. And, of course, there's the relaxation factor. Results of a Danish study also suggest wine drinking is associated with improved social, intellectual, and personality functions.

The Bad

But along with the good, comes the bad. Wine contains negative components that can damage your health and well-being. Alcohol, for example, is a toxin. Beyond moderate levels, it has a damaging effect on the body.

Fortunately, a hangover is entirely preventable. Besides drinking less when you drink, have a glass of water before, during, or after each glass of wine. And never drink on an empty stomach. Food slows down the rate of alcohol absorption into the bloodstream and makes it easier on your system.

Alcohol consumption, which has long had an association with fetal alcohol syndrome, is not advised for women who are pregnant, or for nursing mothers.

Finally, be aware that the alcohol in wine makes it full of calories—ranging from 90 calories for a light-bodied red or white still wine to 135 calories for a glass of port or sweet wine.

Wine and allergies

Other than a hangover, does drinking red wine ever give you a headache? Or perhaps you avoid white wine because it makes you break out in hives? If so, you may have sensitivities to certain components in wines, which cause an allergic reaction.

An allergic reaction to red wine is likely due to the naturally occurring amines known as histamines (which dilate the blood vessels in the brain) or tyramines (which constrict them) in the wine. White wines are generally lower in amines than red wines, although you can experiment with red wines to find ones with lower levels of this allergen.

Allergic reactions to white wine are more likely caused by the presence of sulfites in the wine. Sulphur dioxide is used as a preservative in wines—white wines especially—to inhibit oxidation and the growth of molds and bacteria. Your reaction to sulfites in a wine may be due to either high sensitivity or excessive use of sulfur in the winemaking process.

To find out whether you have to rule out white wines altogether, try cool-climate wines, or, if available, biodynamic wines (which eschew the use of any chemical additives whatsoever). If you still have a reaction, you're the sensitive type and it may just be best to avoid them.

The Ugly

Well, you may think you're clueless about wine, but you shouldn't be about drinking and driving. It goes without saying that *any* amount of alcohol, whether beer, liquor or wine, is unsafe if you are driving.

It's worth knowing that 5 oz (140 ml) of wine is equivalent to 1½ oz (45 ml) of spirits and 12 oz (340 ml) of beer. This formula is based on an average 12% alcohol wine. Adjust accordingly if you're drinking an 8% German Riesling or a 15% glass of Zinfandel.

Take Your Time

The liver processes alcohol at the rate of about one hour for every standard alcoholic drink. If you have two glasses of wine with dinner, allow for at least two hours for it to be out of your system.

When consumed in moderation as part of a healthy diet and lifestyle, wine can be beneficial to your health. On the other hand, only your doctor can tell you whether moderate alcohol consumption will bring benefits or pose risks. To quote the Chinese proverb, "Wine should be taken in small doses, knowledge in large ones."

Where in the World Does Wine Come From?

Around the Wine World in about 60 Pages

Until such time as all wine stores and restaurant wine lists are organized by grape variety or style, you'll need to know something about the places where grapes are grown and wine is made. About 60 countries produce a meaningful amount of wine, and at most half of those have wines represented in typical large urban wine stores. We're not going to cover everything—we'll focus on those that you are most likely to encounter, and what's important to know.

Old World vs. New World

Frankly, it is amazing we've made it this far in the book without using the terms *New World* and *Old World*. In geographic terms, Old World refers to Europe and the Mediterranean basin while New World refers to the Americas, South Africa, Australia, and New Zealand. It's more than about geography, however. In winespeak, Old World and New World are used to emphasize differences in winemaking techniques or styles rather than geographic borders.

The Old World, in a wine context, is about tradition and place. Growers and winemakers have had about 4,000 years to identify which grape varieties are the best to grow and make into good wine. The Old World also captures the culture of wine drinking. Wine is considered an everyday drink rather than something kept for special occasions. It's less often drunk as a cocktail and more to accompany a meal.

In contrast, the New World is more about science than tradition. Grape growing and winemaking are relatively less established (only about 400 years) and the lack of tradition and rules has allowed the ready adoption of new technologies. With a few exceptions, wine is the alcoholic beverage of choice for a small percentage of the population (for example, less than one third of North Americans drink wine regularly), and the culture of food and wine is only now catching up to the rest of the world.

These differences are less clear-cut than they used to be. Old World producers are embracing technological innovations and New World producers see the value—if only a marketing one for some—of what the French call *terroir*.

Deciphering All Those Initials

Most Old World wine producing countries have some way of classifying their wines. A number of New World countries—Canada, United States, Australia, New Zealand, and South Africa, for example—are also getting around to doing this too. Essentially what these classification systems do is guarantee to the consumer that the wine you are buying comes from the region (the rules define or *delimit* the region), possesses the character of the region (e.g., Bordeaux wine smells and tastes like Bordeaux wine), and has been made in accordance with the rules and regulations of the region. Wines are submitted to governing bodies (either local, regional, or national) in order to qualify for the classification.

Each classification system has a hierarchical series of levels or categories. The chart below indicates the names and initials used by the major Old World wine-producing countries:

Terroir

The French word *terroir* describes the unique expression of the vineyard's soil, site, and microclimate in a wine. It can also include human factors like tradition. Combined, these qualities are what's believed to make one wine distinctive from another. There is no equivalent word in English.

Classification	France	Italy	Germany	Spain	Portugal
Table Wine	Vin de table	Vino da tavola	Tafelwein	Vino de mesa	Vinho de mesa
Regional Wine	Vin de pays	IGT—Indicazione Geografica Tipica	Landwein	Vino de la tierra	Vinho regional
Quality Wine	AOC—Appellation d'Origine Contrôlée	DOC—Denominazione di Origine Controllata	QbA—Qualitätswein bestimmter Anbaugebiete	VCIG—Vinos de Calidad con Indicación Geográfica and DO—Denominación de Origen	DOC—Denominação de Origem Controlada
Quality Wine with Distinction	DOCG—Denominazione di Origine Controllata e Garantita	QmP—Qualitätswein mit Prädikat	DOCa—Denominación de Origen Calificada and DO de Pago	

Table wine is the lowest level of classification and there is no reference to place of origin, vintage, or even the grapes on the label.

Regional wines or "country wines" indicate the place of origin on the label. Responding to international demand, producers are listing the grape varieties as well.

Table and regional wines usually represent a large proportion of each country's wine production—sometimes more than half. Prices for these wines are good and they usually deliver fair value for money. Some of Italy's IGT or vino da tavola wines, for example, can be superior to other wines in the same category where producers have chosen to not be included in the higher Quality category, or because, according to officials, they do not conform to local regulations and have been banned from being included in the higher category.

Quality wines are usually the highest-level classification for wines. They conform to the strictest regulations and offer the best guarantee of authenticity.

Wines with distinction are unique or historically defined wines (e.g., Rioja in Spain). Occasionally the regulations are higher, and tighter, than that for Quality wines, but the distinction is simply for political or historical reasons. France is considering the addition of an elite designation; this would be the first major change to the AOC system since 1935.

Each country or region has its own spin on these classifications. It is important to remember that these classifications *do not*, despite their intentions or names, provide a guarantee of quality. That's left up to you to decide.

In the New World, the classification systems are usually one-tiered. A wine is either in the classification or it isn't. But in all cases the intentions are essentially the same: the wine/grapes come from the region, have been made in accordance with the rules and regulations of the region, and to some extent possess the character of the region (although that is less of a feature in the New World.) In United States AVAs (American Viticultural Areas) are used to delimit wine regions, in Canada it is VQA (Vintner's Quality Alliance), in Australia they use GIS (Geographic Indications System), and in South Africa it's WO (Wines of Origin.)

Judging Wine by Its Label

Wine labels differ greatly from country to country, even region to region. New World wineries tend to feature the grape name prominently on the front label: "Chardonnay" or "Cabernet Sauvignon." Some Old World regions—Germany, the Alsace region in France, Friuli in Italy, and most Eastern European countries—also use the grape name approach. As New World wines gain market share around the world, more and more Old World wine regions are considering at least adding grape varieties to the back label to make them more consumer-friendly.

Old World wineries tend to use geographic or regional or *terroir*-based labelling styles: for example, Chianti Classico (Italy) or Ribera del Duero (Spain). The strict laws of these regions dictate which grapes can be grown there, so it's assumed you know which grape or grapes were used in making the wine.

The third type of wine label omits both varietal and geographic information. Some examples are Gentil (a blend of white grapes from Alsace), Ornellaia (Merlot from Italy), and Noble One (botrytisized Semillon dessert wine from Australia). In some cases, these are higher-end wines made by producers who want to use grape varieties not permitted by local authorities, and for others it's simply to differentiate their products.

They say you can't judge a book by its cover, but you usually can tell a lot about a wine from its label. Here are the key things you'll find on most wine labels and what they mean:

- **Producer's name.** If you are familiar with the producer, this can be an indication of the wine's style and quality.

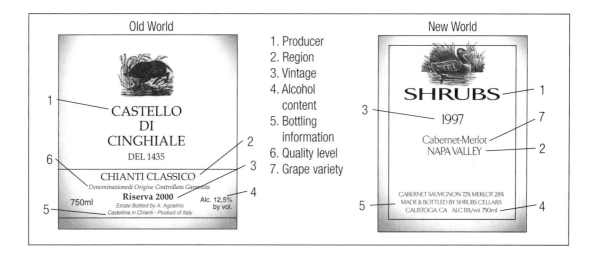

- **Vintage.** The wine's age tells you whether to expect something youthful or mature. If you know the vintage was good or bad in the wine region, this may be an indicator of the wine's quality.
- **Region.** This is where the wine comes from. The more precise the region (e.g., a single vineyard), the higher the quality and likewise the price.
- **Grape variety.** You will always see this stated on a New World wine, and also on some Old World wines.
- **Alcohol content.** Stated as a percentage of volume. Most still wines will be around 12.5%. Fortified wines will be higher.
- **Bottling information.** This indicates where the wine was actually bottled (the winery or a large commercial factory.) You might see *mise en bouteille au château* or *domaine* or *à la propriété* on French labels, and *imbottigliato* on Italian labels.
- **Classification.** For those countries with a classification system for wines, these usually appear as an acronym on the label. For example, VQA, AOC, AVA, DOCa, QmP, or DOC.

Spin the bottle around to see what else the winery has to say about its wine. You may find a little map of the winery's location, some information on the grape varieties in the wine, how dry or sweet the wine is, how much oakiness to expect, foods to pair with it, or serving temperatures. Some regions, for example California wines, require a health warning label on the bottle.

Understand what you read on the back label is there to help sell you on that wine over another. Some of the more famous wines provide no back label information, presuming the wine speaks for itself.

France

1. Bordeaux
2. Burgundy
3. Rhône
4. Champagne
5. Alsace
6. Loire
7. Languedoc-Rousillon
8. Jura-Savoie
9. Provence
10. The Southwest

For many years, France has held the standard for fine wine production. While some of the sheen has worn off its reputation, and New World competitors are nipping at her heels, France still produces over 20% of the world's wine and is home to some of the world's greatest wine brands and regions (champagne, for example). France is also the Old World benchmark for six of the Top Seven wine grapes: Cabernet Sauvignon, Chardonnay, Syrah, Pinot Noir, Merlot, and Sauvignon Blanc. Perhaps only in Italy is the link between wine and culture as strong as it is in France.

Wine Classification

France was the first country to establish regulations for wine production. Among other things these regulations delimit areas of production, approve method of production, and control yields, alcohol levels, and grape varieties. While the current appellation system is under review, each region in France has it's own spin on the AOC rules and regulations.

Vintages

Vintages matter in France because its weather is quite variable, especially in regions like Bordeaux and Burgundy. An exceptional vintage can produce exceptional wines that will last decades, while in a so-so year the wines may be okay but may not be age-worthy. Prices can spike in outstanding vintages, like 2000 and 2003.

Producers

Although price may be an indicator of quality, the most reliable way to guarantee quality is to know something about the producer. Even in bad vintages, good producers can make good wine. In some regions wine brokers—*négociants*—buy grapes, juice, or even finished wine and bottle it under their own label.

Regional Identification on the Label

There are a dozen major wine regions in France and the focus of French wine is on the area of production—the *appellation*—and not on the grape variety. This is important because most bottles of French wine show only the appellation on the label, not the type of grape used. Only AOC wines from Alsace and some regional wines (for example, Vin de Pays d'Oc) include the grape variety on the label.

Due to soil, site, and climate, some appellations will produce better wines than others, and the more specific the information on the bottle, the easier it is to figure this out. When a village or vineyard name appears on the label, the wine will be much better than if it, for example, says Burgundy, or even just France.

As a place to start, you'll need to know four regions: Bordeaux, Burgundy, Rhône, and Champagne. These are the most influential internationally.

Buying Tip
In good vintages, pick a lesser producer. In lesser vintages, pick a good producer.

Main AOC Regions
Alsace
Bordeaux
Burgundy
Champagne
Languedoc-
   Roussillon
Loire
Provence
Rhône

Bordeaux

Located in the southwest, not far from the Atlantic Ocean, Bordeaux is the France's largest quality wine-producing region, producing about a quarter of the country's total output of AOC wine. Traditionally all French wines benefit from the international reputation of Bordeaux. Some of the most expensive and sought-after red wines in the world are produced here, as well as one of the world's greatest sweet wines—Sauternes. However, despite the region's exalted reputation, the majority of wine produced in Bordeaux is just basic AOC Bordeaux.

Location, Location, Appellation!

In Bordeaux, location matters. Each of its 10 districts are characterized by soil composition, climate, the grapes that are grown there, vineyard owners, and traditions. The price and quality of the wine vary accordingly. Simply being on the wrong side of a dividing line can mean the difference between selling a wine for $300 or for $30.

> **Key Districts**
> Left Bank: Haut-Médoc, Graves, and Sauternes
> Right Bank: St-Émilion
> Middle: Entre-Deux-Mers

The wine districts of Bordeaux hug the banks of three rivers—the Gironde, Garonne, and Dordogne. Vineyards to the south of the Gironde are said to be on the *Left Bank* and those on the north side are on the *Right Bank*. In the middle, between the Garonne and Dordogne rivers, is *Entre-Deux-Mers*—literally "between two seas." The Bordelais always think big!

While each district produces different wines, some generalizations can be made about wines from each of these larger areas:

- **Left Bank** red wines are more austere, age-worthy, and tannic. The dry whites are big, powerful wines, while the sweet wines are decadent nectar.
- **Right Bank** red wines are richer, fruitier, and more approachable. They are the best introductory red wines for Bordeaux. They are also safer choices on restaurant wine lists, especially if they are at least five years old. The Right Bank is not known for its white wines.
- **Entre-Deux-Mers** is better known for its crisp, fresh, and dry white wines but it also produces oceans of straightforward easy drinking reds. These can be good value on a wine list.

The districts are further subdivided into *communes* (meaning "villages")—the highest level of appellation possible. It is at this level that the biggest distinctions in terms of price are made. The top wines are made in the top communes.

Bordeaux Wines Are Blends

Bordeaux wines aren't made from one grape. They're usually blends of grapes—reds with reds and whites with whites.

Red Bordeaux is generally a blend of Cabernet Sauvignon and Merlot with quantities of Cabernet Franc, Malbec, and Petit Verdot added depending on harvest conditions and the style of the winery. Cabernet Sauvignon is the dominant grape in the Left Bank and Merlot is more dominant in the Right Bank, but Merlot is the most planted overall.

With all the fuss about Bordeaux's red wines, it is easy to overlook its excellent white wines. Sauvignon Blanc is used on its own to make inexpensive, crisp, dry, and citrus-flavored whites or is blended with Sémillon and Muscadelle to create more lush and smooth wines. The best dry white wines come from Pessac-Léognan.

Bordeaux also makes decadently sweet wines: the most famous being Sauternes. These are made primarily with Sémillon but with some Sauvignon Blanc and Muscadelle blended in for acidity, aromatics, and structure. Lesser-known, good value sweet wines are also produced in Cadillac and Loupiac.

Top Communes
Left Bank: Pauillac, Margaux, St-Julien, and Pessac-Léognan
Right Bank: Pomerol

Key Bordeaux Grapes
Red wines: Cabernet Sauvignon, Merlot, and Cabernet Franc
White wines: Sauvignon Blanc and Sémillon

Bordeaux Wines Are Classified

For easy identification, Bordeaux wines are usually bottled in easily recognizable high-shoulder bottles. It's classification system for AOC wines has three levels:

- **Regional** (e.g., Bordeaux or Bordeaux Supérieur). These are inexpensive wines with a consistent style but don't expect quality. The larger producers may label their wines with a proprietary name (e.g., Mouton Cadet).
- **District** (e.g., Entre-Deux-Mers). This is a step up in quality. The name of the district will appear on the label.
- **Commune** (e.g., Margaux). This is the highest-level appellation within a district.

But now it gets a bit more complicated. The Médoc and Sauternes-Barsac districts (on the Left Bank) are further classified according to properties, known as Châteaux. This classification ranked all properties according to the price of their wines in—get this—1855. Of the five ranks, or *cru classés* (classed growths), the best and most famous are the *premiers crus* (first growths) followed by *deuxièmes crus* (second growths), and so on.

Not to be outdone, the Right Bank came up with a separate classification system (created in 1955), as did Graves on the Left Bank four years later. To further complicate things, not every property is classified under any one of these systems: there are now several hundred *cru bourgeois* wines that are part of a further three-level classification system (exceptionnel, bourgeois supérieur, and cru bourgeois). Some cru bourgeois are excellent wines that represent, at times, better value for money than some of the cru classés. Perhaps Bordeaux wines should be *certified*, not classified!

Is Bordeaux Affordable?

With all this talk of Châteaux and premiers crus, Bordeaux sounds expensive. Well, it doesn't have to be. Top crus like Château Petrus (from Pomerol in the Right Bank) can cost you over $2000 for the 2000 vintage, but a humble AOC Bordeaux wine will set you back less than $15. Between the two there are thousands of different Bordeaux wines, at all price points.

Here are a few buying tips:

- District wines, for example Entre-Deux-Mers, are usually good value but drink them right away. André Lurton is a good producer.
- Cru bourgeois wines are often well-made, good quality wines, and not nearly as expensive as the cru classés.
- Look for the "second label" of a major Château. Carruades de Lafite, for example, is the second label of Château Lafite

Did You Know?

In Bordeaux, the name of the Château that makes the wine can be important. Generally, wines from these producers represent the best quality and command the highest prices. Châteaux aren't always grand castles—although some are—but are more likely more simple estates. Some are hundreds of years old and look quite magnificent.

Rothschild and may include wine that would normally go into their top cru. Mouton Cadet, however, is not the second label for Château Mouton Rothschild: Le Petit Mouton de Mouton Rothschild holds that distinction.

- Buy from lesser known districts or communes. The commune Moulis, for example, is right next door to the famous Margaux and some of its producers are also capable of making full-bodied, age-worthy wines.

Burgundy

Burgundy lies southeast of Paris and forms a long strip, much of it an escarpment, some 115 miles (185 km) long. It shares Bordeaux's distinction of producing some of the most expensive and sought-after red and white wines in the world.

Burgundy's climate is often cool and damp with the occasional hot summer. There can be even greater variations in vintages than in Bordeaux. Soil composition, exposure to the sun, altitude and steepness of the slope (the better vineyards are situated around the mid-point of the slopes and face due east) also contribute greatly to the diversity of the wines from this region.

Hooked on Classics

Unlike wines from Bordeaux, Burgundian wines are made from essentially two grapes—Pinot Noir or Chardonnay—and there is no blending. When conditions are perfect, the wines produced from these two grapes may be the most sublime anywhere. When the conditions are poor, it's a good time to look elsewhere. Vintages really do matter in Burgundy.

Red Burgundy is Pinot Noir. At its prime, this wine is sensuous and silky with exotic raspberry, plum, and earthy truffle aromas, but in poor vintages it can be thin and tart. When winemaking follows more traditional ways, Burgundian Pinot Noir is more subtle than New World versions. Basic Burgundy (Bourgogne Rouge) will be less complex but still nice and fruity. Unless you're sure of the vintage, Pinot Noir from Burgundy is a risky choice on a wine list.

White Burgundy is Chardonnay and, like Pinot Noir it too is at its best in Burgundy. Done well, it has few equals. Burgundian Chardonnay, however, appears to take on multiple personalities based on the area where the grapes are grown:

- In the north, wines from Chablis are austere and crisp with appley aromas.

Bargain Districts
Côtes de Bourg
Côtes de Blaye
Fronsac
Entre-Deux-Mers

Key Grapes
Red wines: Pinot Noir and Gamay
White wines: Chardonnay and Aligoté

- Farther south, Chardonnay can be rich and buttery (in Meursault) or creamy and nutty (in Puligny-Montrachet).
- Even farther south yet, in Mâcon, Chardonnay is medium-bodied, fresh, and lively. And the price will be much less. Mâcon-Villages is an excellent starting point for white Burgundy and makes a safe choice on a wine list.

Another white wine grape, Aligoté, was once an important grape in Burgundy but now is relegated to the production of sparkling wine (crémant) and as an ingredient in an aperitif called *Kir* (white wine and crème de cassis).

Pyramid Power

Burgundy wines are usually bottled in slope-shouldered bottles. The classification system here—originally drawn up in 1861—is a four-step hierarchical system, based on local practices and natural factors such as soil type. It seems simple enough, but when you throw in 10,000 or so vineyards it gets kind of wacky. Almost 25% of France's AOC wines come from Burgundy.

It's easier to think of Burgundy's classification system as a pyramid. As you move up the pyramid, quality and price increases while availability decreases:

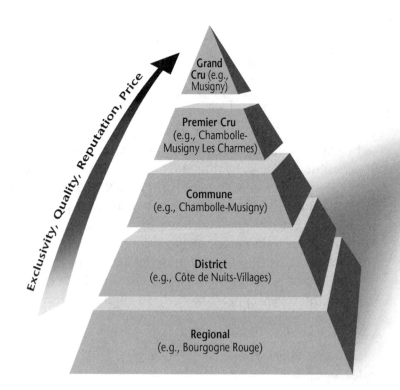

- *Regional* wines, red or white, can be made from grapes grown anywhere in Burgundy. The simplest are called AOC *Bourgogne* (French for Burgundy). Grape names (e.g., Bourgogne Aligoté) and districts (e.g., Mâcon) may be added to the label as long as the wine meets certain requirements. Regional wines represent just over half of total AOC production in Burgundy.
- *Commune* or *village* appellation wines indicate that the grapes come from a particular wine-producing commune. The name of the commune (e.g., Gevrey-Chambertin or Pommard) will appear prominently on the label. Village wines represent about one third of total production.
- *Premier crus* (1er Cru) aren't specifically appellations but are better categorized as a special class of commune. At last count there were 562 premiers crus. The label shows both the commune, in larger letters, followed the specific vineyard where the grapes were grown (for example, Volnay *Les Caillerets*). About 10% of total production is Premier Crus.
- *Grand cru* represents the very best vineyard locations and each one has its own appellation. There are 33 grand cru appellations and they represent only about 2% of total wine production. Only the vineyard name (e.g., *Le Montrachet*) appears on the label.

Key Communes

Gevrey-Chambertin
Morey-St-Denis
Chambolle-Musigny
Vougeot
Flagey-Échézeaux
Vosne-Romanée
Nuits-St-Georges
Aloxe-Corton
Puligny-Montrachet
Chassagne-
   Montrachet

Who's Who?

Here's where Burgundy gets confusing. A quirk of history combined with French inheritance laws means that more than one wine-maker may have access to the same vineyard. With an average

The Roots of Burgundy

At one time, the Grand Duchy of Burgundy covered much of eastern France, and was considered the center of power, knowledge, and wealth. It was monks, however, who planted the first vineyards in Burgundy.

After the French Revolution, the monasteries were disbanded, and while some aristocrats managed to hold on to vineyard land, much more was parceled off to peasants. These vineyards were divided and merged over generations of marriage and inheritance law, until the point that growers today might own several small plots of vines in many different villages; the grapes from each plot made and bottled into separate wines. To use the 125 acre Grand Cru vineyard Clos de Vougeot as an example, it had one owner before the Revolution, and today it has over 80!

vineyard holding of about 15 acres (6 ha)—only enough to produce about 2,600 cases of wine—much of the output from these small plots is sold off to larger wineries or *négociants*—individuals or companies who buy grapes, juice, and/or wine and bottle it under their own name. Over three quarters of Burgundian wine is sold through négociants. Some of the top, or more reputable, négociants you will see in wine shops and restaurant wine lists include Joseph Drouhin, Bouchard Père et Fils, Louis Jadot, Jaffelin, and Louis Latour.

And Where's Where?

Burgundy isn't one contiguous region—Chablis is separated from the rest of Burgundy by about 60 miles (100 km), as is Beaujolais to the south. Burgundy is made up of five diverse districts: Chablis, Côte d'Or, Côte Chalonnaise, Mâconnais, and Beaujolais.

- **Chablis** is the most northerly district and is mainly known for Chardonnay. But these Chardonnays may be different than you are used to—nervy, flinty with quite high acidity. They become more likeable as they age.
- **Côte d'Or** is the spiritual center for Burgundian wine lovers. Here are the vineyards that produce arguably some of the best Pinot Noir and Chardonnay in the world. It is further broken into two subdistricts with the city of Beaune as roughly the dividing point:
  - **Côte de Nuits**, north of Beaune, is known for glorious Pinot Noir. Here you'll find classic communes such as Nuits-Saint-Georges, Vosne-Romanée and Gevrey-Chambertin, as well as the world famous Domaine de la Romanée-Conti—owner of perhaps the most expensive piece of vineyard property in the world.
  - **Côte de Beaune**, surrounding and south of Beaune, produces great red wines (for example, Pommard and Volnay) but is best known for exquisite Chardonnay. The communes of Meursault, Puligny-Montrachet, and Chassagne-Montrachet are where white wines hold court. Here you will find the most prestigious Chardonnay in the world—Le Montrachet.

    Santenay, just to the south and west of Côte de Beaune, produces bargains compared to the other, more famous, commune wines.
- **Côte Chalonnaise**, south of Côte d'Or, is an affordable alternative to its expensive neighbors. The communes of Rully, Mercurey, and Givry are worth looking for on wine store

shelves and are best known for their red wines. Montagny and Bouzeron are white wine appellations.

- **Mâconnais**, even farther south, is best known for affordable Chardonnays. It also produces three times more white wine than the whole of Burgundy, so there should be lots of it around. Here you will find the famous and elegant wines of the Pouilly-Fuissé appellation.
- **Beaujolais**, at the very south of Burgundy, produces more than half of the entire region's wine. This is where the Gamay grape rules.

An Undemanding Wine

While Burgundian Pinot Noir and Chardonnay expect so much of wine drinkers, the Gamay grape made into Beaujolais expects nothing. Instead it routinely gives us simple, fresh, fruity, unpretentious, and inexpensive wines—especially Beaujolais Nouveau. Yet Gamay is also capable of producing more serious and substantial wines. The ten village *crus*—including Juliénas, Moulin-à-Vent, Brouilly, Morgon, and Fleurie—produce richer, full-bodied red wines with a unique character and the potential to age.

Beaujolais-Villages or Cru Beaujolais is a good, safe bet on a restaurant wine list. Easy drinking, it goes well with most foods. With its trademark high acidity, low tannin, light body, and low alcohol, Beaujolais is the red wine that thinks it's a white wine.

Georges Duboeuf is one of the most reliable producers in Beaujolais.

Bargain Districts

White wine:
Mâconnais
Red wine:
Côte Chalonnaise,
Beaujolais-Villages

Beaujolais Nouveau

Technically a *primeur*—a wine that is released between the harvest and the following spring—Beaujolais Nouveau is released every year on the third Thursday of November. Following a quick harvest and even quicker fermentation and bottling, over 65 million bottles of the new wine (about half of the area's production) are rushed to almost every corner of the globe to coincide with specially-planned, and sometimes a bit unusual, Beaujolais Nouveau celebrations.

The Rhône

The Rhône River winds south from its source in the Swiss Alps before it opens out into the Mediterranean, south of Avignon. The last 250 miles (400 km) or so run through the Rhône wine region—one of the oldest in France.

The Rhône is France's second-largest AOC wine region; only Bordeaux is bigger. This is serious red wine country—almost 98% of wines produced here are either red or rosé. Here the international benchmark for Syrah was established.

Easy AOC

Compared to Bordeaux and Burgundy, the Rhône's AOC structure has three straightforward steps:

- At the base is the generic AOC Côtes du Rhône. This mainly applies to vineyards in the southern part of the region and covers about three quarters of the region's total output. These are good value-priced wines but they aren't meant for serious aging. Drink up!
- Next are Côtes du Rhône-Villages, a big step up in quality. There are 16 villages, and these may be the best value wines in France. If the actual name of the village appears on the label it is usually a better wine than the more generic Côtes du Rhône–Villages. Some of the better villages include Rasteau, Visan, Cairanne, and Valréas.
- At the top are the 13 crus—eight in the northern Rhône (Condrieu, for example), and five in the south (Châteauneuf-du-Pape, for example).

A "typical" Rhône wine may be difficult to describe because most Rhône wines are blends—even blends of red wine and white wine grapes. Neighboring wines often bear no resemblance to each other.

North vs. South

The Rhône is really two distinct regions: the North—with about 5% of the production and almost all the best wines—and the South with the rest of the production. (It doesn't get much simpler than that.)

The smaller Northern Rhône is really a narrow valley with steep granite slopes. The vines are planted on these slopes, almost defying gravity, using the reflected light of the river to help the grapes ripen.

Northern Rhône red wines can be quite dense, beefy wines in youth and many take years to come around. Even the white wines, while perfumed and fragrant, are often robust and full-bodied. Here are some useful things to know about the Northern Rhône:

- Syrah is the principal red wine grape.
- Viognier is the principal white wine grape. Roussanne and Marsanne are also grown but mainly for blending.
- The top appellations (crus) are Cornas, Hermitage and Côte-Rôtie. These wines can be pricey; however, Crozes-Hermitage

(another cru) offers good quality wines at a lower price, which are also more widely available

- The top producers include Paul Jaboulet-Aîné, M. Chapoutier, E. Guigal, and Auguste Clape.

The Southern Rhône, in contrast, is flat and exposed, and highly influenced by the Mediterranean. In a word, it's hot! Southern Rhône wines are lighter than those from the north. Côtes du Rhône or Côtes du Rhône-Villages wines are good entry-level wines for novices and safe bets on a wine list. The region also produces crisp and dry rosé wines that make excellent summer sippers. Here are some useful things to know about the Southern Rhône:

- A wider variety of grapes are planted here, including Syrah, Mourvèdre, Grenache and Cinsault for the red wines.
- The most notable white wine grape is Muscat, which is used to produce exotic sweet wines like Muscat Beaumes-de-Venise.
- There are five crus; the more notable are Gigondas, Châteauneuf-du-Pape, and Tavel (for rosé). Prices are generally lower in the south and the wines are also more widely available— especially AOC Côtes du Rhône.
- The most famous appellation is Châteauneuf-du-Pape, with the dual distinction of having the highest minimum alcohol strength of any French wine (12.5%) as well as being the first appellation to be regulated under the AOC system.
- The top producers include J. Vidal Fleury, Château Rayas, Delas Frères, and Perrin Brothers (who follow organic practices and are responsible for making Château de Beaucastel, Coudoulet de Beaucastel, and the very affordable La Vielle Ferme).

> **Key Rhône Grapes**
> Red: Syrah and Grenache
> White: Viognier, Marsanne, and Rousanne

> **Did You Know?**
> Châteauneuf-du-Pape is a wine but it was also the summer home for the popes in the fourteenth century when nearby Avignon, not Rome, was the center of the Catholic Church. Nowadays, it lends its name to a full-bodied red wine made from a blend of up to 13 different grapes. You will still find the papal coat of arms embossed on every bottle of this wine.

Champagne

Champagne is about 90 miles (145 km) northeast of Paris and is France's northernmost wine region. It is essentially known for one wine—champagne—the most famous sparkling wine in the world. Unlike any other wine, champagne has established itself as a brand name associated with quality, prestige, and celebration. And it has vigorously protected its brand: no other sparkling wine in the world can be called champagne.

Did You Know?

Before the seventeenth century, the wines made in the cold climate of Champagne rarely finished fermenting in the fall. Fermentation would start up again with the warmth of spring. Since the wines were already in bottles, the second fermentation would create gas and the bottles would explode. Since the other monks who made the wine weren't happy losing so much of it, Dom Pérignon started investigating a better (and safer) way to contain the bubbles in the wine. The English, who had actually "invented" sparkling wine some 25 years earlier, sold Dom thicker bottles and cork stoppers. The rest, as they say, is history.

The Blend's the Thing

Champagne is made from Chardonnay or Pinot Noir, or combination of the two with a little Pinot Meunier thrown in. Because its grapes are grown so far north, the region's wines are usually too light and acidic to sell on their own. But when made into champagne, they are magically transformed into an elegant wine with millions of tiny, persistent bubbles. The blend of grapes determines the type of champagne:

- *Blanc de Blancs* is made from Chardonnay.
- *Blanc de Noirs* is made from from Pinot Noir and Pinot Meunier.
- *Rosé Champagne* could have a *little* Pinot Noir wine added to the original *cuvée*, or blend.

Key Classifications

Champagne is essentially one appellation. But like all French wine regions, there as some vineyards, or crus, that are considered better than others, and these are ranked. Since much of the wines are blends of grapes from different sites, and even of different years, little of this information ends up on the label. Mainly it is used to establish the prices the growers are paid for the grapes.

Villages that obtain the highest grape prices—considered to be the best vineyards—are called grand cru and the next level down are premier cru. There are 17 grand crus and 38 premiers crus. One of the most sought after champagnes—Krug's Clos du Mesnil—is a single-vineyard, premier cru.

From a consumer's point of view, the distinction between *vintage* and *non-vintage* champagnes is more relevant. Vintage champagne is made only in years that are "declared" to be exceptional, and most producers age these wines for a much longer period than their other non-vintage wines.

All champagne corks must have the word champagne stamped on them, and only vintage champagnes can have the year stamped on them. Generally, champagne should be consumed when you buy it. Vintage champagne can keep, but why wait?

What's Dry?

Champagne can be made dry (Extra Brut, Brut, Extra Dry), sweet (Sec or Demi-Sec), or extra sweet (Doux). These words refer to the dosage and one of them should appear somewhere on the label.

Hitting the Marques

Large champagne houses or *Marques* produce champagne in the regional towns of Epernay and Reims. There are about 100 Marques and only a handful of *grandes Marques*. The most famous of the grandes Marques is Möet & Chandon, which makes the renowned *préstige cuvée* called Dom Pérignon.

A bottle of top *préstige cuvée* will easily break the $150 mark, and some sell for two or three times that amount. However there are many excellent non-vintage, and even vintage, champagnes selling for much less.

The top Marques include: Moët & Chandon, Mumm, Pol Roger, Perrier-Jouët, Piper-Heidseck, Bollinger, Taittinger, and Veuve Clicquot. Each Marques has a house style based on the grapes in the blend. For example, Pol Roger and Perrier-Jouët are light-bodied and elegant while Bollinger and Veuve Clicquot are full bodied and toasty. Try some of these and see which style you prefer.

The Rest of France

We're not finished with France yet. There's more to French wines than just Bordeaux, Burgundy, the Rhône, and Champagne. Here's what to look for from some of it's other wine regions.

Alsace

Alsace is a picturesque region—about 105 miles (170 km) long—in the extreme northeast of France, along its border with Germany. A mixture of French and German traditions flourish in this region and, in fact, mainly Germanic grape varieties are grown. The wines, however, are more French than German—well-suited for food, slightly higher in alcohol, and generally drier than their German counterparts.

While Riesling is the most-planted grape in the region, and perhaps the true Alsace wine, the exotic Gewürztraminer is the "poster-grape" of Alsace. Pinot Blanc is the second most-planted

The Noble Grapes of Alsace

Riesling, Gewürztraminer, Pinot Gris, and Muscat—only these grape varieties receive the Grand Cru designation.

grape, and although it isn't one of the grapes designated as *noble*, it nevertheless produces excellent wine. Gewürztraminer and Pinot Blanc are good starter grapes for exploring the region for the first time. There is renewed interest in Pinot Gris—the grape formerly known as Tokay d'Alsace—as a full-bodied white wine representative of the region. Few Alsace wines need aging but the better, and sweeter wines can last for decades.

Alsace wines are mostly white. The grape variety is indicated on the label and AOC wines must be bottled in a tall, narrow flûte bottle.

Did You Know?

Edelzwicker literally means "noble mixture" in German and is used to describe a blended white wine of two or more noble grape varieties. Winemakers invent fantasy names (e.g., Gentil) for these wines. Quality varies but some versions are outstanding.

Classy Wines

The Alsace classification system is straightforward:

* *Grand cru* refers to top-rated vineyard sites—50 at last count—but not necessarily the top wines. (Some great Alsace wines come from non-rated vineyards.)
* *Vendage Tardive* indicates a late harvest wine made from noble, usually botrytis-affected, grapes. These are usually sweet but some may be dry.
* *Sélection de Grains Nobles* indicates wines made from selective pickings of botrytis-affected grapes. There's little room for doubt here; these are *very* sweet.

Growers sometimes add other terms like *réserve* or *cuvée exceptionelle* to the label but these don't have any legal standing. These terms usually indicate the winemaker is much more pleased with this wine than in previous vintages.

What to Look For

While over 2,000 growers bottle and sell their own wine, this represents slightly less than 20% of the total regional output of wine. About 175 companies bottle the rest. Some of the more reliable and readily available merchants or shippers include: Hugel et Fils, Domaine Weinbach, F.E. Trimbach, Léon Beyer, Domaine Marcel Deiss, and Domaine Zind-Humbrecht.

The Loire

The Loire is France's longest river and on its banks are some of the most diverse and unique wine areas in all of France. Its cool maritime climate suggests this is white wine country, however it is also known for its light, food-friendly red wines and inexpensive sparkling wines.

The Loire—the third largest wine producing region in France—is a very long (635 mile/1020km) and diverse region. The influence of the Atlantic decreases as you follow the Loire River inland; as result, the grapes that are grown along this region, and the wine styles that have developed, are quite different. The region as a whole is best characterized as four sub-regions:

- *Pays Nantais,* where the River Loire opens to the Atlantic Ocean, is known for crisp, dry white wines made from the Muscadet grape.
- *Anjou-Saumur* is best known for its sparkling wine (in Saumur), and some of the world's best sweet wines made from the Chenin Blanc grape (in Anjou).
- *Touraine* is also known for Chenin Blanc (Vouvray), though a drier version, and really good Cabernet Franc (Chinon).
- The *Upper Loire*, or *Center* as it is sometimes called, includes the famous appellations of Sancerre and Pouilly Fumé. Sauvignon Blanc is the key grape. This is where some of the best goat's cheese is made (Chavignol), which interestingly is a perfect match for Sauvignon Blanc.

The Loire's white wines are crisp and dry and great with food. The reds are light yet elegant and are also food-friendly. Better still they're all afford-able so they make good choices on a wine list.

Chenin Blanc can also be used to make luscious sweet (*moelleux*) wines that can be amazingly long-lived. The best sweet wines come from Anjou-Saumur, and two appellations in particular: Quarts-de-Chaume and Bonnezeaux (pronounced *bonzo*).

Sur Lie

Muscadet wines may have the words "Sur Lie" appended to their name. This tells you the wine was aged on the lees (spent yeast cells) and bottled straight from the tank. The result is a fresh, crisp and lively wine with a slight spritz. A great wine to have with steamed mussels.

Key Grapes

White: Sauvignon Blanc, Chenin Blanc, and Muscadet

Red: Cabernet Franc, Pinot Noir

No Class?

The Loire's wines are classy, and their classification system simple. Just look for the name of the sub-region or appellation (e.g., Sancerre) on the label. At last count there were almost 90 AOCs in total, the most of any wine region in France.

What to look for

In such a large and diverse region, there are many, many producers we could name. Here are a few of our favorites and the AOC they are associated with: Henri Bourgeois (Sancerre), Didier Dagueneau (Pouilly-Fumé), Charles Joguet (Chinon), and Domaine de Vieux Chai (Muscadet de Sèvre-et-Maine).

Languedoc-Roussillon

This is the region—often called the Midi—in the south of France that everyone is talking about. Winemakers here have successfully shed years of tradition and inefficiency to produce exciting wines from both traditional and non-traditional grapes. Without the burden of archaic appellation laws, the Old World and the New World seem intent on coming together in the Midi to produce food-friendly, but more importantly, consumer-friendly wines.

Languedoc-Roussillon is the biggest wine region in the world—just over twice as large as Bordeaux. While there are many AOC wines from this region, you are more than likely to see "vin de pays" on the label, and more often than not the grape variety. There are about 100 vin de pays and the largest, Vin de Pays d'Oc, has the better producers. Some of these wines are great and some are less so—but they are all good value.

Over 90% of the wine made here is red, based on traditional Rhône-style grapes such as Syrah, Grenache, Cinsault, and Mourvèdre, while Carignan is the traditional local choice. Viognier is used for white wine. Like the Rhône, many of the wines are blends. Increasingly, however, the fashionable Cabernet Sauvignon, Merlot and Chardonnay are being used.

Appellations to Buy:
St-Chinian
Corbières
La Clape
Pic St-Loup
Fitou

Putting a Wrap on France

There are few other regions you might come across in a local bistro-style restaurant or specialty wine shops.

Jura and **Savoie** are two small regions in the east of France bordering Switzerland. Very little gets exported but be on the look out for the sherry-like curiosity from Jura called Vin Jaune.

Provence is probably best known for its rosé wines, and the savory AOC Bandol wine made from the Mourvèdre grape.

The Southwest is often tacked on to Bordeaux, its northern neighbor. This huge area, covering almost all of western France, includes some of the quirkiest wines in the country—full-bodied, tannic monster reds from Cahors and Madiran, Bordeaux-esque beauties from Bergerac and Buzet, and superb sweet wines from Jurançon. It's not too late to be the first on your street to try wines from these regions.

Italy

Many people, when they think of Italian wine, think of Chianti and Soave, and maybe even Valpolicella. Trust us; there is much, much more to Italy. Italy is usually in a dead heat with France for the title of leading wine producer worldwide. This relatively small country produces an enormous quantity and variety of wines in almost every corner of the country. Vines grow everywhere and wine is an entrenched part of everyday life, along with bread and olive oil.

Italy's white wines tend to be bone-dry, fresh, and neutral while the reds are mouth-watering and juicy. The red wines cry out for food while the whites make a perfect apéritif on a hot summer day. Italy also makes big, bold, and age-worthy red wines that are world class in every way.

Wine Classification

Like France, Italy controls its wine production; however the current laws are more recent (although the rules governing Chianti are almost 200 years old). Over the past 30 years or so, the Italian wine industry has been in a state of flux, and is only now emerging as a country that consumers can start to trust for quality and consistency.

The first three levels in Italy's classification system are similar to the French AOC system. Perhaps not wanting to be outdone, Italy has class step higher—*Denominazione di Origine Controllata e Garantita (DOCG)*. *Vino da tavola* (table wine) and IGT (regional wine) represent about 85% of all Italian wine production, compared to less than 50% in France. There are just over 310 DOC (quality wine) regions, and 33 wines in the DOCG category. In 1980, the first wine promoted to DOCG was Vino Nobile di Montepulciano in Tuscany.

1. Piedmont
2. Tuscany
3. Veneto
4. Trentino Alto-Adige
5. Fruili-Venezia Giula
6. Lombardy
7. Emilia-Romagna
8. Umbria
9. Marches
10. Abruzzo
11. Apulia
12. Sicily
13. Sardinia

But it isn't all that straightforward—the best wines aren't necessarily all in the DOC or DOCG categories. Some high-end producers, unhappy with the rigid restrictions placed on them by the Consorzio, or the different ways the rules and regulations can be interpreted, have chosen to label their wines "Vino da Tavola" out of protest. These versions, which are some of best wines in Italy, can be expensive and certainly much higher quality than the classification suggests.

The Italian classification system is not as good an indication of quality as perhaps price is (that is, not all Chianti Classico DOCG is top quality). Better still is to know some good producers. Particularly those who passionately embrace tradition while recognizing the beneficial technological advances in winemaking.

Regional Style

Most of the grapes grown in Italy don't grow anywhere else in the world. While these grapes can be used to make high-quality wine—and many are—they just aren't familiar to most of us. Over 2,000 grape varieties are grown in Italy, in hundreds of different locations within the 20 designated wine regions. Even under the DOC system over 900 varieties are approved for production, so it is much more useful to learn about the notable regional styles than grape names.

So how do you navigate through the wine regions of Italy? In a Ferrari would be nice, but here's another way.

Piedmont

Piedmont, which means "at the foot of the mountains," is tucked into the far northwest of Italy. One of Italy's most important and influential wine regions, Piedmont produces one of the most renowned red wines in Italy, Barolo. It also produces one of the most fun, Asti.

Piedmont is currently home to nine DOCGs and 45 DOCs, the most in Italy. Some of the *denominazione* are named for places (e.g.,

Barolo or Asti) while others are grape names (e.g., Barbera or Dolcetto). In the case of grape names, a town or commune name is usually affixed to the name of the grape, as in Barbera d'Alba—meaning Barbera from Alba. The denominazione appears on the label.

> ## Key Piedmont Grapes
> Red: Nebbiolo, Barbera, and Dolcetto
> White: Moscato, Arneis, and Cortese

Long Live the King

Barolo—"The Wine of Kings, and King of Wines"—and the less famous Barbaresco, are not grapes but rather DOCG wines. They are named for villages around which the tannic Nebbiolo grapes that make up these wines are grown. Nowhere else in the world does this grape produce such impressive, long-lived, wines.

How do Barolo and Barbaresco compare?

- **Barolo** may not look like it from its light color but it's a tannic monster of a wine—lots of acidity with complex and wild aromas of cherries, chocolate, violets, and even truffles (the ones that grow in the ground).
- **Barbaresco** is a similar style, but regulations require less aging time in the barrel so the wines are usually less full-bodied. In most vintages you can usually drink Barbaresco earlier than Barolo.

Good, traditionally-made versions of either wine can be pricey and don't even think of drinking them until they are 10 years old. Some modern-style producers are making wines for earlier drinking. And a few producers release single-vineyard *crus*. Reliable producers of Barolo include: Ascheri, Elio Altare, Luciano Sandrone, Elvio Cogno, Aldo Conterno, and Giacomo Conterno. For Barbaresco: Gaja, Bruno Giacosa, and, Marchese di Gressy.

Nebbiolo (which actually means "little fog") is sometimes called Spanna. More approachable and less expensive Nebbiolo wines come from Langhe, and Alba, where the name of the village is affixed to the grape name, as well as Roero, Ghemme, and Gattinara, where you will see just the DOCG name on the label.

Sweet-tarts

As you get used to drinking Italian wine, you will notice that the hallmark red wine taste is a combination of sweet and tart in the same mouthful. This is the case for two other important grapes in Piedmont, Barbera and Dolcetto.

- **Barbera** has nice acidity, is lighter-bodied, and generally low in tannin—mouth-watering and easy drinking at the same time.
- **Dolcetto**, which means "the little sweet one," is even juicier and fruitier than Barbera.

Barbera and Dolcetto that have spent some time in barrel or come from special vineyards (this should be indicated on the label) can age, but most versions should be consumed young and with food. They are often less than half the price of Barolo or Barbaresco and definitely wines to seek out on a wine list. The grape name often appears on the label or might be added to a place (for example Barbera d'Alba or Dolcetto d'Alba). Good producers include: Ascheri, Deltetto, Elvio Cogno, Luciano Sandrone, Gaja, Aldo Conterno, and Prunotto.

Some wines just gotta have fun

Although Piedmont is famous for its red wine, don't overlook the sparkling wines, made using the tank method, from the Muscat grape. This is Asti country. Noticeably sweet, this wine has wonderful aromatic qualities. In fact, it actually smells and tastes like grapes. Asti is inexpensive—not bad for a wine that lights up in your mouth.

Asti is usually sweet, and bubbly (*spumante* is the Italian word for sparkling). For fewer bubbles, try Moscato d'Asti. Refreshing and low in alcohol (usually around 5%), it's a great wine to have if you are opening more than one bottle.

Piedmont does have some serious white wines. If you check around you might find some *Gavi*, made from the Cortese grape. Good versions are usually dry, full-bodied with nice citrus, green apple, and honey aromas. We also quite like Arneis, particularly versions from the Roero denominazione.

Herbalicious
Piedmont is also famous for the aromatized wine called Vermouth

The Rest of the Northwest

Lombardy is an underrated region, just east of Piedmont, that also makes excellent red wines from the Nebbiolo grape. Lighter-bodied and less expensive than Barolo and Barbaresco, these wines are nevertheless gaining an international reputation. The best wines come from the Valtellina Superiore DOCG: look for sub-districts Sassella, Grumello, Inferno, and Valgella on the label. The region also has a reputation for excellent sparkling wines, made in the classic méthode traditionelle style, called Franciacorta DOCG.

The wines of **Val D'Aosta** and **Liguria** are rarely seen as much of them are consumed locally.

Veneto

Veneto may lack the flair of Tuscany and Piedmont, but it too is an important wine region. Tucked into the Italy's northeast, around Romeo and Juliet's hometown of Verona, Veneto produces the most recognized white wine in Italy and also one of the more distinguished red wines. It's a safe bet that if Chianti wasn't the first Italian wine you drank, Soave or Valpolicella probably were, or still are.

Veneto is the third largest region in Italy—after Apulia and Sicily—in terms of wine production but the largest in terms of DOC output. Despite the output, it has only three DOCG wines and 21 DOCs.

> **Key Grapes**
> White: Garganega, Trebbiano, and Prosecco
> Red: Corvina, Rondinella, and Molinara

Suave Soave

Soave is a bone-dry white wine that generally doesn't offend, and some versions can be quite remarkable. Soave (named after a town in the region) is made from the Garganega grape with some undistinguished Trebbiano thrown into the blend. Not allowed in the past, Chardonnay and Pinot Bianco (Pinot Blanc) are now authorized for use in the blend.

> **Did You Know?**
> Veneto's first DOCG wine was Recioto di Soave—a sweet dessert wine made from semi-dried grapes.

At its best, Soave has lovely aromas of nuts and honey, and a long lemony finish. Wines from the *Classico* zone—the older "heart" of the region—are usually even richer. Producers like Anselmi, Balestri Valda, and Pieropan all make good Soave, while Masi offers excellent value, and lots of wine.

Bubbles Anyone?

Veneto also has some excellent but underrated dry sparkling wines, made from the Prosecco grape. Prosecco is a DOC wine, and the name of the grape on the label. Better versions will also have the villages of Conegliano and Valdobbiadene indicated prominently. Prosecco, made either in a *frizzante* (slightly bubbly) or *spumante* (fully sparkling) style, is an excellent aperitif and a good match for appetizers. Ask for one next time you are in the mood for something bubbly. Masottina is an excellent producer.

Valpolicella

The principal red wine grapes of the Veneto region—Corvina, Rondinella and Molinara—aren't exactly household names, but the wines they are blended together to make are. You'll probably recognize them as Valpolicella and Amarone.

- **Valpolicella** DOC is a light, fruity (cherry), entirely gluggable wine that is best when young. These are moderately priced wines and are good picks on any wine list. There is also a Valpolicella Classico DOC, as well as Ripasso versions.

- **Amarone della Valpolicella** DOC (or Amarone for short) is made from fully fermented semi-dried (*recioto* in Italian) grapes. This produces a rich, dry, intense wine, bursting with chocolate and dried fruit (plum) aromas, and a long bitter—(*amaro* means "bitter")—almond finish. Since Amarone is fermented fully dry (though it definitely smells sweet) it has a fairly high alcohol (14%–15%) content. You can drink them early, but better versions are great with five to 10 years aging.

- **Recioto della Valpolicella** DOC is made like Amarone (grapes are semi-dried) but the wine is not fully fermented to dryness. The wine, therefore, is slightly sweet and rich, but still with that classic bitter finish.

Ripasso

If you see this on a bottle of Valpolicella, it means the wine has been steeped in vats containing the lees of the previous year's Recioto. The result is a richer, more full-bodied wine—a mini-Amarone.

Buying (good) Valpolicella and Amarone rarely ends in disappointment but it is safer to stick to the top producers: Allegrini, Degani, Nicolis, Tedeschi, Tommasi, Quintarelli, and Zonin. Some of these producers also make single-vineyard wines as well as IGT wines. Masi produces a full range of good-quality Veneto wines, and at all price ranges.

You can also find good Cabernet Sauvignon and Merlot from the eastern part of the region (Piave DOC). The grape variety often appears on the label.

The Rest of the Northeast

Friuli-Venezia Giula (often just called Friuli for short), just east of Veneto, has a strong reputation for high-quality, dry white wines made from local and international grape varieties. In addition to the DOC information, the grape variety usually also appears on the label. If you see "colli" on the label (Colli Orientali for example) that means hill—wines with a little more character come from these areas.

The Tocai Friulano grape is used to make nutty, full-bodied white wines, while Ribolla and Verduzzo are even more flavorful and aromatic. You will also see Pinot Bianco, Chardonnay, Sauvignon Blanc, and Müller-Thurgau. The red wines are generally lighter in body and flavor. Merlot is the leading grape in terms of production but the local red grape Refosco, makes more interesting wines.

Friuli's most famous wine is a sweet wine called Picolit, made from late-harvested or air-dried grapes.

Trentino-Alto Adige is Italy's most northern wine-growing region—on the other side of the Alps from Austria. Due to the cooler climate, this mountainous region is ideal for white wines. In fact, along with Friuli, Alto Adige produces some of Italy's best white wines.

The white wines are generally fresh, light, crisp, and dry. They are excellent with food or just on their own. Usually the label indicates the grape variety. These include Pinot Bianco, Pinot Grigio, Riesling, Gewürztraminer (said to have originated in this region near its namesake town Termeno—Tramin in German), Chardonnay, Sauvignon Blanc, and Müller-Thurgau. The region also makes excellent sparkling wine from the area near the city of Trento.

Trentino makes excellent red wines from indigenous varieties: Teroldego, Schiava, and Vernatsch. So good are these wines that they rarely make it beyond local consumption.

Emilia-Romagna is perhaps better known in gastronomic terms for its balsamic vinegar, Prosciutto de Parma, and of course Parmigiano-Reggiano cheese than for its wine. The best-known grape variety here is Lambrusco, which makes light-bodied, thirst-quenching red wines that are low in alcohol and sometimes even slightly fizzy (frizzante). For whites, Albana sports lovely nutty aromas and vibrant acidity making it a perfect match for the local cheeses and handmade *salume*. The region is gaining a reputation for growing the Sangiovese grape, and top producers can make wines that rival those of Tuscany to its south.

Tuscany

Probably no region in Italy conjures up more romantic images than Tuscany. Its rolling hills and historic towns—Florence, Siena, Montalcino, and San Gimignano—have inspired countless artists, writers, and filmmakers. Here, too, winemaking has been elevated to an art form.

Tuscany, in central Italy, has the largest area under vines, and is home to six DOCGs, 34 DOCs, and where you will find the so-called *Super-Tuscans*. Its most famous red wine is Chianti—a DOCG, as is its oldest zone, Chianti Classico. But Tuscany also produces Brunello di Montalcino—one of the most expensive DOCG wines in Italy—as well as Vino Nobile di Montelpulciano DOCG. Vernaccia di San Gimignano is a white wine DOCG, and is worth checking out.

Chianti's Not Some Fiasco

You might think of Chianti as pizza wine (some of you may also remember it as the wine that came in the funny straw-wrapped bottle—called a *fiasco*). In the right hands, though, it can be a concentrated and stately wine that in good vintages can last for decades.

Did You Know?

The Chianti blend was created over 135 years ago by Italy's second Prime Minister, Baron Ricasoli.

Traditionally, Chianti is a blend and the principal red wine grape in it is Sangiovese. For political reasons, other grape varieties—including even white wine grapes—were allowed in the Chianti blend, but in practice this isn't done any longer. Now you can find Chianti made with 100% Sangiovese.

Like all Italian red wines, Chiantis have that hallmark sweet-tart taste. They are dry, with nice acidity and aromas of cherries, plums, herbs, and even a hint of tobacco or leather. They can be light, medium, or even full-bodied with a good amount of tannin and a touch of bitterness on the finish.

Chianti is vast region within Tuscany, and is actually made up of eight different zones. The climate and soils within the region are quite varied and as a result the zones can produce wines of different quality and style. Here's a look at what to expect:

- **Chianti Classico DOCG** is the center and oldest part of the Chianti region. Some of the best Chianti comes from here and the black rooster emblem—the Gallo Nero—on the neck easily identifies the bottles. Producers age these wines for a minimum of two years before release; three if they are designated *riservas*. At their best, Chianti Classico are elegant and earthy wines, with bright red berry fruit flavors, and the characteristic Chianti acidity.
- **Chianti DOCG**, which surrounds Classico, is made up of the remaining seven subzones. The name of the subzone is usually affixed to the name Chianti (e.g., Chianti Rufina). These wines have to be aged for just over two year before release, but some producers wait longer.

- Rufina, Colli Fiorentini, and Colli Senesi produce the next highest-rated Chianti, somewhat elegant, some with the potential for aging.
- The other four—Colli Aretini, Colline Pisane and Montalbano, and Montespertoli—produce lighter, less distinguished wines meant for early drinking.

In better vintages, producers may hold some Chianti in barrel longer and offer it as a *riserva*. In lesser years they will only produce a *normale*. Recently Tuscany enjoyed a long string of excellent vintages for its red wines starting in 1997 and ending with the 2001 vintage.

There are many excellent producers of Chianti. Our favorites include: Antinori, Baggiolino, Carpineto, Fattoria di Felsina, Fontodi, Frescobaldi, Poggio Amorelli, and Sant' Appiano.

Vin Santo

Vin Santo is traditional Tuscan dessert wine made from air-dried grapes. The sweet juice ferments slowly and matured for as many as five to six years—bellisimo!

Big Bruisers

The Sangiovese grape is also used in three other important wines in other parts of Tuscany:

- **Brunello di Montalcino** DOCG, from grapes grown around the hilltop town of Montalcino, is an intense, concentrated wine that needs decades before it is at its best. Some of the better versions are very expensive. Look for Altesino, Biondi-Santi, Castelgiocondo, Il Poggione, La Fornace, or La Lecciaia.

  Most Brunello producers also make Rosso di Montalcino DOC. Less expensive than Brunello; these are lighter versions of their big brothers and can be consumed earlier.
- **Vino Nobile di Montepulciano** DOCG fits somewhere in between Brunello and Chianti. In good years it can be almost as powerful as Brunello, yet elegant, like Chianti. Look for Avignonesi or Carpineto.

Super-Tuscans

Many Tuscan producers make prestige wines by blending the local Sangiovese grape with non-traditional grapes, like Cabernet Sauvignon and Merlot, or make wines from these international varieties alone. Because these grapes are not allowed under the current rules, or the wines are produced outside the Chianti zone, they don't qualify as DOC or DOCG. In protest, producers simply labelled their wines Vino da Tavola or IGT. The rules are changing and one

The Super-Tuscans

Tignanello, Sassicaia, Solaia, La Gioia, and Ornellaia

more famous Super-Tuscan wine (Sassicaia) has now been awarded its own DOC status—Bolgheri Sassicaia.

Super-Tuscans can command price tags well over $100. They usually bear a proprietary name (Tignanello for example), and the style of these world-class wines varies depending on the grapes in the blend (Tignanello, for example, is a Cabernet-Sangiovese blend) and the producer. Many are New World in style due to the extended aging in new oak barrels.

What Else Is in the Middle?

Umbria is best known for the widely exported, dry white wine called Orvieto. Made from the Trebbiano grape, these can be somewhat neutral wines. Stick with the better producers or the Classico versions.

Red wines to watch for include the Chianti-like Torgiano DOC—better known as Rubesco (made only by Umbrian producer Lungarotti)—or the rich and intense Sagrantino di Montefalco DOCG.

Marches is most famous for its grape Verdicchio, or, rather, the green amphora-shaped bottle the wine is sold in. Don't think this is just pretty packaging—the dry, white wine inside is quite good.

You'll also find excellent red wines in the Marches region, particularly from the Rosso Piceno DOC, made from a blend of Sangiovese and Montepulciano grapes.

Lazio also known as Latium, is where Rome is located. It is best known for a white wine called Frascati DOC, a wine made from Malvasia and Trebbiano. Some versions have character (the ones with more Malvasia) but many are simple.

Abruzzo's claim to fame is the inexpensive Montepulciano d'Abruzzo. This low tannin, easy-drinking red wine is a favorite of banquet halls everywhere. The grape has nothing to do with the town of the same name, however, which is in Tuscany.

Molise wines are rarely exported, and for many years it didn't even have any DOC wines. If you can find them, look for the beefy red wines from Biferno DOC.

The South

This is currently where the action is in Italy. Some of the more exciting Italian red wines are being produced in the South, and stepped-up investment in the wineries means the quality is improving, too. The climate is reliable, so vintages aren't really an issue here. Expect to get consistently good-value wines with big and unrestrained flavor.

Puglia (Apulia)

When you look at a map of Italy, Puglia is the "heel" of Italy's "boot." Wine has been produced here for over 4,000 years and more wine is produced here than anywhere else in Italy. But it isn't just about quantity: there are some great quality wines here too, although less than 10% of Puglia's wines fall into the DOC category. When we checked last, there were no DOCG wines. The better wines come from the Salento Peninsula: Salice Salentino, Copertino, and Squinzano.

Get acquainted with wines made from the grape called Negroamaro, meaning "bitter black". It can make deep, rich and flavorful wines that can take five or so years to come around. Better still, these wines are a real bargain.

Nero d'Avola, Primitivo—now proven to be the same grape as Zinfandel—as well as international grape varieties like Chardonnay are also grown in this region.

Sicily

At one time the island of Sicily was best known for the fortified wine known as Marsala. It was also the source of bulk wine destined for other regions in Italy, and even France. Things have changed dramatically in recent years and Sicily is gaining an international reputation for some very exciting table wines (although about 80% of Sicily's output is still bottled off the island or distilled).

Sicily is hot, so the better wines come from the higher elevations or closer to the coast. Grape varieties are being planted in the areas where growers feel they should do well, from a quality and not a quantity perspective. There are high hopes for the Nero d'Avola grape to do well, making excellent, full-bodied, intense red wines. International grape varieties are also gaining a reputation in Sicily, and particularly look for great wines from the Syrah grape for red

> ## Did You Know?
> Sicily has more land under vine than any other region in Italy, and is second only to Puglia in terms of volume. By comparison, Sicily produces nearly the same amount of wine as all of Australia.

wines, and possibly Chardonnay for the whites (from cooler areas). On an island off the Sicilian coast—Pantelleria—you will find lovely fortified dessert wines made from the Moscato (Muscat) grape.

Producers to look for include Planeta, Zonin, Biondi, Duca di Salaparuta, Fondo Antico, and Tasca d'Almerita.

Campania, Basilicata, and Calabria

We seldom see wines from these three regions. Campania has a slight lead on the others with the soft and delicate dry white wine called Greco di Tufo DOC and the more aromatic, hazelnutty Fiano di Avellino DOC. The plummy red wine called Taurasi DOC also makes it to our shores.

Sardinia

This island isn't really in the south, but west of Rome in the Mediterranean, Sardinia is gaining a reputation for excellent red wines made from the Cannonau grape—the Italian name for the Grenache grape. DOC versions have been aged in oak and the name of the grape appears on the label.

Germany

Compared to France and Italy, or many other countries for that matter, Germany is rarely considered to be a winemaking power-house or even a wine-drinking culture. It ranks a respectable eighth in terms of wine production and only sixteenth when it comes to per capita wine consumption (the average German drinks about eight times more beer than wine.) So why does Germany merit so much coverage in our book?

In our opinion it is because Germany produces some of the best white wines in the world, and in particular is the world standard for one of the Top Seven grapes, Riesling. German winemakers achieve this in conditions so extreme—many of the vineyards lie as far north as grapes will ripen and on terrain almost as inhospitable—that you wonder how this is possible. For some time German wine has been unfashionable (sweet wasn't "in") and, judging by the labels, even out of step from the rest of the world; nevertheless, this is changing and excellent wines are begging to be discovered.

It's Riesling

Believe it or not, there's only one grape to worry about—Riesling. Better still, even on the most gothic labels, the word Riesling will show up somewhere on the bottle.

Riesling represents about a quarter of total production. As a wine, it is low in alcohol (less than 10% for drier wines), has nice acidity, smells fruity (green apple, apricot, or peach) and sometimes even minerally or smoky when young. It can be made in a range of styles from dry to lusciously sweet. When it ages, Riesling acquires a highly prized quality—an aroma reminiscent of petrol.

The second most-planted grape is the early-ripening Müller-Thurgau, used for lower-priced blends like Liebfraumilch. Red wine grapes make up about 20% of production, led by Spätburgunder (meaning "late" Burgundy, a.k.a. Pinot Noir).

Germany is also known for a value-priced sparkling wine called *Sekt*.

It's Not Only Sweet

The terms *trocken* (dry) or *halbtrocken* (off-dry) indicate the total amount of residual sugar in the finished wine at time of bottling. About half of German wines will be either trocken or halbtrocken and the trend is to use these words on the label so it's easier to pick them out. If you don't see either on the label, assume the wine is going to be sweet.

But the real secret to quality German wines is their hallmark acidity. Even a halbtrocken wine seems drier when balanced with acidity. And as foodies know, this makes German wines probably the most food-friendly of all white wines, or at least the most versatile.

It's All on the Label

German wine laws may appear to be the most complex in the world—and the confusing labelling doesn't help either—but once you learn the basics, they are probably the most consumer-friendly. Everything you need to know is on the label.

German wines are classified according to the sugar content—or *must* weight—of the grapes at harvest (called the *Prädikat*), not after they are made into wine, as is the case in most other countries. In any given year, in theory, any of Germany's 2600 or so vineyard locations is capable of producing high quality wine, and many do. More than 90% of Germany's wine is in the quality category, *Qualitätswein*.

At the bottom of the scale are *Tafelwein* and *Landwein*. Next is *Qualitätswein bestimmter Anbaugebeite* or QbA for short, meaning "quality wine from a particular area or region." Natural ripeness levels are usually so low that these wines are routinely chaptalized (sugar is added during fermentation).

Qualitätswein mit Prädikat or QmP is where it gets interesting. QmP means, "quality wine with special attributes." In cooler vintages, not much QmP wine is made, as the grapes haven't ripened enough. In warmer years, production is higher. QmP wines are considered better wines as the grapes have to be fermented as harvested, and no sugar can be added.

QmP wines are further classified (we said it was complex) into six levels, but you'll more likely encounter only the first three:

- *Kabinett* wines are the lightest of the QmP wines with an often-perfect balance of sweetness and acidity. There aren't any limits on sugar levels or alcohol content in the finished wine so these wines can be dry or off dry, but never sweet. The best Kabinett wines come from the Mosel or Nahe regions.
- *Spatlese* means "late harvest." The grapes are more mature at harvest than Kabinett grapes, and so the wines are fuller. Spatlese wines are generally made in a sweeter style, and the best dry versions come from the Pfalz and Baden regions.
- *Auslese* means, "selected harvest." These wines are made from grapes that have started to shrivel up or have been botrytized. These are rarely made dry and are the more expensive of the three levels.

If you want even sweeter wines, then look for *Beerenauslese*, *Eiswein* (icewine), or *Trockenbeerenauslese* on the label. Only the most mature grapes have been fermented for these wines and they will be sweet, and expensive.

German wines are bottled in the traditional tall, narrow flûtes, with one exception: the wines that come from the Franken region.

Focus on Four

Germany is a big country with some of the most northerly vineyards in Europe. Grapes ripen only in a few choice areas—mainly along a few large rivers like the Rhein, Mosel, and Main.

Since the re-unification of Germany, there are 13 regions (called *Anbaugebeit*). You need to know just four:

- The *Pfalz* is the biggest region in terms of production and has some of the most interesting and exciting wines. Some of the most famous estates include Bürklin-Wolf, von Buhl, and Müller-Catoir.
- The *Mosel-Saar-Ruwer* is really three regions. The vines are grown on the steep slopes of the rivers of the same name. The region produces a lot of average wine but is also home to some of the most Germany's most famous vineyards (called *Einzellagan*.) Mosel wines are bottled in green bottles, as opposed to the more commonly seen brown bottles.
- The *Nahe*, while eclipsed by the Pfalz and Mosel-Saar-Ruwer in terms of production, makes classic Riesling of distinction and elegance.
- *Baden*, the most southerly wine region, is the region on the rise. There is a lot of modernization taking place in the wineries; expect to see more of these wines in the future.

The other regions are Ahr (known for red wines despite being Germany's northernmost wine region), Franken (known for dry white wines made from the Silvaner grape), Rheinhessen (known for blends), Württemberg (known for red wines), Hessische Bergstrasse, Mittelrhein, Saale-Unstrut, and Sachsen.

Using Your Words

Some German wine labels are intricately designed and the type is often hard to read (although we find that is changing). On the other hand, German wine labels can be extremely consumer-friendly—everything you need to know about the wine is provided on the label.

Here's what you get:

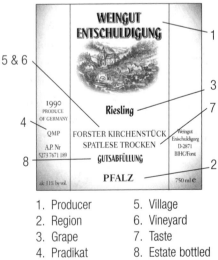

1. Producer
2. Region
3. Grape
4. Pradikat
5. Village
6. Vineyard
7. Taste
8. Estate bottled

- The name of region will always appear on the label, either at the bottom or top of the label, or prominently written in the middle if it's a QbA wine.
- If it is a QmP wine, immediately after or below the vintage you'll see the name of the district (*Bereiche*) or village (*Gemeind*), or group of vineyards (*Grosslage*), followed by the name of the vineyard (*Einzellage*). The first word will have—"er" affixed to it meaning it is "from" that place. For example, *Forster Pechstein* indicates

the grapes are from the vineyard called Pechstein, near the village of Forst.

- Elsewhere on the label you'll find the producer's name, the grape variety, the Prädikat if it's a QmP wine, and perhaps the sweetness level in the finished wine. Remember if it doesn't say trocken or halbtrocken, assume it is sweet.

Buying Tips

Stay with the regions we've mentioned, and the style of wine you like, and you won't go far wrong.

Look for wines with QmP on the label; they are only slightly more expensive but you'll have a good idea of what you are getting.

Buy from trusted producers: Selbach-Oster, J.J. Prüm, Dr. Bürklin-Wolf, Lingenfelder, Müller-Catoir, Reichsgraf Von Kesselstatt, Reichsrat von Buhl, and Kurt Darting.

Spain

Spain has more land under vine than any other country, and its reputation for quality wine has improved in recent years. A sort of wine renaissance has hit Spain; Spanish wine, like the country's food, is becoming popular again.

The image of musty old wines is being pushed aside by a desire to produce pure, modern wines. While still working with traditional grape varieties, producers are also experimenting with international grape varieties and new winemaking techniques. The results of this transition have been nothing short of amazing. Spain produces some lovely juicy gluggable red wines, and fresh, clean, dry white wines that can give the rest of Europe, and even the New World, a run for its money. Spain also produces wines for serious collectors.

Spain's better wines are made from local grapes like Tempranillo (Spain's premier red grape variety), Garnacha (Spain's most widely planted red grape), and Albariño, but increasingly, international varieties like Cabernet Sauvignon and Chardonnay are being added to the mix. They may be harder to find but Spain is also making exciting wines from less common native grape varieties like the Godello (white wine in DO Valdeorras) and Mencía (a red wine in DO Bierzo and DO Valdeorras).

One of Spain's biggest challenges is lack of rain. Some parts of Spain are the driest in Europe. Since irrigation has been allowed, beginning in 1996, Spain has enjoyed a run of good vintages.

Spain's Wines Are Classified

Spain's system resembles Italy's, including wines of distinction, *Denominacion de Origen e Calificada* (DOCa) for the highest category of wines. So far only two regions—Rioja and Priorata—have been awarded this distinction. A higher DO category has been added to the classification—*vinos de pago*—awarded to wineries ("pago" roughly translates into estate) making distinguished wines for a period of time under exceptional circumstances (for example, climate, soil, and tradition).

> **Did You Know?**
> The first vinos de pago was awarded in 2003 to Dominio de Valdepusa in Castile La Mancha (central Spain, southwest of Madrid).

The system seems simple enough, except Spanish wines also have aging requirements. These requirements (the amount of time the wine has to stay in the barrel and bottle) apply to white and red wines, though red wines usually have longer requirements. There are variations across the regions but this is what the following words mean on the label:

- *Joven* wines (pronounced HO-ven), meaning "young", have the minimum aging requirements. These wines are usually released within a year of harvest and until recently received no time in barrel. *Roble* somewhere on the label (means "oak") indicates the wine has been in a barrel for a few months before bottling.
- *Crianza* wines (pronounced CREE-an-tha) must be aged for 24 months before release, and at least six of which are in barrel. Crianza are usually pleasant, medium-bodied red wines that are drinkable right away, but can benefit from further aging.
- *Reserva* wines are aged for a minimum of 36 months, with at least one year in oak and two in bottle before release. Made only in better vintages, Reservas are usually very good wines and the ones to buy if they are available. Smooth and silky.
- *Gran reserva* wines are made only in the very best vintages and have even longer aging requirements: five years before release with at least 18 months in barrel. As a result, the prices are usually higher. Gran reservas are highly sought out by collectors, and those who appreciate something special.

Distinct Regions

Spain lies between the humid, cold Atlantic Ocean and the warm Mediterranean Sea. It's a very large country and the geography varies considerably from region to region. The many different soils, elevations, climates, and microclimates result in a huge range of wines, and wine styles.

Spain's classification system is evolving and at last check there are 60 DO designations and two with DOCa. Most of the best wine regions are located north of Madrid with one exception: Andalucía, where sherry comes from. Here are a few of the more notable regions:

Rioja

Probably the best known wine region in Spain, Rioja (pronounced REE-oh-ha) has undergone major changes in terms of its style. The more rustic style is being replaced by well-made, deep, intense, and fruity wines. A more modern, international profile is emerging.

Red Rioja wines are traditionally made from Tempranillo grapes, with Garnacha and some other local varieties in the blend. American is the oak of choice for barrels, but French oak is also used.

White Riojas are made from the local Viura grape. Modern versions are crisp and neutral while traditional versions are bold and flavorful.

Rioja producers to look for include: Bodegas Montecillo, Bodegas Palacio Remondo, Bodegas Tobía, Marqués de Riscal, Marqués de Murrieta, Muga, Contino, and Artadi.

Ribera del Duero

Much smaller than Rioja (about one third the production), Ribera del Duero also uses Tempranillo (known here as Tinto Fino or Tinto del Pais) for its red wines. The climate can be more favourable and as a result the wines of Ribera can be richer, rounder, and even more elegant than Rioja.

Ribera's three most famous producers are Vega Sicilia—whose wine *Unico* is aged longer than any other red wine in the world and never released before ten years after the harvest—Dominio de Pingus, and Alejandro Fernández (Tinto Pesquera), but there is usually a fair amount of Ribera around from other producers. Look also for the wines of Bodegas Mauro, Bodegas Pingon, and Viña Pedrosa.

Navarra

Located just above Rioja, Navarra is a culturally rich and geographically diverse region. The mountainous northern part of

Navarra is the area Hemingway immortalized in his novel, *For Whom the Bell Tolls*.

At one time Navarra was famous only for its *rosado* (rosé) wines made from the Garnacha grape. As if overnight, Garnacha plantings were reduced by half (to 40% of total production) and replaced with the more popular native Tempranillo, as well as international varieties such as Cabernet Sauvignon and Merlot. Now Navarra produces exciting bold red wines, some of which can give Rioja a run for its money. Continued innovation and experimentation suggests this is also a region to watch. Bodegas Julian Chivite and Guelbenzu are reliable producers, but also look for Palacio de la Vega, Bodegas Nekeas, and the organic family winery Bodegas Lezaun.

Cataluña

Catalonia has long been an important center for cork production. As a wine region it produces a variety of wines from traditional, powerful reds to cool-fermented dry whites to value-priced sparkling wines. There are two important appellations within Catalonia: Penedes DO and Priorato DOCa.

Lying to the southwest of Barcelona, **Penedès** is the most important of the Catalan appellations. It is the principal center for sparkling wine (Cava DO) production. Within the region a large selection of grape varieties are planted, most especially the local Parellada, Xarel-lo and Macabeo grapes (which go into Cava production) as well as Garnacha and Monastrell for red wine production. Penedès is also where the internationally recognized producer Torres is based. Torres wines are some of the best value, well-made wines coming out of Spain at the moment.

Priorat is one of the rising stars of Spain's wine regions, having been recently awarded the second DOCa in Spain. This region produces spicy, inspiring, full-bodied wines that are in high demand, with prices to match. The region is dominated by small growers (co-operatives) but an increasing number of estates are making fine red wines. Native (Garnacha and Cariñena) and international (Cabernet Sauvignon, Merlot, and Syrah) varieties are planted, many on very inhospitable terrain and poor soils. Wines must reach minimum alcohol strength of 13.5% to qualify for the DO. Alva Palacios makes probably the most sought after Priorat wine—L'Ermita.

The Rest of Spain

Rueda, in the historic Castilla y León region, makes wonderfully crisp, aromatic white wines from the native Verdejo and Viura grapes. **Bierzo**, in northwest Spain, makes elegant red wines from the local Mencía (men-THEE-a) grape. And **Rías Baixas** (REE-as by-shuss), on the Atlantic coast, is the home of the deliciously aromatic white wine made from the Albariño grape. Make sure the version you buy is from a recent vintage (ideally no more than two years old) and look for better producers like Terras Gauda. Near the Mediterranean port of Cádiz, **Jerez** and **Manzanilla Sanlúcar de Barrameda** are the two most important DO's for sherry.

Other Old World Countries

France, Italy, Spain, and Germany together make up over 80% percent of Europe's production (and over half of total world production), which is why they deserve the extra attention. The wines from these four countries are the ones most likely to show up on restaurant wine lists and wine shop shelves. But what about the other Old World countries—what do you need to know about them? Here are a few other wine regions that you might come across in your local markets, and what to expect if you pick up a bottle of their wine.

Portugal

Portugal is probably most famous for its great fortified wines, port and madeira, and in the past a rosé wine better known as Mateus. In recent years, Portugal has demonstrated that it can produce very good red and white table wines, albeit from lesser-known local varieties. The better red wines come from the regions of **Douro** (using the same grapes varieties used to make port), **Dão**, and **Bairrada**. While many of these wines were traditionally rustic and sometimes tannic in style, recent advances in winemaking and vineyard selection have resulted in the wines becoming more accessible to international palates. Give one a try with a meal and you'll see what we mean.

Portugal's most distinctive white wine is the **Vinho Verde** from the very northern reaches of the country. Bone dry, this wine is fairly aromatic (think peaches) with a piercing acidity and a little "spritz" on the finish. Not for keeping, drink this wine as soon as you buy it.

Hungary

Hungary is making a name for itself on the international scene. No longer wishing to be solely reliant on its full-bodied *Egri Bikaver* (means "bull's blood from the town of Eger") or the softer and spicier *Szekszárdi*, producers started to plant international varieties and you can now find many good value examples of Chardonnay and Pinot Gris. Hungary has a lot of potential—especially with native varieties like Kadarka, Kékfrankos, Furmint, and Irsai Olivér—and recent investments in the wineries mean we can expect more and better things to come.

Coverage of Hungary would be incomplete without a mention of Tokaji Aszú, in particular *Essencia*, one of the world's best sweet wines.

Greece

Winemaking as we know it started in Greece. Despite its lineage, Greece didn't kept up with the times and it's only in the last 15 years or so that its wines have begun to take their place on the international stage. Most people still think of *Retsina* (a wine flavored with pine resin) when they think of Greek wine. This is unfortunate as Greece now makes some excellent full-bodied red and tangy white wines using native varieties, from appellations like **Naoussa**, **Nemea**, and **Zitsa**, as well as the sweet liqueur wines (made from dried Muscat and Mavrodaphne grapes) from **Patras**.

Austria

Austria is a small wine-producing country but it makes some very good wines. Like Germany, Austria is mainly white wine country. It has a similar classification system to Germany (with a couple of exceptions); however, the wines themselves have more alcohol, body, and are generally drier.

The leading grape is Grüner Veltliner which can make excellent dry and off-dry white wines. The best comes Grüner Veltliner comes from Niederösterreich (lower Austria), but you can also get nice versions—including well-made Riesling—from the Kamptal, Kremstal, and Wachau regions. For red wines, try Blaufränkisch, Saint Laurent, or Zweigelt.

Eastern Europe

The wines of Bulgaria, Romania, Czech Republic, Slovakia, Slovenia, and the Balkan States are emerging as sources of good, inexpensive wines if you are selective. Ask a trusted wine clerk for advice before grabbing a $6 bottle of Laski Rizling from Velika Morava.

Wine production may suffer as countries enter the EU, so Bulgaria is probably the safest bet right now—especially for Merlot and Cabernet Sauvignon. You likely won't find Bulgarian wine on many restaurant wine lists yet, but look for Boyar Estates at your local wine shop. Good value.

And don't count out Romania, the world's thirteenth-largest wine producing region. Wines from Carl Reh can be quite good. If investment continues, we could see quality wine from countries like Moldova, Georgia, Azerbaijan, and even Russia in the future.

England

Due to its cooler climate, or obvious geography, you might be surprised to learn that England produces wine at all. In relatively small amounts England is developing somewhat of a reputation for its sparkling wines, which is quite fitting given its connection to the invention of the wine in the first place.

Switzerland

Very little Swiss wine is exported; the best being the dry white wines made from the Chasselas grape. There's an enjoyable Swiss red wine called Dôle—a blend of Gamay and Pinot Noir—and in the Italian-speaking part of Switzerland (Ticino) they make very good Merlot.

Eastern Mediterranean Countries

The eastern Mediterranean is thought to be where wine was first made. Grapes are still important to this region but not necessarily for making wine. Turkey for example is the fourth largest producer of grapes in the world but most of them are for eating. Cyprus is best known for its fortified wine *Commandaria*, and Tunisia, Israel, and Lebanon export wines but in small quantities. Most remarkable is the internationally renowned Château Musar, which makes a Bordeaux-like blend from Cabernet Sauvignon and Cinsault, in Lebanon's Bekaa Valley.

United States

Outside of Europe, United States is the most important wine producer in the world. It ranks fourth in the world in terms of wine production—about half of what France and Italy each produce—but is the technological leader in both grape growing and winemaking, with much of the development driven by the University of California at Davis. While it was the Roman historian Pliny the Elder who wrote *in vino veritas*—in wine there is truth—it was probably a Californian winemaker who coined the phrase—*in vino monetas*—in wine there is money. (Okay, we made up the last part!)

The United States is one of the few New World countries to classify its wine production. In 1983 it adopted an appellation system (American Viticultural Areas or AVAs) to define the geographical boundaries of the wine areas. Currently there are about 160 AVAs, and more than half of them are in California.

The AVA system doesn't work the way European classification systems do. There are no rules concerning what grapes can be grown in which AVA, or how the wine is made. You might have to experiment a little to find the grape, style or producer you like.

The federal government also imposed guidelines to bring some honesty to wine labelling. The wine must now include at least 75% of the grape variety identified on the label, and 85% if it's an AVA wine.

There are wineries in all 50 States (though grapes are grown in only 20), and four States—California, Oregon, Washington, and New York—account for two-thirds of the wineries. In the other states, with a few exceptions, most vineyards are planted to cold-hardy French hybrids or native *Vitis labrusca* vines. Depending on where you live, availability from certain state wineries is probably limited. For example, don't expect to see the sweet-style Jungfraulich from Valiant Vineyards—South Dakota's oldest winery—in your local market.

Look for Wines From
Arizona, Idaho, Missouri, Texas, and Virginia

California

While the first commercial winery in the United States was actually in Cincinnati, it was California that put the United States on the world map with respect to wine. Much of the credit goes to the brothers Gallo—Ernest and Julio—who, after Prohibition was repealed, built the world's largest wine-producing company, known for its inexpensive "jug" wines (remember *Hearty Burgundy*?) and now a line of premium quality wines from Sonoma County. Robert Mondavi also should receive credit, as his dedication to quality wine production and tireless promotion earned him the international respect of his peers as well as domestic success. Stag's Leap's Cabernet Sauvignon beating top Bordeaux in a blind tasting in the early 1970s didn't hurt the image of California wines either!

While there are many different grape varieties grown in California, the major classic Bordeaux and Burgundy varieties—Cabernet Sauvignon, Chardonnay, and Pinot Noir—are favoured for quality wines, albeit with a distinct Californian style. Stylistically, the emphasis is on BIG—there is nothing subtle about Californian wine. It's all about ripe, fruit-driven character.

- **Cabernet Sauvignon** is intense, sweet blackberry and plum fruit with ample tannins and vanilla oak.
- **Pinot Noir** has bright cherry fruit flavor, sometimes jammy, with nice elegant structure.
- **Chardonnay** exudes ripe, sweet fruit, with toasty and buttery qualities from the oak.

Other grape varieties include: Zinfandel (which is used to make fruity gluggable wines as well as hearty, peppery wines with lots of bramble fruit); Sauvignon Blanc; Rhône grapes like Syrah and Viognier; and Italian grapes like Sangiovese. The climate is so conducive to grape growing that pretty well everything can grow.

California produces an incredible range of wines from the low-end "Two Buck Chuck" (literally $2 for a bottle of wine) to pricey "cult" wines. Expect to pay more for *reserve* wines as well as vineyard-selected wines from prestigious AVAs (Howell Mountain, for example). Relative to Europe, vintage variation isn't much of a problem in California, and currently the region is enjoying string of good to excellent vintages. To be safe, only the best California wines age.

While **Napa Valley** has a big reputation, it's actually as small wine-producing area (only representing about 5% of total production). But what it does do is produce most of California's most prestigious wines, the most important of which are Chardonnay and Cabernet Sauvignon. In a

Cult Wines

A number of wineries have appeared whose small-production wines have earned them a cult following. These include Colgin, Harlan Estates, and Screaming Eagle. Even if you can afford the hundreds of dollars these wines cost, don't expect to just walk into a wine shop and buy one—they are usually sold on a strict allocation basis only, and waiting lists—if they even exist—are long.

supporting role you'll also find Sauvignon Blanc (sometimes seen as Fumé Blanc), Merlot, and Pinot Noir (from the cooler Carneros AVA).

Temperatures can vary by as much as 10°F (6°C) along Napa's 30-mile (45-km) length. That means there can be a considerable difference between wines grown in the cooler Carneros (in the south) than those in the much warmer Calistoga (in the north). Many of the better AVAs are located at higher altitudes, away from the burning heat of the valley floor. Diamond Creek, Spring Mountain, Stags, Leap, Howell Mountain, and Rutherford are examples of excellent AVAs.

While there are far too many excellent Napa producers to list, here's a few you might want to give a try: Chateau Montelena, Clos du Val, Clos Pegase, Duckhorn, Robert Pecota, Beringer, and Whitehall Lane.

There are also many excellent sparkling wine producers in Napa (although some are actually in the Carneros region) including: Domaine Chandon, Schramsberg, Gloria Ferrer, Mumm Napa Valley, and Domaine Carneros.

Sonoma County grows more grapes, is larger and has more microclimates, especially cooler ones, than Napa Valley. Sonoma originally had a better reputation for fine wine than Napa, but Napa has taken the lead in recent years. In Sonoma County, Pinot Noir, Zinfandel, Chardonnay, and Sauvignon Blanc take center stage. Some of the best Pinot Noir outside Burgundy comes from Sonoma, particularly from the cooler Russian River Valley AVA. Dry Creek Valley AVA—where Gallo has a major presence—is especially good for Zinfandel. Other notable AVAs include the warmer Alexander Valley and Knights Valley. There are still many excellent producers including: Chateau St. Jean, Gary Farrell, Paul Hobbs Cellars, Ravenswood, Buena Vista, Gundlach-Bundschu, and Marimar Torres

Sonoma County may be responsible for the success of Chardonnay in the United States. A typical Sonoma Chardonnay has lots of body, a rich texture, and lots of ripe fruit flavors. The style varies from crisper, complex, more tropical examples from the cooler Carneros in the south, to more full-blown, rich-textured versions from the warmer Alexander Valley in the north. Because Sonoma Valley is so big and geographically diverse, the region offers many other styles in between, from AVAs like the Russian River Valley, Bennett Valley, Sonoma Valley, Sonoma Coast, and Chalk Hill. Try Somona Chardonnay from Le Crema, Ferrari-Carano, Matanzas Creek, and Sonoma-Cutrer.

In the **Bay Area** (near San Francisco), there are a couple areas worth noting. On the east side of the Bay is **Livermore**. Wente Bros. is here—one of California's oldest wineries. South of San Francisco are the **Santa Cruz Mountains**, which have attracted some of the best and most eclectic winemaking in the state. Chardonnay, Cabernet and Pinot do well here. Bonny Doon Vineyards—lead by iconoclastic owner Randall Grahm—routinely pushes accepted winemaking practices, by emphasizing Rhône grapes in its wines and by its highly original, sometimes whimsical, marketing ideas. In addition to irreverent wine names and labels, the wines are always worth seeking out. Other notable Santa Cruz producers include: David Bruce, Bargetto, and Ridge Vineyards.

Continuing south, **Monterey County** is slightly larger than Napa Valley. Although generally a cooler region, Monterey County is quite geographically diverse. The wines of region are beginning to get attention: look for Bernardus, Chalone, and Robert Talbott.

Closer to Santa Barbara is an area called the **Central Coast**. While the wineries in this area haven't yet achieved the status of Napa and Sonoma, nevertheless they produce excellent wines. The movie *Sideways* gave this area, and Pinot Noir in particular, an incredible boost in 2005. The Central Coast includes Edna Valley, Paso Robles, Santa Ynez Valley, and Santa Maria Valley

- Cooler **Edna Valley** is better known for Pinot Noir and Chardonnay.
- **Paso Robles** is best known for Zinfandel, as well as Rhône varieties like Syrah. Every year Paso Robles also hosts the Hospices du Rhône—the world's largest celebration of Rhône variety wines.
- Within Santa Barbara County is the **Santa Ynez Valley**. The region is quite warm, allowing Syrah to do well, while Pinot Noir has gained critical acclaim in this versatile AVA.
- Still within Santa Barbera is the cooler **Santa Maria Valley**. Here Chardonnay, Pinot Noir, and Syrah are world class.

Central Coast producers to look for include Corbett Canyon, Talley Vineyard, Castoro Cellars, Tablas Creek, Sandford, Qupe/Au Bon Climat, The Gainey Vineyard, Richard Longoria, Lane Tanner, Foxen, Byron, and Io.

Oregon

Oregon vineyards are west of the Cascade Mountains where the climate is cool and damp. Good weather isn't reliable so there is considerable variation between vintages. Recent good vintages include 2001, 2002, 2004, and 2005.

It may be a generalization but Oregon wines to be more European (that is, lighter and more subtle) than Californian in style. The Oregon climate is better suited to Burgundian grape varieties and Pinot Noir is the star. Chardonnay is the second most-planted grape but is being rapidly replaced by Pinot Gris. Growers are still experimenting with grape varieties so don't be surprised to see Zinfandel, Syrah, Viognier, or even Albariño, if you're visiting the region.

Currently there are 10 AVAs, but the **Willamette Valley** remains the most important. Most of the best Pinot Noir comes from the Willamette Valley, where many of the more celebrated producers are located. There are over 200 wineries in Oregon, but the wines from Adelsheim, The Eyrie Vineyards, Bergström Winery, Brick House, Cameron, Cuneo Cellars, Chehalem, Domaine Drouhin, St. Innocent, and Sokol Blosser are worth looking for.

> ### Wine Pioneer
> In 1970, David Lett, owner and winemaker of The Eyrie Vineyards, released the first Pinot Noir from Oregon. David had the insight and courage to believe that world-class Pinot Noir could be made in Oregon. The rest, as they say, is history.

Washington

Washington State's vineyards are mostly east of the Cascade Mountains and here the climate is semi-arid, even desert-like. The weather is more reliable than Oregon's and vintages are consistently good.

Bordeaux grapes (Cabernet and Merlot) thrive here and produce big, rich, flavorful wines with considerable aging potential. Syrah is also doing well here. White wines don't have the profile of the reds, but there are good Chardonnays as well as Sauvignon Blanc and Semillon.

> ### Did You Know?
> Washington State is roughly on the same line of latitude (46°N) as the great French winemaking regions of Bordeaux and Burgundy.

Washington has eight AVAs. **Columbia Valley** is the largest, **Yakima Valley** has the most wineries, and **Walla Walla Valley** is where you find most of the premium wineries. Look for Chateau Ste. Michelle, Canoe Ridge, Columbia Crest, L'Ecole #41, Hedges Cellars, The Hogue Cellars, Leonetti, and Woodward Canyon.

New York State

Grapes have been grown in New York State since about 1860, and it has the fourth highest number of wineries in the United States.

It has one of the world's largest wineries—Canandaigua Wine Company—as well as many small "boutique" operations

New York State is a cool, climate grape-growing region. Probably the only reason grapes grow at all here is due to the moderating influence of Lake Ontario, the Atlantic Ocean, and the Finger Lakes. Although New York State is better suited to growing white wine grapes, in good vintages it also produces impressive red wines. Riesling does very well, as do French hybrids like Vidal and Seyval Blanc. As for the reds, Merlot and Pinot Noir do well in good vintages. There is a lot of vintage variation although 2001 and 2002 were highly rated.

Finger Lakes, **Hudson River Valley**, and **Long Island** are the most important AVAs. While New York State has a long tradition with winter-hardy French Hybrid grapes, the Finger Lakes AVA produces excellent white wines from international varieties (including Chardonnay), and the milder Long Island AVAs are gaining stride with red varieties including Cabernet Sauvignon, Merlot, and Cabernet Franc. Producers like Dr. Konstantin Frank, Atwater Estate, Fox Run, Casa Langa Vineyards, Osprey's Dominion Vineyards, and Lamoreaux Landing are worth seeking out.

Canada

Canada is a small wine-growing country, it ranks thirty-fourth between Slovakia and the Czech Republic. But there is nothing small about its attitude towards making and selling world-class wine. Canada produces excellent wines, including world-famous icewine. Canadian wines are starting to show up on wine lists in major cities like New York, Chicago, Los Angeles, and London.

Most of the country is above the fiftieth parallel, outside the ideal range of production for grapes. And while Canada's Niagara region is on the same line of latitude (43°) as Tuscany, here the similarity ends. Canada is a cool-climate wine region with a much shorter growing season.

Canada is in the process of establishing a national classification system that both identifies geographical location and sets standards of production. Currently only Ontario and BC have adopted the Vintners Quality Alliance (VQA) system. Ontario has three approved Designated Viticultural Areas (DVAs)—**Niagara**

Did You Know?
It is believed that the Viking Leif Ericsson landed somewhere on Canada's east coast around 1000 AD and found so many vines growing that he named his discovery Vinland (Land of Wine).

Peninsula (which also includes 12 approved sub-appellations), **Lake Erie North Shore**, and **Pelee Island**—while British Columbia has four—the **Okanagan Valley**, **Similkameen Valley**, **Fraser Valley**, and **Vancouver Island**. Prince Edward County, east of Toronto, is expected to become Ontario's fourth DVA once the local grape harvest reaches required levels.

VQA wines can only be made with *Vitis vinifera* grapes and the wine must contain at least 85% of the specified grape variety. Further, a wine must be 85% from the DVA *and* 100% from the vineyard to carry that vineyard's designation. All VQA wines are subject to an independent tasting panel and wines meeting these standards are allowed to bear the VQA seal.

There are grape wineries (we make the distinction as there are fruit wineries in other provinces) in four of Canada's ten provinces (Nova Scotia, Quebec, Ontario and British Columbia). On a consistent basis, the best quality wines currently come from Ontario and British Columbia.

Ontario

Ontario's vineyards are close to either Lake Ontario or Lake Erie. These large bodies of water act as heat sinks and moderate the often-harsh winter temperatures. The winters are often too cold for sensitive vines; however, the long, cool growing season is excellent for grape development as it encourages the production of natural grape acids. The variable climate, however, means that vintages can be variable as well.

Ontario produces excellent white wines—especially Riesling and Chardonnay—but also high-quality reds from Cabernet Franc, Pinot Noir, and Cabernet Sauvignon. Baco Noir, a French hybrid grape, makes interesting wines in the right hands.

Niagara is probably most famous for its Riesling and Vidal icewines. Few places in the world have both the quality of grapes and the ideal conditions for making icewines on a consistent basis.

While much of development of the Ontario wine industry has taken place in the last 15 or so years, there are a number of excellent well-established wineries in Ontario, as well as some terrific up and comers. Established producers include: Andres, Inniskillin, Jackson-Triggs, Cave Spring Cellars, Vineland Estates, Henry of Pelham, Chateau des Charmes, Hillebrand, Konzelman, and Pelee Island Winery. The wineries to watch for include: Tawse, Stratus, Daniel Lenko, Lailey Vineyard, Thirteenth Street, Peninsula Ridge, and Malivoire.

British Columbia

British Columbia's four DVAs range from the desert-like southern Okanagan Valley to the maritime climate of Vancouver Island. Like Ontario, the climate can be variable, which means that vintages can be variable as well. However, British Columbia has enjoyed a series of excellent vintages since 2001.

Although still a young industry, British Columbia wineries are producing excellent white wines from Pinot Gris, Pinot Blanc, and Chardonnay. Some exciting white wines are also being made from less common grapes such as Madeleine Sylvaner, Siegerrebe and Auxerrois. World-class red wines are made from Pinot Noir, Merlot, and Cabernet Sauvignon. There is a lot of experimentation in BC so don't be surprised when you come across Syrah and Sémillon.

BC also makes icewines—including a Pinot Noir icewine—and some incredible *méthode traditionelle* sparkling wines.

Producers to look for include: Blue Mountain, Mission Hill, Burrowing Owl, Poplar Grove Farm Winery, Quail's Gate, Stag's Hollow, Summerhill Estate Winery, Venturi-Schulze, La Frenz, and Black Hills.

Nova Scotia

Nova Scotia's wineries are mainly in two areas—the Annapolis Valley and the Northeast Shore—where the proximity to water has a moderating effect on winter temperatures. Although the number of wineries fluctuates, Jost Vineyards and Domain de Grand Pré are the largest, and probably the easiest to find on wine lists. Despite the tough climate, Nova Scotia wineries persevere and put out award-winning wines.

Quebec

Quebec wineries are mainly in the Eastern Townships near the Vermont border. The industry is tiny and relies mainly on winter-hardy French hybrid grape varieties. The wines, which can be good, are mainly sold within the province.

Mexico

Don't be surprised if Mexico doesn't spring to mind as a wine pro-ducing country. Tequila or cervezas are probably what you think of first. But actually Mexico was the starting point for grape growing in the Americas some 400 years ago.

While much of the country is simply too hot for growing grapes, the cooler North Baja Peninsula—just over the border from San Diego—as well as the higher altitude Querétaro region have proved to be well suited to the task. Here traditional French varietals like Chardonnay, Merlot, Cabernet Sauvignon, and Pinot Noir do well. Some Californian varietals like Zinfandel and Petite Sirah have also adapted well, as has Nebbiolo.

Although there are some quality-driven, boutique-style wineries, Mexico also produces value-priced wine in relatively large quantities, some with rustic, jammy qualities. We don't get to see lot of Mexican wine but LA Cetto and Monte Xanic are good bets.

South America

The strong European influence of South America's immigrants has helped shape a wine industry based on international varietals. If you are looking for good value, look no further. Stricter controls on labelling (what it says on the label is now what's inside the bottle!) and huge investments in upgrading production facilities have helped this region gain a substantial share of the market in North America—if not the world. It doesn't hurt that many good wines from South America are inexpensive. Quality, flavor, and value—what more can you ask for?

Six of the 13 South American countries produce wine. At one time Brazil was the fourth largest wine-producing country in the world, but not any longer. Uruguay makes good wines, including the beefy and tannic Tannat, but they're rarely found outside the country. For now, the wines you're most likely to see are from Chile and Argentina.

Chile

Currently the eleventh largest producer of wine in the world, Chile is also regarded as the leading producer of fine wine in South America. Its near-perfect climate and relative political and economic stability indicate this is a wine country with potential. A surge in investment in Chilean vineyards from Europe and the United States is also contributing to the rapid growth in quality and quantity.

Did You Know?

Chile is one of the only countries in the world that is phylloxera-free. The combination of sandy soil and geographic isolation has kept the vineyards uncontaminated. As a result, *Vitis vinifera* vines grow on their own rootstocks. Many of the wines are therefore older than their counterparts in the rest of the world, and can produce better fruit.

From north to south, the main growing regions are:

- **Aconcagua** is known for its intensely colored red wines from Bordeaux varieties.
- **Casablanca** does well with Sauvignon Blanc and Chardonnay for white wines, and Pinot Noir for red wines.
- **Maipo**—probably the most famous region—has a great reputation for Cabernet Sauvignon and Merlot, and gaining attention for Syrah.
- **Rapel,** which includes the Colchagua and Cachapoal sub-regions, does well with full-flavored Bordeaux and Rhône varieties. Cabernet Sauvignon is the most-planted grape variety in the region.
- **Curicó** produces lively white wines and full-bodied reds.

Chile is known for fruit-forward, easy-drinking red wines. Cabernet Sauvignon has long been the star, though other red varietals, like Syrah, are gaining a profile internationally. The red grape Carmenère, which for many years was bottled in error as Merlot, is also becoming quite popular because of its soft, ripe fruit flavors. While many Chilean wines are inexpensive, a number of premium-priced red wines are being produced, some the result of joint ventures with European and US winemakers (Seña, for example).

> ### Key Grapes
> Red: Merlot, Cabernet Sauvignon, Carmenère, and Pinot Noir
> White: Chardonnay and Sauvignon Blanc

The quality of Chilean white wines has lagged behind the reds, often due to overly enthusiastic irrigation or high yields. Stick with whites from the cooler regions (Casablanca in particular) to be sure of quality.

Chilean wine labels indicate the grape and usually the region. Grape growing conditions are so perfect that vintages are rarely an issue. You should always find good value Chilean Merlot and Cabernet on wine shop shelves. Prices have been going up in recent years as quality increases, or as more expressive wines come on the market. Producers to try include: Vina Santa Rita, Errazuriz, Montes, Cousino-Macul, Undurraga, Los Vascos, Concha Y Toro, Mont Gras, and Casa Lapostolle.

Argentina

Argentina ranks fifth in the world in terms of production—about double that of its neighbor to the west, Chile. Yet Argentina exports only a fraction of what Chile does: most of the wine is consumed locally. Argentina is planning to turn this around, and, like Chile, quality is on the rise while prices remain accessible to the average consumer.

There is really only one wine region of note—**Mendoza** (which produces about 80% of Argentina's wine)—although **Salta** and **Rio Negro** are also developing reputations for good wine.

Argentina is red wine territory but with many different grapes. While everyone in the New World makes Cabernet Sauvignon and Merlot, only Argentina makes great soft and juicy wine from Malbec (its leading quality grape variety). It also works with Italian varieties—Barbera, Bonarda, and Sangiovese—and Spanish varieties like Tempranillo. Syrah is also gaining a reputation.

White wine production is taken less seriously with the exception of wines made from the wonderfully aromatic Spanish grape Torrontés. Other white grape varieties include Chenin Blanc, Chardonnay, and Sémillon.

Argentinean wineries are making a name for themselves on the world stage and a number of reliable producers ship to export markets. Don't assume only value-priced wines leave the country—Argentina also produces premium-priced wines that receive high scores with the international press. In both price brackets, look for: Bodegas Catena Zapata, Bodegas Norton, Trapiche, Susana Balbo, Luca, Etchart, Familia Zuccardi, Valentin Bianchi, and Bodegas Lurton.

Did You Know?

Argentineans consume more wine per capita than any other country except tiny Luxembourg, and Spain.

Australia

In global wine terms, Australia is a relatively small wine-producing nation—ranking sixth in the world in terms of production but still only about one-seventh the output of Italy. In geographic terms, Australia is larger than all of Europe and can produce literally any quantity and style of wine imaginable, from cool-climate steely whites to big, jammy, warm-climate reds. Australia has ambitions to be the world's most influential supplier of wines by 2025 so get ready for more "fruit-to-the-front" wines in your local wine shops.

While Australia has a tradition of winemaking from as far back as the early 1830s, its calling card is technology and innovation. Much of this innovation has gone into increasing economies of scale—both in the vineyard and in the winery—and the result is gallons and gallons of clean, well-made wines at all price levels. But unless global consumption picks up again, the glut of

1. Barossa Valley
2. Coonawarra
3. Clare Valley
4. Padthaway
5. Hunter Valley
6. Yarra Valley
7. Tasmania
8. Margaret River

Australian wine caused by increased plantings could be a problem for producers, but good news for consumers. Prices have already started to fall in some markets.

Australia's appellation system (Geographic Indication or GI) identifies the source of wines. The first level is *Produce of Australia*, followed by *South-Eastern Australia* (a catch-all designation for most export wines), then the five *States of Origin*. Each of these states is broken into *zones* and then *regions*. Like in Europe, the more specific the GI, the more distinctive the wine. The Australian Label Integrity Program (LIP) requires that wines with varietal labelling (the norm in Australia) must contain at least 85% of that variety, from the region (if specified).

Red grape production outnumbers white grape production two to one, and these three grapes make up about 60% of the total plantings in Australia. Here's what to expect:

Critter Wines

Riding the crest of the big wave of Australian wine exports, the sweet, fruity, value-priced, Casella Yellow Tail, hit North America markets with a wallop in 2001. The number #1 selling wine in the United States (Casella is also Australia's #4 exporter), Yellow Tail has spawned a bunch of other uncompli-cated, entry-level wines with cute "critters" on the label.

- **Shiraz**—with almost a quarter of total plantings (and over a third of total red grape acreage), Shiraz comes in a variety of different styles. From elegant, spicy, chocolaty, blackberry fruit versions in cooler-climates (Coonawarra, Margaret River) to more muscular, powerful, and rich, ripe, jammy blackberry fruit versions inland where conditions are warmer (Barossa, Hunter Valley).
- **Chardonnay**—the increased popularity of Australian Chardonnay has resulted in its recent rise to second place in terms of total plantings (just over 20%). Perhaps the success is due to the fact that the over-oaked style of past decades has been replaced by cleaner, fresher, more food-friendly versions. Now you will find more rich and complex wines, backed with nice ripe melon, peach and citrus (grapefruit and lime) aromas and flavors. Warmer regions (Riverland) offer richer, tropical fruit aromas, while cooler regions (Tasmania) are more subtle, with more citrus aromas.
- **Cabernet Sauvignon**—once the second most-planted grape, Cabernet's popular has waned in recent years. Look for cooler regions (Coonawarra and Margaret River) where the minty, blackcurrant aromas and flavors are pronounced and the

wines more elegant and full-bodied. In slightly warmer areas (McLaren Vale) the wines are equally elegant but offer richer blackcurrant fruit aromas, with hints of chocolate and spice.

You can also find good Pinot Noir, Merlot, and Grenache for red wines and Sauvignon Blanc, Riesling, Semillon, and Verdelho for the whites. There's also growing excitement around traditional Spanish (Tempranillo) and Italian (Sangiovese, Barbera, and Nebbiolo) varietals.

Stickies

Australia's focus on fresh and dry table wines is fairly recent. Up to about 40 years ago, Oz wines were more likely a sweet port-like wine (a.k.a. "stickies") or came in a box (although some still do.) Now you can select fruity, well-made wines from many different grape varieties at all different price points: from $10 to ones costing hundreds of dollars.

Believing that it provides a more consistent, higher quality product, Australian winemakers love to blend: either by blending two or more grapes together, or blending wines from different regions. It's common to see Cabernet blended with Merlot or Sauvignon Blanc with Semillon, while some of the best Australian wines (Penfold's Grange, for example) are blends of vineyard wines from different regions.

Australia has over 60 wine regions, positioned between its hot, arid, red center to the north, and the cold ocean to the south, each reflecting a unique range of climates, soils, and grapes. It's hard to generalize about this vast country, or for that matter about the over 1,500 producers that make wine, but here's roughly what you can expect from the major wine-producing States, as well as some producers to look for from each region.

South Australia

The largest wine producing state, South Australia makes over half of all Australian wine. The best wine regions include: **Barossa Valley** for big, bold Shiraz (Penfolds, Peter Lehman, Torbreck, Barossa Valley Esetate); **McLaren Vale** for elegant Shiraz and Cabernet (Geoff Merrill, Hardy Reynella, Wirra Wirra, d'Arenbreg, Haselgrove); **Coonawarra** for Cabernet (Majella, Brand's Balnaves); **Eden Valley** (Henschke, Yalumba); and **Clare Valley** for elegant Riesling and Shiraz (O'Leary Walker, Annie's Lane, Jeffrey Grossett, Wendouree). South Australia also includes the vast **Riverland** region—the highest volume wine-production area in Australia—responsible for much of the value-priced wines that dominate the export market.

New South Wales

One of the warmest wine grape growing regions in Australia, this state produces about a quarter of all Australian wine. New South Wales is considered the ancestral home for Australian wine production; some of the first vineyards planted around Sydney by early settlers in the 1830s. Look for wines from the **Hunter Valley**, the lower valley better known for Semillon and Shiraz, while the upper, drier, valley is known for Chardonnay. The Hunter Valley is considered on of the best regions in the world for Semillon (at one time erroneously called Hunter River Riesling) particularly when it is at least three years old. Producers to look for include Tyrell's, Lake's Folly, Brokenwood, Tulloch, De Bortoli, and Rothvale.

Victoria

Victoria has the most wineries and the most individual styles of any state. In geographic terms it is also quite diverse, from the very warm **Murray Darling**, **Swan Hill**, and **Rutherglen** regions in the west to the cooler **Yarra Valley** and **Mornington Peninsula** regions to the east. Even cooler still is the **Alpine Valley** region to the northeast of the State. Rutherglen is famous for sweet, fortified-style Muscats, while some of the most elegant Pinot Noir and long-lived Chardonnay in Australia come from the **Yarra Valley**. While there's lots to chose from, producers like Yering Station, Coldstream Hills, Badger's Brook, and Paringa (Mornington Peninsula) are worth seeking out.

Tasmania

The island of Tasmania is the most southern wine-growing area in Australia, and the smallest of Australia's six States. It is a cool-climate region, and can produce excellent, elegant Pinot Noir and Chardonnay, fresh and crisp Riesling, as well as exciting sparkling wines. Tasmania is a single GI, and most of the wine production is centered on its north coast. There are fewer than 100 wineries on the island and much of their wine is sold locally. Producers to look for include Moorilla Estate (the oldest commercial winery on the island), Tamar Ridge, and Pipers Brook (the island's largest winery).

Western Australia

In Australia's largest state (making up about one third of the continent), most of the wine regions in Western Australia are tucked into a tiny corner in the southwest: around and south of Perth. This state is known for its high-quality wines especially those from **Margaret River**. Blessed with a climate similar to the top regions of Bordeaux, Margaret River is an excellent source of Cabernet Sauvignon and Merlot, and is forging a reputation for complex Chardonnay. In fact Leeuwin Estate is credited with making one of Australia's best Chardonnay. There are many other excellent Margaret River wineries to recommend, and Vasse-Felix, Voyager, Cape Mentell, Evans & Tate, Pierro, and Moss Brothers are often near the top of everyone's list.

The **Swan District** predates Victoria and South Australia in viticultural terms, and is home to the state's largest winery, Houghton. In the extreme southwest corner of the state (east of Margaret River), are the **Pemberton**, **Manjimup**, and **Great Southern** regions. Pemberton is better known for Pinot Noir and Chardonnay (look for Picardy and Salitage), while Manjimup has a reputation for Cabernet Sauvignon and Merlot (look for Chestnut Grove and Fonty's Pool). The Great Southern is large and diverse, and appears capable of making excellent wines from almost every major grape variety. Among the many quality producers, look for Alkoomi, Frankland Estates, Howard Park, and Goundrey.

New Zealand

New Zealand may be a small country, in both geographic and wine-production terms, but it produces its share of quality wine, at least judging by international acclaim showered on its wines, especially Sauvignon Blanc.

If New Zealand were in the northern hemisphere, parts of it would lie in roughly the same area of latitude as Italy or Spain. New Zealand, however, is a temperate, maritime climate, with mostly coastal vineyards. New Zealand is made up of two main islands and the climate varies between the two islands—the harvest in the north often precedes that of the south by six weeks. The fact that the wine regions can be separated by as much as 1000 miles (1600 km) contributes to the diverse range of wines that come from New Zealand.

New Zealand has 10 main wine regions and government regulations are minimal. There's no system yet to certify the origin of the grapes or the wine, or even delimit wine regions. What is grown where, how it is grown (yields, for example), and quality standards are essentially left up to individual producers. New Zealand law does, however, require that a varietally-labelled wine must include at least 75% of that variety.

The regions are located in basically two distinct areas: the North Island and—wait for it—the South Island. In the warmer North Island, you will find **Martinborough** (where some of the best Pinot Noir comes from), **Hawke's Bay** (best known for Cabernet Sauvignon and Merlot, and now Syrah), **Gisborne** (for Chardonnay). On the cooler South Island, **Marlborough** (New Zealand's biggest and most important region and home of the famous Cloudy Bay winery) is the source for more than 80% of New Zealand's Sauvignon Blanc, while **Central Otago** (the most southerly wine region in the world, and more semi-continental than other regions), is gaining a reputation for Pinot Noir. Together, Marlborough, Hawke's Bay, and Gisborne represent over 90% of New Zealand's annual harvest.

New Zealand Sauvignon Blanc is acclaimed as providing the New World's benchmark style: zingy and zesty, with distinctive aromas of grapefruit, green melon, lemongrass, gooseberry, and passion fruit. The wines are, in general, clean and lean, with balanced fruit and acidity. Worldwide demand for this style is increasing, and vineyard plantings have more than doubled in the past five years. Chardonnay used to be the most widely planted white wine grape, but not any longer.

As for reds, Pinot Noir, currently New Zealand's third most-planted grape (in a virtual tie with Chardonnay but growing at a faster rate) shows the most promise. It's hard to generalize about the New Zealand style (due to site and vintage variation), but it does lean more toward Burgundy than elsewhere. You'll find more of the elegant, earthy, cherry, spicy, chocolaty aromas and flavors reminiscent of Old World Pinot Noir, rather than big jammy fruit aromas and flavors common in some New World regions. Merlot shows promise, as does Cabernet Sauvignon and Syrah, especially in Hawke's Bay where they can ripen properly.

There are over 500 licensed wineries in New Zealand, and one—Montana, or Brancott as its known in the UK and US—dominates wine production, with over 60% of the market. Other producers worth checking out include: Palliser Estate, Ata Rangi, and Te

Kairanga from Martinborough; Cloudy Bay, Koura Bay, Dog Point, Seresin, and Forrest from Marlborough; and, C.J. Pask and Matariki from Hawke's Bay.

South Africa

As its wine industry continues to evolve and improve, South Africa is quickly becoming an important wine region on the world stage. As the industry moves from volume production to quality wines, its rank in terms of production has dropped (now ninth) but you can expect to see much better wines on wine shop shelves, and on restaurant wine lists.

> **Did You Know?**
>
> In the New World, South Africa has the longest tradition for producing quality wine. The Dutch planted vines as early as 1654.

Almost half of South Africa's vineyards have been replanted in recent years, and the historically high percentage (85%) of white grape plantings has given way to more balanced plantings. To reflect the demands of the export market, white grape plantings now only make up about 55% of all plantings. Most of the new plantings have been to Cabernet Sauvignon, Merlot, Syrah, and Sauvignon Blanc, with Syrah and Sauvignon Blanc thought to be the future stars, quality-wise.

Chenin Blanc (once better known as Steen locally) is still the most-planted wine grape and accounts for almost a fifth of total plantings. It's used to produce a variety of different styles from dry, everyday wines to late-harvest sweeties.

Cabernet Sauvignon is the most widely planted red wine grape, and Syrah is now second. Many winemakers think Syrah (also bottled as Shiraz) may be the grape of the future. South Africa makes quite interesting Pinot Noir but the quantities are very small. More than half of red wine vineyards are less than 10 years old (part of the replanting), so it's a good idea to buy the youngest vintages available to take advantage of the quality improvements of recent years.

Cinsaut (once called Hermitage) used to be the leading red variety, and at one time, most South African red wine on wine shop shelves would have been Pinotage (a crossing of Cinsaut and Pinot Noir which is grown only in South Africa). However both have lost their appeal and have fallen dramatically in terms of red grape plantings.

South Africa has a well-established Wines of Origin (WO) system. The system guarantees the origin of what's in the bottle—100% from the place the grapes are grown; 85% of the grapes that are listed on the label; and, 85% from the vintage indicated on the label—as well each wine is tasted and certified by a tasting panel.

South Africa's vineyards are mostly situated in the Western Cape, near the coast, where the potentially high temperatures are tempered by cool ocean breezes. There are five (at last count) large wine regions but it is the 18 or so districts that you will see on the label. There are also about 50 smaller wards covered by the WO. The more notable districts are **Stellenbosch, Paarl** (the two most established districts which represent about one-third of all production, including Cabernet Sauvignon, Pinotage, Syrah, Chardonnay, and Chenin Blanc), **Robertson** (for Chardonnay, Syrah, and Cabernet Sauvignon), and **Overberg** (slightly cooler and good for Sauvignon Blanc, Pinot Noir, and Syrah).

Of the over 370 wineries operating in South Africa, here are a few you should check out: Tukulu, Winds of Change, Hamilton-Russell, Bouchard-Finlayson, Neil Ellis, Cape Point Vineyards, Klein-Constantia, Mulderbosch, Freedom Road, and Fariview, with its tongue-planted-firmly-in-cheek Goats Do Roam and Goats Roti wines.

Rest of the World

What have we missed? Did you know that wine is made in China, India, Korea, Japan, and even Thailand? Some of these wines may have reached your wine shop already—we've tried a pretty good Chinese Riesling however the Korean wine we sampled wasn't so good.

Total production is still very low in most Asian countries, and production is mainly intended for domestic markets. Japan has its own *Vitis vinifera*, Koshu, which makes a crisp, delicate white wine.

China

Is it the Old World—or the New World? Wine has been made in China for over 2,000 years, though only in the last decade or so has the potential for quality wines been recognized. There are about 400 wineries operating in China today, and 100 of these are serious producers of grape-based wines.

China's wine regions remain largely undefined. Most production comes from two areas: the provinces south and west of Beijing;

and the coastal provinces to the east. One promising new winery—Suntime—is situated in the remote western reaches of the vast Gobi Desert! Great Wall and Dragon Seal are wineries to watch.

It's still too early to comment on the wines. Regulations are non-existent, and quality is variable. Some growers reduce yields to get better wines, while others chaptalize heavily to gain high alcohol levels. Wine labels may also be misleading, or at minimum unhelpful. As investment continues to pour into the wine industry, much of it foreign, expect things to change. Maybe in the next edition of this book we will have more to add.

India

Buoyed by increased local demand and a severe 250% tax regime on imports, India's wine industry is flourishing. India grows a lot of eating grapes, but wine production is tiny—about two million bottles in total. The eight or so wineries currently registered are in the states of Maharashtra and Bangalore (Karnataka). While there is a preference to grow Bordeaux varietals, many wines are blends of local grapes like Arkeshyma and Bangalore Blue.

Chateau Indage is the largest winery (200,000 cases) and produces the famous Omar Khayyan sparkling wine. Other producers to look for include Sula and Grover.

The Art of Tasting Wine
Or Learning How to Spit

As of yet, we haven't had to teach anyone how to drink in our tasting events. That seems to come naturally—and very naturally to some. What we do instead is teach people how to *taste*.

Don't worry; you don't have to adopt some pretentious ritual just to be able to enjoy wine. Professional winetasting is for professionals. But tasting like a pro opens up a whole new dimension to wine that you might not even know exists.

Tasting anything is a multi-sensory experience, whether it's a plate of french fries or a glass of wine. While you think you're using only your mouth to taste, your other senses actually play a bigger role. Just try to taste those fries with a cold.

When you taste wine you use your senses in order: sight, smell, touch, and taste. We'll leave out hearing because we have yet to meet someone capable of differentiating between the sound of '89 Bordeaux sloshing around in a glass and a Starbucks' grande Americano.

Wine tasting is easy to learn and a bit like cooking. At first you're stumbling around in the kitchen, then before you know it you're making spaghetti Bolognese. And in no time at all you're inviting everyone over for Thanksgiving dinner.

With a little practice, and some patience, you too will be tasting like a pro and inviting your friends to wine parties.

The "Eyes" Have It

Just as we expect milk to be white and opaque, we should expect our wine to look a certain way. Even before we get to the wine, visual clues on the bottle and the label tell us a lot about the wine inside: where it's from, what grape or grapes it's made from, how old it is.

The cork itself—once it's out of the bottle—can give clues as to the age and care of the wine. If it's a relatively young wine, there won't be much to look at: the part of the cork that touched the wine is probably wet but not much else. Older corks, however, will be much darker. If the cork is in bad shape, maybe the wine wasn't stored properly.

And what about the wine itself? Why do pros stare at their wines for so long? Essentially they are looking at three things: clarity, color, and intensity.

Clarity

Is the wine bright and clear or dull and hazy? At one time this was very important but these days we don't see as many badly made hazy wines. Brightness, though, is important, as it indicates the presence of acidity and quality.

If the wine is a sparkling wine, then obviously you should expect to see bubbles. Some still wines (Muscadet sur Lie, for example) may have a slight spritz, but otherwise bubbles, where there aren't supposed to be any, aren't a good sign.

And there shouldn't be anything floating in your wine or resting on the bottom of the glass. Chunky bits are okay for orange juice but not wine.

Crystals

You may find sugar-like tartrate crystals sticking to the bottom of the wine cork or as part of the sediment at the bottom of the bottle—or your glass if you poured it in. They are harmless and indicate the wine has been stored in cold conditions. Many winemakers cold-stabilize their wines before bottling to eliminate these crystals.

Color

Certain wines have certain colors. You can use any term you want to describe the color of a wine—and some people do—but here are a few colors, or more precisely *hues,* you should expect to see in wine:

White Wines	Red Wines	Rosé Wines
Green	Purple	Blue-pink
Lemon	Ruby	Orange-pink
Straw	Cherry	Salmon
Gold	Garnet	
Amber	Brick	
	Mahogany	

Did You Know?

In addition to oxidizing as they age, red wines polymerize—a $10 word used to describe how color molecules link together over time to form larger molecules. Eventually they get too heavy to stay soluble and fall to the bottom of the bottle as sediment. If you ever open a 20-year-old port, for example, you will see the sediment that has formed on the side of the bottle (if the bottle was stored on its side). The first to go are the purple molecules (anthocyanins), leaving the more reddish-orange tannins behind. Knowing how and when these changes occur are a professional taster's "party trick."

In addition to helping you describe the wine, here's what else the color suggests:

- **Age**—White wines gain color as they age (from greenish tints to amber), while red wines lose color (from purple hues to mahogany). As they age, wines oxidise just like an apple core left on the countertop overnight. A very young Chardonnay, for example, shouldn't be amber. If it is, it could mean there's something wrong with the wine.
- **The grape type**—Fuller-bodied wines are deeper colored. Cabernet Sauvignon produces a darker-colored wine than Pinot Noir, and certain grape varieties (e.g., Grenache) brown more rapidly than other varieties.
- **Origin**—Cool-climate regions produce lighter-colored wines and warm-climate regions produce deeper-colored wines.
- **Winemaking technique**—Overripe grapes, longer skin contact during fermentation, and oak aging all result in more deeply colored wines.

Intensity

Depth refers to the intensity of the color. In the glass, this isn't uniform: the deepest color is usually at the center of the glass, getting paler towards the rim. Here are a few key words, and the order in which they would be used, to describe depth:

Watery ➔ Pale ➔ Medium ➔ Deep ➔ Opaque

For example, a young German Riesling wine will have a watery intensity, while a young Shiraz will look opaque. As the Shiraz ages it will start to lighten at the rim first (where the wine meets the edge of the glass).

Taste—It's All in Your Nose!

For the enjoyment of wine, your nose—your sense of smell—is the most important tool you have. When you *taste* a wine, you actually *smell* it. Your tongue is capable of differentiating only four main tastes—sweet, sour, bitter, and salty—while your nose is sensitive to over 10,000! Since there are 200 or so known odorous com-pounds in wine, it's no contest—the nose wins.

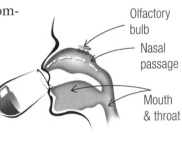

Olfactory bulb

Nasal passage

Mouth & throat

We will not go into detail on how the nose works, but essentially what goes up your nose when you inhale are molecules in a gaseous state. Everything, except maybe rocks, gives off these gaseous molecules. The molecules are trapped in your nasal cavity, in the mucous layer, and the odors are transferred through impulses to the olfactory bulb and eventually to the brain. Here it triggers your memory of the smell and tells you "Ah, raspberries!"

That assumes you have smelled raspberries before of course. If you don't have a memory for the smell of raspberries, you won't be able to put a name to it.

Practice, Practice, Practice

Professional tasters have very good smell memories. For some, it's a gift, but for most it's learned. Becoming more aware of how things around you smell can strengthen your memory.

People who smell certain things on a regular basis (florists or donut makers, for example) find the intensity of familiar smells diminished when they encounter them elsewhere. This is called *adaptation*, and it also happens with wine.

First let's talk about what to look for when *describing* the smell of a wine, and then we will show you how to actually smell a wine.

Wines Have Noses, Too.

You will hear people refer to the "nose" of a wine. This refers to the "smell." Instead of saying your wine "smells" of strawberries, you say, "I detect strawberries on the nose". If a wine has a "big nose," it means the smell is intense.

Aroma

Let's get this straight at the outset—there are no raspberries, or any other fruit (other than grapes), in wine. It just may smell like raspberries. Wine odors come from three sources: the grape, fermentation, and aging.

Aroma refers to odors associated with the grapes. Aroma is more obvious in young wines and pungent-smelling wines like Sauvignon Blanc or Muscat. Pros call it the *primary aroma*.

It's fairly easy to describe wine aroma. Wine people use common items—plants, fruits, and flowers especially—partly because they belong to similar chemical groups (that's why things smell similar) but mainly because they provide a common vocabulary. On the next page are some examples of wine aromas.

Aroma		Grape
Fruity	Citrus	Riesling
	Black fruits (e.g., blackcurrants)	Cabernet Sauvignon
	Red fruits (e.g., raspberries)	Pinot Noir
Floral	Violets	Nebbiolo (Barolo)
	Roses	Gewürztraminer
	Orange blossom	Muscat
Vegetal/ Herbal	Asparagus or cut grass	Sauvignon Blanc
	Bell pepper	Cabernet Franc
Spicy/Nutty	Black pepper	Syrah/Shiraz
	Almonds	Garganega (Soave)

Bouquet

Bouquet not only sounds more sophisticated than aroma, but also describes more sophisticated and complex odors. These are the odors associated with fermentation and aging. They add a layer of complexity that leads directly to our overall enjoyment and appreciation of wine.

During fermentation, yeasts and bacteria act to create a new set of odors. Certain yeasts create their own aromatics, some good and some bad. (Wild yeasts can induce some less desirable odors.) Wooden barrels, if used, make their own individual contribution to the wine's bouquet. All of these add to the wine's primary aromas and create an expanded odor profile. Barrel-fermented Chardonnay, for example, smells quite different from Chardonnay made in stainless steel tanks.

In wines that have been aged—in barrels and/or bottles—a different set of changes occurs. In barrels the wine oxidizes and certain components of the wood (oak, for example) are dissolved in the wine. This is the origin of the smell of vanilla in oak-aged wines. Newer barrels contribute more to the bouquet than older barrels. In the bottle, the wine has very little contact with oxygen, so the process is more or less *reductive*. Harsher odors slowly become muted and more harmonized.

Some wines take longer than others to develop their bouquet, however, for most of the wines on the market the winery has made this decision for you. They are ready to drink when you buy them. For the others, check vintage charts or ask for advice.

Follow Your Nose

What else might your nose lead you to? Here are a few clues:

- **Cleanliness**—Wine should be free of unpleasant odors. You wouldn't drink a glass of milk that has soured, would you?
- **Grape variety**—Noble varieties (e.g., Cabernet Sauvignon and Riesling) are more distinctive.
- **Grape quality**—Poorer quality grapes are usually overly intense (e.g., North American labrusca grapes) or "foxy." And overcropping any vine produces grapes of weaker character or less intensity.
- **Age**—Recently bottled wines often suffer from something called "bottle fatigue": the wine is "dumb" and you can't really smell anything. Older wines can be "closed" at first, and need some time to open up. A few minutes in a decanter can speed this process along.

Is It OK to Touch?

The touch factor in wine refers to its *texture*, sometimes called mouthfeel. When you slosh the wine around in your mouth, it feels a certain way. Some wines are smoother (e.g., Pinot Noir), some are harsher (e.g., a young Cabernet Sauvignon), and some are mouthfilling (e.g., a California Chardonnay). What's going on and what does it mean?

- *Astringency* is the puckering or drying sensation you feel on your teeth and gums. Astringency comes from tannins, either from the grape itself or from the barrels in which the wine was aged. Try a mouthful of very strong tea and you'll get the idea of what astringency feels like. High acidity in a wine will accentuate the sensation of astringency. Astringency is often confused with bitterness, but they are two separate things. One is a feeling and the other is a taste.
- *Body* is a more difficult term to define. It's the feeling of weight and richness in your mouth as a result of alcohol, sugars, and intensity of flavor. Think about it in terms of fabrics (silk, velvet, wool) or viscosity (watery, thin, full, or thick).
- High levels of *alcohol* will produce a hot sensation down the center of your tongue and can be perceived both as a sweet and bitter sensation. That is why some dry red wines like Amarone, with high alcohol levels, are thought to be sweet. Alcohol also coats the surface of your mouth and distributes flavors around your palate.

Let's not forget bubbles—that "prickle" on the tip of your tongue that comes from sparkling wine. While drinking sparkling wine is more commonly associated with happier occasions, the dissolved carbon dioxide in the wine is actually creating a mild pain sensation in our brains. This sensation puts our taste buds into overdrive and intensifies the flavors in the sparkling wine, or the food we are eating with it.

Finally, the serving temperature of the wine can have an impact on the perception of astringency, body, and alcohol. Cool serving temperatures will de-emphasize a wines texture; too warm, and the alcohol in particular will be overemphasized.

Listening to Your Mouth

The texture of a wine in your mouth can suggest the following:

- **Grape variety**—Red wines, especially young red wines, have more tannin. Certain grape varieties (e.g., Nebbiolo) are more tannic than others (e.g., Merlot), while some varieties (e.g., Riesling) feel lighter-bodied.
- **Origin of the wine**—A wine from a warm-climate region will feel fuller-bodied than one from a cool-climate region, and the sensation caused by higher alcohol levels will be stronger.
- **Fermentation technique**—If the wine has been fermented in oak for a period of time, you will detect tannins or astringency from the oak. Oak tannins are softer than grape tannins, and are more apparent on the checks and the back of your mouth (as opposed to grape tannins, which are apparent on your teeth and gums.)

Stick Out Your Tongue

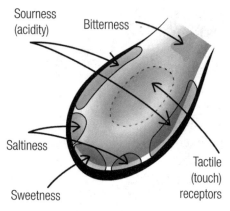

Sourness (acidity)
Bitterness
Saltiness
Tactile (touch) receptors
Sweetness

Different parts of your tongue are more sensitive to certain tastes than other parts. That's why the pros slosh the wine around in their mouths. When you taste something sweet, for example, you should pick it up on the tip of your tongue. You'll taste sweet elsewhere, but the tip is the most sensitive. Sweetness, then, should be the first thing you notice in a wine.

Acidity (tartness) is sensed at the sides of the tongue and will probably make your mouth water, just as it does when you drink fresh-squeezed orange juice. Acidity gives wines their "zing."

Bitterness—like the taste of tonic water or strong black coffee—is mainly sensed at the back of the tongue. This explains why some people comment on the "bitterness" of a wine once they've swallowed it—it's the last thing they taste. A touch of bitterness is considered to be an attribute in young red wines, and in particular some Italian red wines.

> **Did You Know?**
> Our sensitivity to sweetness is the lowest of all the tastes. Bitterness is the highest and sourness is in the middle. And in case you're wondering, salt occurs in such minute quantities in wine you shouldn't be able to detect it.

Speaking of Tongues

Once the wine is in your mouth, what will your tongue tell you?

- **Balance**—Acidity should offset sweetness, otherwise the wine will be cloying. Any one component is excess will make the wine taste unpleasant.
- **Grape variety**—Certain grapes (e.g., Sauvignon Blanc and Barbera) have more acidity than others.
- **Origin of the wine**—Grapes grown in cool-climate regions generally have more acidity. Italian wines tend to have a touch of bitterness on the finish.
- **Fermentation technique**—Some winemakers prefer to leave a little residual sugar in their wines, some a lot, making the wines off dry, sweet, or lusciously sweet.

> **Did You Know?**
> There's another taste—umami. Savory foods (shellfish, meats, cooked tomatoes, and cheeses) are said to be high in umami and may increase the sensation of bitterness in a wine.

Who Gets the Last Word?

Remember, all you can discern at this time is sweet, sour, and bitter. You don't *taste* raspberries in wine, you *smell* them. Now if you swallow the wine, you might actually think you taste raspberries. That's because there is a secondary route to the olfactory bulb at the back of your throat called the *retronasal passage*.

As you breathe out after swallowing, wine odors are volatized by the warmth of your mouth and pushed out over that mucous layer again. So when you think you are *tasting* raspberries, you are actually *smelling* them again. Your nose always has to have the last word.

Putting It All Together

When it comes to tasting wine, you have to pull all of your senses together. When you do you can start to make decisions or even assessments about the wine. Do you like it? Should you drink it? Should you give it to your sister for her birthday? Is it good value and should you buy more?

Here are three things to consider as you combine your senses:

- *Finish* is the lingering impression a wine leaves long after you have swallowed it. If the wine has a "short" finish (a few seconds) the flavor disappears quickly. Ten seconds is considered medium and 15 seconds long. Too long and the wine has overstayed its welcome. If a wine was inexpensive and it had a long finish, buy more!
- *Balance* describes the harmony between fruit, acidity, sugar, alcohol, and tannins, in the wine. This isn't the exclusive domain of superior wines; even humble table wines can exhibit balance. It's the best indicator of good winemaking.
- *Quality*, of course, is subjective. What really matters is what *you* think of the wine. It isn't about price, expert reviews, or even what your friends say. If you like the wine, then just say so.

Getting Ready to Spit

Now we get to the good part. Wine tasting requires a little preparation, so here are a few things to do before getting started.

Put yourself in the right frame of mind. If you just spent two hours battling rush hour traffic, maybe this isn't a good time to taste wine. Your senses are most acute in the morning, say around 10 a.m., or mid-afternoon before you have dinner. Tasting when starving or after a full meal isn't a good idea, either—especially after a double anchovy and garlic pizza! Even tasting wine after drinking a coffee will have an effect on how the wine smells and tastes. If you taste for fun—say as part of a get together with friends—then you'll probably be doing it in the evening. In this case just avoid strongly flavored foods.

Avoid using cologne or perfume too. It will have an effect on what you smell. And don't brush your

Blind Tasting

In a blind taste you are given a sample (or more) of wine and asked to evaluate it without knowing where it was made or what grapes were used. That way price, the producer or any other factor does not influence your assessment of the wine.

It's also a fun party game.

teeth just before you taste. If you do, all the wines will taste minty fresh.

Make sure the lighting is good. Remember, you have to see the wine. Save the dim lights for the romantic dinner afterwards.

Create space. A nice big table is better than a small corner of your kitchen—especially if this is a social affair. If possible, use a white surface. A tablecloth would be great but you may not like the inevitable red wine spills. A sheet of white paper works fine—anything that you can put the wine against to see its true color.

Wine-tasting checklist:

- Make sure the wines are at the right temperature (about 50°F/10°C for white wines and 60°F/16°C for reds.) You should be able to get about 12 samples from each bottle.
- Unless the bottles have screwcaps, don't forget the corkscrew.
- Clean, clear glasses—preferably all the same size and shape if you're going to taste more than one wine or have friends over. Make sure the glasses have stems and hold about 6 to 8 oz (220 ml).
- Have something to take notes with when you taste. That way you have a record of what you thought about the wine. It will come in handy when you taste a whole series of wines and want to remember something about them later. For a copy of the tasting sheet we use, go to www.thewinecoaches.com.
- If you're tasting lots of wines, you might want to have plain bread, breadsticks, or room-temperature mineral water (not the fizzy kind) handy to neutralize your palate. If it's one or two wines, don't bother. Definitely hold the Gorgonzola or salmon dip until after you've finished tasting the wine.
- You'll need something to spit in if you aren't planning on swallowing all the wines. Preferably something opaque as no one likes to look at someone else's spit. It also needs to be large enough so that you don't have to worry about being overly accurate. The pros use spittoons but a paper coffee cup or plastic beer cup work just fine.

Getting the Wine Out

Now comes the fun part: opening the bottle. Before the days of screwcap bottles, getting the cork out of a bottle required a bit of skill. Like shuffling a deck of cards, with practice, it's easy to look impressive using a corkscrew.

What's Between You and the Wine?

Well, usually just the traditional cork. But nowadays there are many different closures being used. Metal screwcaps are becoming very popular, especially with wineries in the New World. You might come across synthetic corks (sometimes hard to get out), glass stoppers (not widely used yet), and even crown caps (like beer bottles) on wine bottles. Wine is also sold in Tetra Pak® containers, with plastic spouts to pour the wine from.

While their use has been decreasing in recent years, corks, made from the bark of cork trees in Spain and Portugal, are still the most popular means of sealing bottles of wine. Over 80% of wines sold in bottles still use a natural cork. Corks hold the wine inside, yet allow a minute amount of oxygen to enter the bottle. For quality wines, this is said to help the development of the wines. The jury is still out on whether wines sealed with a screwcap offer the same conditions for longer-term aging.

Corks aren't perfect, however, and occasionally a contaminated one will give the wine off-odors. Some say as many as one in 12 bottles are contaminated by bad corks. Until cork producers find a way to combat this defect, and some are working very hard to produce cleaner corks, winemakers will continue to use screwcaps rather than subject their wine to an unpredictable little chunk of bark.

As consumers, we should be concerned about quality as well. Next time you see a screw top or crown cap on a quality wine, don't sneer but instead appreciate that the producer thought enough about you to make sure you received their wine in the best possible condition. But then again, opening a bottle of wine has its traditions. Twisting off the metal cap of the wine bottle at your table maybe isn't the same experience as that provided by a skilled sommelier removing the cork with a hand-crafted corkscrew.

Did You Know?

Corks are usually bleached prior to washing. Occasionally the chlorine reacts with molds in the cork and can produce off-odors in the wine.

If you detect an eau-de-musty basement smell in the wine, it is "corked" and you shouldn't drink it.

Where's the Cork?

Unless the bottle you're about to open is sealed with a screwcap, there's a good chance that the first thing that's between you and the wine is a plastic or aluminum *capsule* covering over the top of the bottle neck.

- If there's no capsule, just a wide bottle lip or flange and a cork covered with a wax or plastic seal, skip ahead to the next section on using a corkscrew.
- If there's a capsule, cut if off below the second lip of the bottle. Most corkscrews have a little knife or cutting edge to help you do this. Run the knife completely around the neck of the bottle, cutting through to the glass. Use the point of the knife to pull up the piece of the capsule you've just cut off.
- Plastic capsules often have a little tab sticking out: it's okay to pull the tab to remove the capsule top.

Check out the top of the cork. If it's an older wine, there might be crud on top of the cork. This is okay because it indicates the wine has been stored in a humid place. Don't worry, the crud won't have gone into the wine, and to make sure it doesn't, just wipe it off with a clean damp cloth or paper towel.

With screw cap closures there is no cork, simply twist the cap, breaking the seal that holds the cap on, and you're ready to pour the wine.

The Pointy End Goes in First

It's hard to believe that a little piece of cork can cause so much trouble. We've had to open wines with corks wedged in so tightly that the force of yanking the cork out pulled some wine out with it. And we've opened wines with corks that have compressed so much over the years so that they slipped down the neck of the bottle and into the wine below.

How you get the screw part of the corkscrew into the cork will depend on the design of the corkscrew you use. There are three that we recommend. They all cost under $25 and do the job nicely:

- **Waiter's Corkscrew**—Most people in the restaurant business use this compact corkscrew, hence its name. Tucked into its handle is a small knife that folds out for cutting the capsule foil.

    Waiter's corkscrew

    To use one, make sure the bottle is on a solid surface. (Experienced servers can open a bottle in the air but they've had lots of practice.) Remove the foil or plastic capsule first, or if there is a little plastic tab on top of the cork, just prepare to drill through it.

    Gently press the point of the spiral (called the *worm*) into the center of the cork, holding the corkscrew at a 45-degree angle. As you begin twisting the worm into the cork, straighten it up so it goes in vertically. Twist it in a clockwise direction about four or five turns, until it is almost completely in the cork. Teflon® worms are best—you won't believe the difference it makes.

Push the bottom of the handle downwards now, in order to hook the hinged metal piece of the corkscrew onto the lip of the bottle. Hold the metal piece on the lip with your free hand while you pull up the handle and the worm with your other hand. This should draw out the cork. Ease up near the end of the process otherwise you might draw out some wine if the bottle was overfilled.

On some waiter's corkscrews, the hinged metal piece is in two parts (two-phase). You use the middle stage first, to bring the cork half way out, then release and use the end stage to bring the cork fully out. The two-phase models are particularly useful for wines that have longer corks. Our favorite model is PullTaps®.

Probably the best way to learn how to use a waiter's corkscrew is to watch your server next time you're at a restaurant.

Screwpull

- **Screwpull® Corkscrew**—This is an excellent corkscrew for home use: it's simple and fast to use. It has a longer Teflon®-coated worm that works on almost every cork, but since it doesn't come with a built in knife you will need an extra accessory (foil cutter) to cut the capsule.

  Expose the cork and place the Screwpull® on top of the bottle with a plastic leg resting on each side of the neck. The point of the worm should be sitting on top of the cork. Hold the legs against the top of the bottle and begin twisting the handle clockwise, twisting the worm into the cork. Keep turning, and the cork slides right out of the bottle neck. No pulling required.

  We find the Screwpull® only works for standard 750 ml bottles. Some larger format bottles have too large a neck for the device.

Butler's friend or Ah-So

- **Butler's Friend**—For older bottles with fragile corks we recommend a corkscrew called the Butler's Friend or the Ah-So. This unique corkscrew gets the cork out without piercing a hole in it. It requires technique and a lot of practice, but once you get the knack, you'll love using it.

  Holding the handle, slide the longer prong between the cork and the bottle top, gently working it down just enough to allow you to insert the other prong against the cork on the other side. Use your free hand to get both prongs in the bottle. Rock the prongs back and forth, with a gentle downward push, until the handle is close to the top of the bottle. Twist and pull up the opener until the cork is freed. If the cork is loose, however, it may just push the cork down the neck and into the wine—that's where patience comes in.

Lever-type openers have become quite popular lately. With the patent expiring on the Rabbit® opener, many different lower-cost alternatives flooded the market. Essentially they all work on the same principle by removing the cork from the bottle in one easy movement. More expensive than the three versions we just described, lever-type openers also take up more storage space and are not very portable.

Busted!

Everyone breaks a cork now and then—don't worry about it. Sometimes the cork is flawed or is just very old. If there's still enough of the cork left in the neck of the bottle gently reinsert the corkscrew at an extreme angle, and ease the cork out. If it doesn't work, simply poke the broken piece into the bottle.

A little bit of cork isn't harmful, just don't serve your guests first. Corks floats and the first pour usually has more bits. If it's really bad, pour the bottle of wine into a decanter through a coffee filter.

How to Not Drink the Gunk at the Bottom of the Bottle

If you just opened a bottle of older red wine, there is a good chance that it will have some sediment on the bottom of the bottle. You don't really want that in your glass. It won't kill you but it will make the wine less brilliant and hazier. To keep this from happening, you—or your server—will have to *decant* the wine.

There are three reasons for decanting a wine:

- To separate the wine from the naturally forming sediment or deposit. This is more common in older, full-bodied tannic red wines and in vintage ports. There shouldn't be sediment in a white wine;
- To aerate, or help a wine breathe or open up; and,
- For show!

At home, you don't really need a special decanter for this purpose—any clean, clear glass or crystal jug will work just fine provided that it's large enough to hold the contents of a bottle and has a large surface area to expose the wine to air. We use a glass pitcher as a decanter. It looks great, works well, and is easy to clean.

If you are decanting for aeration, just open and empty the wine vigorously into the decanter. Do this about half an hour before the meal and enjoy.

Decanting for sediment is a little trickier.

- First, make sure the bottle has been upright for a few hours to let the sediment settle down to the bottom of the bottle. If the wine has been stored for a number of years (vintage port, for example) you may want to keep it upright for a day or so.

- Open the wine as you normally would but take extra care not to shake the bottle. Hold the bottle of wine in one hand and the decanter in the other. With a light source (a candle or a mini flashlight) below the neck of the bottle, slightly tilt the top of the bottle and the decanter towards each other and *slowly* pour the contents of the wine into the decanter.

- Continue pouring until you see the dark sediment pass into the neck of the bottle. It'll be near the end of the wine, and therefore is easier to see in the light. Stop decanting at this point, and you're ready to start enjoying the wine. We usually don't recommend drinking the ounce or so left in the bottle, but you can run it through a coffee filter if you don't want to waste a drop.

Does Wine Breathe?

I'm not coming out 'til I'm good and ready!

Aeration, or letting a wine breathe, gives it contact with air to improve the aromas and taste of the wine. This is for full-bodied, higher alcohol, or tannic, young red wines that need time to be at their best—Cabernet Sauvignon, Syrah, and Barolo for example. Older white wines (Burgundy, for example) also seem to benefit from a little aeration.

If wines didn't get the time they needed in the bottle, you can help them along by getting oxygen into the wine as quickly as possible. Give the wine in your glass a few good swirls, or decant it as we just described. There are some who insist that the aromas and flavors of a wine are lost by decanting it, and they prefer to aerate the wine by simply swirling it in their glass.

You can go too far with this breathing thing, however. Wines left too long exposed to air can become flat and dull, or worse, oxidized. Oxygen improves the wine to a point, but then steadily causes it to decline into something un-tasty.

How to Open a Bottle of Sparkling Wine Without Killing Your Guests

Opening a bottle of wine is quite different and much more challenging. Despite what you see at the Formula One winner's circle and in the movies, sparkling wines aren't supposed to be opened with a loud pop and a gush of foam. And as funny as it may seem in the movies, the cork can be a dangerous little projectile. Some of the unique things about a champagne bottle—like the wire cage over the cork and the thicker glass—were designed to protect you and your guests from harm.

Opening a bottle of sparkling wine is easy if you maintain control of the bottle and let the escaping pressure do all the work. Here's how you can open a bottle without putting your guests or your pets at risk.

- *Never use a corkscrew.*
- Make sure the wine is well chilled (under 50°F/10°C). This will suppress some of the pressure that can cause it to open explosively. If the bottle has been in an ice bucket, dry it off—the bottle that is.
- Tear off the foil to reveal the wire cage that wraps over the cork. Press one of your thumbs over the top of the cage and hold it there while you undo and remove the cage with your other hand. This can be tricky so point the wine away from your loved ones, Aunt Mabel's china collection, and that big window in the front room. Even while removing the cage, always try to keep your thumb on top of the cork at all times.
- Now grasp the cork tightly with one hand (the one with the thumb that's been on the cork), while holding the bottom of the bottle firmly with your other hand. Hold the bottle at a 45° angle and gently start turning the base of the bottle away from you (clockwise if you are using your right hand to turn) while holding the cork steady. The pressure in the bottle will slowly begin to push the cork out. Control the pressure

Ready to Punt?

One extra special bonus with champagne and many other sparkling wines is the chance to pour using the punt, that indentation at the bottom of the bottle. This really impresses people. Just put your thumb into the punt and rest the underside of the bottle against your fingers as you pour.

while slowly easing out the cork. You should hear a soft hiss if it's done properly. It's okay to stop for a few seconds to prevent any foaming incidents. Have the glasses ready just in case.

Do You Need Glasses?

Why spend money on glasses, why not just spend it on more or better wine? Better glasses improve the look, the smell, the taste and the feel of the wine. Sadly, they won't turn a $20 wine into a $50 wine. But if they improve the tasting experience, perhaps that's all that matters.

Do you have to spend a lot to get good glassware? You can if you want. Riedel, a brand of Austrian crystal glassware, makes wine glasses for every grape type and wine style imaginable, but they can be expensive.

To start off, you might be happier with an all-purpose, and inexpensive, glass that will still enhance the appearance, aroma, and taste of the wine you drink. If you are thinking of buying a set of these glasses, here's what to look for, and what to avoid:

	Go For:	Avoid:
Color	Clear	Tinted or cut glass
Weight	Light, with thin rim	Heavy, with bead on rim
Size	10–12 oz (300–350 ml)	Shooter glasses or goldfish bowls
Shape	Tulip	Parallel sides, like a hi-ball glass.
Other	Has a stem	Logos

- Clear glass allows you to see the color of the wine, without it being distorted by the appearance of the glass itself.
- A lighter-weight glass lets you concentrate on the feel of the wine in your mouth, not the feel of the glass.
- A larger size gives you the room you need to swirl your wine without having it slosh over the sides.
- The shape, tapered in toward the rim, concentrates the aromas and enhances the taste experience. You might want to buy a different set of glasses for sparkling wine– tall flutes and not those saucer-type glasses from the sixties—as they concentrate the bubbles more in the glass.
- The stem lets you hold the glass without getting fingerprints on the bowl, or warming up the wine.

Filling the Glass

Don't be disappointed when you are served a glass of wine that isn't filled right to the rim. When serving wine with a meal, glasses should be filled to the widest part of the glass bowl, about 4 or 5 oz (110–140 ml) per glassful. This allows for more aeration, for the wine to open up and release its aromas into the air. It also gives you enough room to swirl the wine, again to release those aromas into the bowl of the glass so that you can enjoy them. If you are tasting wine, and not serving it with a meal, a couple of ounces is sufficient.

When pouring sparkling wine, you should use a succession of small pours instead of one so the wine won't foam up and pour over the rim.

Tasting Like a Pro

Now that you've successfully opened and poured the wine, you're ready to taste it. While the pros have their rituals, all you need is a system or routine that you are comfortable with, that helps you build the case for or against the wine, yet doesn't require a lot of time. With practice you can perform our program in a matter of seconds. Of course if you become a world-class taster, or you really enjoy the wine, then you'll want to spend more time with each wine.

The 4 S's

Our "Four-Step Program to Taste Like a Pro" is based on—you guessed it—four steps: the 4 S's:

1. See
2. Sniff
3. Sip
4. Spit (or swallow depending on where you are)

These steps follow closely the sensory appeal of wine that we discussed earlier in this section: see relates to sight; sniff relates to smell; and sip relates to touch and taste. The spit or swallow step wraps up the whole experience. Don't worry about the process at first; it is more important to think about the wine and how it appeals to you.

For our program, you'll need about 1 or 2 oz (30–60 ml) in your glass. That way you'll have room to swirl the wine in the bowl without spilling. You might not think this will be enough wine, but trust us, you'll get four to six good sips out of it. Besides, it leaves even more to drink later if you like the wine.

Here's how each step works:

See

Although most wines are pretty clean nowadays, a visual inspection of the wine is still an important part of the process. Here's what the pros do and what they're looking for:

- Looking down at your glass, check for clarity—is the wine bright and clear? Are there any floaters? Bubbles?
- Tilt the glass at about a 45° angle over whatever white surface you're using. You are now looking at the color (hue) and intensity of the wine. Look at the core or center of the wine first, not where it meets the glass (the rim.)
- Use simple words to describe what you see. For example, "pale, greenish-yellow" or "deep, ruby red" are good descriptors. "Crayola #264" may be more accurate, but most people won't know what that means.
- Now look at the rim. If the color extends all the way to the rim this suggests a younger wine. If the rim edge is pale or watery, it's probably a more mature wine. The wider the rim, the more mature the wine.

Sniff

Here's where you get to *swirl* the wine like you've seen the pros do. But before you do, let it settle for a few seconds. Swirling the wine can mask some faults.

- Once it has settled, lift the glass to your nose and take a quick sniff. What do you smell? Is the wine clean? Is what you smell weak or pronounced?
- To swirl, hold the stem or base of the glass and make a few small counter-clockwise circles. At first, do this with your glass on the table. When you get good at it, you can do it in the air like the pros. Now you know why we said to buy large glasses. Swirling takes practice so give yourself lots of space early on and don't wear anything white.

Did You Know?

The streams that run down the side of your glass after you swirl it are called "tears" or "legs." This indicates the evaporation rate of the alcohol in the wine, the surface tension, and other technical things. Wines with more alcohol appear to have more "legs." You can't really draw too many conclusions about the wine from the legs, but they are nice to look at.

- Swirl the glass a few times, then get your nose right into the glass and take a deep but short sniff. What's the first thing that comes to mind? A fruit? A vegetable? Your grandmother's baking? Take a couple more sniffs to see what else you detect. Write down whatever comes to mind.

Smell is personal—whatever is triggered in your brain is yours and no one can tell you you're wrong. Of course, certain smells are associated with certain grapes from certain regions. In a red wine it is unlikely that you are getting a citrus smell and white wines don't smell like blackcurrants. And you shouldn't smell turkey in *any* wine.

Three or four sniffs is enough. Any more and you will tire out your nose or look pretentious. Even if you only came up with a few words don't worry—smelling takes practice.

Sip

You've been patient, now you get to try the wine. You are looking for "touch" and "taste" sensations.

- Take a sip—about a good tablespoonful—and swish or slosh it around in your mouth. Don't swallow (or spit) yet. Try to hold it in your mouth for a few seconds to get the full effect.
- What level of sweetness (on the tip of your tongue) or bitterness (on the back of your tongue) do you detect? How about a tingle on the sides of your tongue? Does it make your mouth pucker or water? Is the wine silky or coarse, light-bodied or full? Are there any bubbles? Does the wine feel balanced—like the way a juicy peach is both sweet and tart? Can you detect alcohol—a burning sensation on your tongue?
- Look for indications of anything out of balance. Write down whatever comes to mind. Does the wine taste different from what you smelled? (The wine smelled sweet but tastes dry, for example). Or does it confirm what you smelled?

Keep in mind certain wines are supposed to have certain characteristics—New Zealand Sauvignon Blanc should be dry and crisp and California Cabernet Sauvignon should feel fuller-bodied, with tannins.

Spit or Swallow?

If you are intending to drink the wine, or you're in a restaurant, it's best to swallow the wine. If you are planning on tasting many different wines, however, and you have a spittoon handy, it's a good idea to spit rather than swallow. You start to lose your objectivity after four or five samples.

- Try another taste. This time let the wine rest on top of your tongue and gently inhale over top of it without swallowing—sort of like a reverse whistle. By drawing air into your mouth you are intensifying the volatile odors in the wine. This can be really tricky at first so wear dark clothes or keep a napkin handy to catch any drips.
- Now swallow, or spit, and after you do so exhale through your nose. What do you smell now? Is it different than when you first smelled the wine? More or less intense? Are there any new aromas?

Now it's time to draw some conclusions about the wine. Did you like it? Don't be afraid to talk about the wine. A few well-chosen words can help place the wine in your memory bank.

Reputable magazines and many wine writers use numerical systems to rate wines, but don't get blinded by 100-point scores or five-star evaluations. Just remember that the only way to evaluate a wine properly is to taste it yourself.

Using Your Words

Most people haven't developed a wine vocabulary. They can describe what an apple pie smells like when it is baking or the smell of sports equipment left in its bag from last season but they can't easily describe a wine. We assume you're in the same boat, so we've put together a table with some words to start thinking about and to use when you want to describe what you taste.

You might think some of the "smell words" should be in the bad words column. However, you can use *herbaceous* or *vegetal* to describe Sauvignon Blanc because its smell is usually associated with asparagus or cut grass. And that's okay in the context of a Sauvignon Blanc, but not a Chardonnay, which doesn't usually have vegetal characteristics. Older Red Burgundies can also smell vegetal, like "rotting leaves." It is all in how you interpret the smell.

Sight Words	Smell Words	Texture Words	Bad Words
Bright	Buttery (mild)	Astringent	Acetone
Bubbles	Clean	Chalky	Ammonia
Clear	Earthy	Chewy	Buttery (strong)
Cloudy	Floral	Creamy	Cheesy
Deep	Fruity	Crisp	Cooked
Dull	Gamey	Dry	Corked
Hazy	Grapey	Delicate	Garlic
Intense	Herbaceous	Fine	Geranium
Opaque	Jammy	Firm	Horsey
Pale	Juicy	Flabby	Leesy
Legs	Mineral	Harsh	Moldy
	Nutty	Heavy	Mousey
	Oaky	Hot	Plastic
	Perfumed	Lean	Putrid
	Pronounced	Light	Sauerkraut
	Ripe	Luscious	Sherry
	Rustic	Prickly	Soapy
	Spicy	Racy	Plastic
	Subtle	Rich	Rotten eggs
	Tired	Robust	Rubbery
	Vegetal	Silky	Sour
	Weak	Smooth	Sulphur
	Yeasty	Soft	Vinegar
	Youthful	Tannic	Wet cardboard
		Thin	

But How Many Words Do I Have to Remember?
People ask us this question all the time. They don't want to say something wrong and the list can be intimidating. If you keep your nose alert to smells around you, you really don't need to memorize a list at all. You're just building your memory.

Certain fruits are called upon more frequently than others, and here's a list of some of them:

In White Wines	In Red Wines
Apple	Blackberry
Apricot	Blackcurrant
Lemon	Cherry
Lime	Plum
Melon	Prune
Peach	Raspberry
Pineapple	Raisin
Tropical Fruit	Strawberry

When Good Wines Go Bad

It happens, good wines go bad. Sometimes they were made that way and sometimes something happens on the way to the wine shop shelf or restaurant. If you didn't store it properly, the wine could even have gone bad while it was under your care. That's learning the hard way!

The only drawback to learning how to taste properly is that it brings out all the good *and* the bad characteristics in the wine. Poorly made or defective wines aren't up to the challenge. While you'll learn to distinguish between something unfamiliar and something defective, you may also learn to uncover some flaws in good wines.

Flaws or defects are what makes a wine undrinkable or diminish the overall experience of drinking the wine. For example, wine shouldn't remind you of vinegar, a musty basement, rotten eggs, or sherry (unless it is sherry, of course). Unusual aromas could be due to bad winemaking, unintentional contamination from the cork, or poor storage.

Even before you put the wine to your nose to sniff, take note of what it looks like. If you notice a haze, prematurely browning colors, or bubbles when there shouldn't be any, pay special attention to the wine when you do sniff it. The following substances occasionally appear in the wine and may affect its appearance. However, they're essentially harmless:

- **Sediment**—These are the solids that precipitate out of tannic red wines as they age. Pour carefully or decant so you don't drink any.
- **Tartrates**—These are more common in white wines. Found on the base of the cork or settled at the bottom of the bottle, tar-

Lychees?

We purposely didn't put lychee on this list because it only comes into play with one wine—Gewürztraminer. Many people, however, are unfamiliar with its smell. If you want to try lychee fruit, go to an Asian grocery store and buy a can of them. It's the closest to what you smell in the wine.

trates look like glass crystals but they aren't. Pour carefully and they won't get in your glass.
- **Cork pieces**—These little bits of cork, from incomplete cork removal, won't hurt you—just have fun fishing them out of your glass.

Even if you are unfamiliar with the grape type or the wine itself, the wine should smell like wine and it should always smell "clean." It's rare: in maybe less than 5% of the bottles you drink will you find an off-odor in the wine. Here are some of the defects you're most likely to encounter:

- *Corked.* Cork taint (2, 4, 6 trichloroanisole or TCA for short) is the most common wine flaw (the average occurrence is said to be about one in every 12 bottles). It's also the easiest to identify again when you've smelled it once. The wine smells of musty, damp basement, or wet, moldy cardboard.

  This is nearly always isolated to one bottle, and not the whole shipment, but it can happen to any bottle that uses a cork. Don't drink "corked" wine; it's not harmful but it's not a pleasant experience.
- When wine is *oxidized* it smells of dried-out fruit or sherry. The wine has been exposed to air, either because it wasn't stored properly or because the cork was defective. The problem could be isolated to one bottle, unless the whole case was stored improperly. If you taste the wine, it will seem flat or unusually weak. Don't drink it. Wine left open too long will get oxidized.
- If a wine becomes overly oxidized, or was exposed to excessive heat, the wine is said to be *madeirized*. The aromatics are reminiscent of the wine called madeira but with more cooked, dried out molasses flavors. It's pretty hard to miss.
- When wine goes bad, it turns to *vinegar*. Because so many wines are treated with sulphur dioxide, it shouldn't happen but it does. And you'll know it. This defect is also probably isolated to one bottle. Don't drink it.
- A *sulphur* smell is a bacterial aroma often due to bad winemaking practices. You will recognize it as rotten eggs. It can affect a whole batch of bottles. Don't drink it even if you can get it past your nose.
- Another chemical aroma that can appear in wine is *acetone* (nail polish remover). Very unpleasant. Don't drink it.

Often mistaken for a fault, but isn't, is the presence of sulphur dioxide—the smell of burnt matches. Sulphur is actually an antioxidant used by wineries to preserve the wine, and while it might be sharp enough to make you sneeze (some are more sensitive than others) it should dissipate after a few minutes.

Stuck With a Bad Bottle?

Recognizing any of these faults, or if the wine doesn't seem right to you, is reason enough to return the wine. Just re-cork the bottle and return it from whence it came. Most reputable wine stores will replace the defective wine no questions asked, assuming you have the sales receipt. Just make sure you return it close to full. Yes they'll notice!

If the wine smells or tastes defective to you in a restaurant, bring it to the attention of the server right away. He or she should replace it without question.

Saving Opened Wine

It may not always be possible to finish a whole bottle of wine at one sitting. Or maybe you have some left over from your dinner party. Instead of pouring it out, or sitting up all night drinking the dregs, here is what you can do to protect your opened wine:

- Use a hand-operated vacuum pump to remove the air. Most pumps come with rubber stoppers that have a one-way valve. You put the rubber stopper where the cork was, place the vacuum pump over it, and pump it a few times to create a vacuum. It helps delay oxidation and extends the life of your opened wine by a few days.
- A slightly more expensive option, but less labour intensive, is to use inert gas. Most wine stores sell this product in a canister—an extremely light canister that almost feels empty. You "spray" the odorless, tasteless gas, using a thin straw-like nozzle, into the top of the opened wine bottle. The heavier gas displaces the oxygen that's in contact with the surface of the wine. You push the cork back into the bottle, and voilà—the wine's life is extended by up to a week.
- The least expensive option is to transfer your partially full bottle into an empty, clean half bottle, then put the cork back in. Save a few half bottles when you come across them, they come

in handy. This alone could buy you one more day, but not much longer.

- Sparkling wines keep their fizz overnight in the fridge if you use a special wine stopper invented for this purpose, sold at most wine stores.

Whatever method you use, put the bottle in the fridge to slow its decline even more. This applies equally to red or white wines. Eventually though, the wine will lose its freshness and won't be as enjoyable as when you first opened it. Any wine opened for more than one week should be either used for cooking (but check first to make sure it hasn't gone bad) or thrown out.

Wine Has Style
What's Yours?

When we ask people what wines they like, they often say things like, "A dry, white wine with no oak," or "Something big and juicy...I love big red wines!" Body, sweetness, and flavor are all important ways to define your preference in wine—we call it the wine's style. Understanding what these terms mean helps you decide if you want something light enough to enjoy on a warm summer day or rich enough to stand up to your mom's superb pot roast.

If you take everything you learned so far—grape variety, wine production, country of origin, and tasting—and pull it all together, you'll be able to find the style of wine you like, in a wine shop, at a restaurant, or wherever you want to buy it.

What's in Style?

Body, flavor, and sweetness are key to defining a wine's style. These terms aren't unfamiliar—they relate to many other food products—but how do they relate specifically to wine? And more importantly, how do they connect to the kind of wine you like?

Body

Body is about how a wine feels in your mouth. There are many ways to evaluate body but first, think about it in terms of *weight*. Alcohol, extracts (for example, sweetness and tannins), and acidity are big contributors to the wine's body, and especially its weight:

- Lower-alcohol, dry white wines (e.g., Riesling) feel watery, or *light-bodied*.
- Higher-alcohol, tannic red wines (e.g., Shiraz) feel more *full-bodied*.
- If the acidity is low, or residual sugar is high (icewine, for example), even lower-alcohol wines will feel *fuller*.

The difference in body isn't found only between white and red wines, however. For example, a low alcohol German Riesling is lighter-bodied than a higher-alcohol California Chardonnay. Now if the Riesling was also an eiswein, the extra sugar could make if feel fuller-bodied than the Chardonnay.

In red wines, lower-alcohol, lower-tannin Beaujolais will feel lighter-bodied than a higher-alcohol, tannic Australian Shiraz.

Besides weight the body of a wine comes from *textures* (silky, velvety, or coarse) and *viscosity* (watery, thin, full or thick). Think milk—skim milk, homogenized milk, and cream—and you'll get the idea.

- Silky, fine wines (e.g., Pinot Noir) seem light-bodied
- Velvety, mouth-coating wines (e.g., Merlot) feel medium-bodied
- Coarse, young, tannic wines (e.g., Cabernet Sauvignon) seem fuller-bodied

What weight, textures, and viscosity appeal to you? Next time you drink a glass of your favorite wine, think about how you would classify it. Think about the other foods and beverages you consume—are you consistent in your preferences?

Flavor

There are hundreds of different flavors in wine, but which ones appeal to you most? Knowing what you like in foods can help you determine your wine flavor profile. For example, do you like juicy, fruity foods? How about ripe or tart-tasting things? Do you prefer spicy, sweet or savoury dishes? Do you like mild or intense flavors?

When deciding what flavors you prefer, it isn't important to be able to distinguish between two similar things, say a mandarin or a navel orange. All you need to know is whether you prefer citrus fruits over tropical fruits, or even that you prefer fruits in general over more savoury things.

Perhaps when you drink a wine you don't want much flavor at all. That's okay; there are many neutral wines to choose from.

Dry to Sweet

Although you can't smell sweetness—sugar is not volatile—you can smell the aromas generally associated with sweet things. An off-dry Riesling, for example, gives off aromas of ripe peaches or apricots, while unoaked Chardonnay (Chablis, for example) reminds some of lemons and wet stones. Peaches *smell* sweeter than citrus, and definitely sweeter than wet stones.

When you taste these wines, they will confirm what you thought when you took your first whiff. You'll notice the sweetness in the off-dry Riesling on the tip of your tongue, while the drier almost tart Chablis will pucker your mouth.

Wines from warmer climates (Australia, for example) sometimes smell sweeter as the fruit is generally riper when it is picked. If you like sweet things but prefer dry wines, then New World wines might be a good choice.

Alcohol also smells sweet, so higher-alcohol wines, like Amarone, may suggest sweetness when in fact they are dry. Though some high-alcohol wines, like port, smell sweet because they are sweet. There's no hard and fast rule here, but there will be no doubt when you taste it.

Finding Your Style

We all have our own threshold or preferences for body, flavor, and sweetness. What is light to one may be full-bodied to someone else. People with a sweet tooth invariably find even off-dry wines too dry, and dry wines seem almost sour to them.

Learn about the styles that appeal to you by trying wines in each category. We'll cover still wines first, followed by rosé, sparkling, fortified, and dessert wines. In the corresponding charts, the grape varieties in each body type are listed, along with some typical countries or regions that make "textbook" examples of these wines. Flavor profiles accompany each chart to help you determine what appeals to you. If you see a wine you already like, look in the same category for something new to try.

Styles are matched to different price brackets. Expect finer textures from the more expensive wines—grand cru white Burgundy, for example, will feel more round and supple on the palate than a less expensive Chardonnay. Winemaking styles and grape ripeness can complicate this, so we are only throwing it out as a generalization.

Dry White Wines

Price	Light-Bodied	Medium-Bodied	Full-Bodied
Under $15	Chardonnay • Mâcon Blanc Sauvignon Blanc • Bordeaux Blanc • Chile Riesling • Canada • German Kabinett Muscadet Orvieto Soave Vinho Verde Verdicchio Vernaccia Pinot Grigio Liebfraumilch	Chardonnay • Mâcon-Villages • St-Veran • Montagny • Languedoc • Chile Sauvignon Blanc • Entre-deux-Mers • South Africa Pinot Blanc • Alsace • British Columbia Gewürztraminer • Chile	Viognier • Languedoc
$15–$30	Riesling Sauvignon Blanc • Sancerre Chardonnay • Chablis • Petit Chablis • Mâcon-Villages Albariño Chenin Blanc Grüner Veltliner Orvieto Classico Pinot Grigio Torrontés	Sauvignon Blanc • California • Graves • Pouilly-Fume • New Zealand • Australia (blends) Chardonnay • South Africa • California • Australia Riesling • Alsace • Australia Gewürztraminer Soave Classico Gavi Pinot Gris • Canada • Oregon • Alsace	Chardonnay • Australia • California • Pouilly-Fuissé • Spain • Canada • Oregon • South Africa Viognier • California • Rhône

Price	Light-Bodied	Medium-Bodied	Full-Bodied
Over $30	Chardonnay • Chablis • Petit Chablis	Chardonnay • Chablis Premier Cru	Chardonnay • Chablis Grand Cru • Côte de Beaune • Burgundy Premier and Grand Cru • United States • Australia Sauvignon Blanc • Pessac-Léognan

Dry white wines fall into three categories: Fresh and Crisp; Smooth and Creamy; and, Attitude. Here's what each category means:

Fresh and Crisp
When you need a wine to drink on its own or to build up an appetite for dinner, reach past the Chardonnay and grab a cool glass of tangy, fresh, and crisp wine. Sounds like a commercial jingle for:

Pinot Grigio	Riesling Kabinett	Verdicchio
Muscadet sur Lie	Albariño	Sancerre

Smooth and Creamy
If tangy just not right for you, perhaps you'd prefer something a little bit smoother. You'll likely pay a little bit more; these wines have probably seen the inside of an oak barrel at some time in their life. Look for:

Burgundy	Pinot Gris	Soave Classico
Chardonnay	Pinot Blanc	Fumé Blanc

Attitude Whites
These are distinctly aromatic wines, that aren't afraid to show it. More often than not, they are actually light-bodied wines, but they pack some delightful fragrances. Check these out and you will see what we mean:

Neutral Wines
Some people prefer white wines that don't smell of oak, tropical fruits, or "cat's pee." For more neutral wines, look to the Old World and basic Orvieto, Soave, Muscadet, or Vinho Verde.

Gewürztraminer   Muscat d'Alsace   Viognier
Sauvignon Blanc   Torrontes

If you prefer your attitude whites to be richer, ripe, and toasty (a.k.a. oaky), look for:

Californian Chardonnay   Australian Chardonnay

Dry Red Wines

Price	Light-Bodied	Medium-Bodied	Full-Bodied
Under $15	Merlot	Bordeaux supérieur	Bairrada
	• Eastern European	Malbec	Dão
	• Chile	Southern Italian Reds	Pinotage
	• Languedoc	Grenache	Baco Noir
	Cabernet Sauvignon	• Australia (blends)	
	• Bordeaux AC	• Côtes du Rhone	
	Pinot Noir	• Italy	
	• Bourgogne Rouge	• Spain	
	• Chile	Vin de Pays d'Oc	
	Gamay	Shiraz	
	• Beaujolais	• Australia	
	• Canada		
	Chianti		
	Montepulciano D'Abruzzo		
	Valpolicella		
	Bardolino		
$15–$30	Pinot Noir	Syrah/Shiraz	Cabernet Sauvignon
	• Canada	• Crozes-Hermitage	• Australia
	• Loire	• Australia	• Canada
	Cabernet Franc	• South Africa	• South America
	• Canada	Pinot Noir	Merlot
	Côtes du Rhone	• Burgundy Villages	• California
	Barbera d'Asti	• Burgundy Côtes	Shiraz
	Dolcetto	• Canada	• Australia
	Ribera del Duero Joven	• United States	Zinfandel
		Cabernet Sauvignon	Vino Nobile de Montepulciano
		• Crus Bourgeois	Châteauneuf-du-Pape
		• Haut-Medoc	Duoro
		• Languedoc	Rosso di Montalcino
		Cabernet/Shiraz Blends	
		• Australia	
		Merlot	

Price	Light-Bodied	Medium-Bodied	Full-Bodied
$15–$30		• Chile	
		• California	
		Gamay	
		• Cru Beaujolais	
		• Canada	
		Zinfandel	
		Rioja Crianza and Reserva	
		Chianti Classico	
		Barbera d'Alba	
		Valpolicella Classico	
Over $30		Merlot	Cabernet Sauvignon
		• Saint Émilion	• Bordeaux Châteaux
		• Pomerol	• Napa, California
		Pinot Noir	• Washington State
		• Burgundy Premiers Cru	• South Australia
		• Burgundy Grands Cru	Syrah/Shiraz
		• New Zealand	• Hermitage
		• Oregon	• Côtes Rôtie
		Ribera del Duero Crianza	• Cornas
		Cabernet Franc	• Australia
		• Saint Émilion	Barolo
		• Ontario	Barberesco
		Chianti Classico Riserva	Super-Tuscans
			Brunello di Montalcino
			Amarone
			Priorato
			Ribera del Duero Riserva
			Rioja Gran Reserva

Dry red wines fall into three categories: Fruity and Mouth-watering; Smooth and Silky; and, Attitude. Here's what each category means:

Fruity and Mouth-Watering

If you prefer your red wines packed with fruit and stuffed with mouth-watering acidity, and with very little tannins, there's a lot to choose from. Better still, you don't have to pay through the nose for them. Many of these red wines come from the Old World, the most famous being Beaujolais. Italy, however, really corners the market on juicy, mouth-watering red wines. Here are a few examples for you to try:

Barbera d'Asti	Dolcetto	Valpolicella
Bardolino	Chianti	Malbec (Argentina)

Smooth and Silky

If you like your red wines to be more mellow and seductive, you may have to pay a little bit more, but we think you'll agree it is worth it. Give these wines a try:

Pinot Noir	Merlot	Chianti Classico Riserva

Attitude Reds

For the extraverts in the group, how about some not-so-subtle wines—those hit-you-over-the-head, big, bold, and spicy wines? Although there are a few bargains out there, be prepared to pay a little more for these intense wines. Many of them will actually improve with age if you have the patience. If you keep them long enough, though, they may become more mellow. In addition to Cabernet Sauvignon from Australia, California and, of course, Bordeaux, try these:

Syrah/Shiraz	Zinfandel	Pinotage
Baco Noir	Barolo	Marechal Foch

Rosé

Rosé has an image problem in North America; it isn't considered to be a serious wine. People in the south of France, even the tourists, don't have this problem. Rosé wine is a way of life. Here you will find a bottle on every table at lunch; it is more popular than white wine.

It might be White Zin—a sweetish blush wine from California—that turned many people off rosé. Rosé can also be light, dry, and refreshing—essentially the perfect wine for lunch.

A great grape for rosé is Grenache (Garnacha in Spain). It produces a wine with a slight mauve or pinkish orange hue in both a crisp and elegant style (Provence in France) or a slightly heavier, higher alcohol style (Navarra in Spain). You can also find excellent dry rosé wines made in other countries, using other different grape varieties.

Here's what to expect when you want to give rosé a try:

Lighter Style	Sweeter Style	Heavier Style
Bandol	White Zinfandel	Tavel
Bordeaux	Mateus Rose	Spanish Rosado
Cabernet d'Anjou	Lambrusco	Clairet

Sparkling Wine—It's Not Just For Breakfast Anymore

Most people don't think about what sparkling wine tastes like. They are too preoccupied with drinking it out of slippers or smashing it against the bows of ships. So why do we bother classifying sparkling wines? Why not just determine the price you are willing to pay and just pop the cork? Actually don't pop—you'll lose all the bubbles.

There are different styles of sparkling wine, and as you drink more of them you will see that there is more to it than price, and bubbles. The body of a sparkling wine is harder to describe than that of a still wine, as you have all those bubbles floating around to distract you. One of the easier ways is to look at the grape variety—as they do in Champagne (where they give body a lot of thought.)

> **Party Hint**
>
> If you are planning a stand-up reception with appetizers, choose a lighter-style sparkling wine. Fuller versions are better served at a meal where the wine may accompany a course or two.

- Lighter-bodied sparkling wines, (e.g., Blancs de Blancs Champagne) have more white grapes like Chardonnay in their blend
- Fuller-bodied sparkling wines, (e.g., Blancs de Noir Champagne) have more black grapes like Pinot Noir in their blend.

Method of production (méthode traditionelle vs. tank), the length of time the wine rests on the lees, and the sweetness of the wine, all have an effect on body. A secondary fermentation of over two years, as with vintage champagne, produces an elegant, rich wine that has millions of fine, and persistent bubbles. When the fermentation of the wine is stopped before the sugars were converted to alcohol, and then the secondary fermentation occurred quickly in a pressurized tank, the resulting sparkling wine would be sweeter, with large, coarse bubbles that don't last very long in the glass.

In Champagne, each producer has its own *house style*, so you can pick the wines that match your style. And best of all, once you determine the style you like, there isn't much variation year over year.

- Lighter-bodied House Style: Laurent-Perrier, Perrier-Jouët, Pol Roger, Pommery, Taittinger
- Medium-bodied House Style: Moët & Chandon, Mumm, Piper
- Fuller-bodied House Style: Bollinger, Heidseck, Krug, Veuve Clicquot

Other countries often use different base grapes in their blends and a variety of different production methods. Even those sparkling wines that use the same grape varieties as champagne, and the same methods, can't seem to get it exactly right. Nevertheless, there are still many excellent sparklers at all price ranges and preferences.

If you want bubbles but don't want to pay for them, try a sparkling wine from the "Cheap and Cheerful" list. If you want champagne, but prefer not to pay the big bucks, try one or more of the "The Pretenders"—made using méthode traditionelle. If you prefer your bubbles slightly sweeter, with dessert, we have included a category for these as well. Of course, we have also included the "Real Thing"—champagne.

Cheap and Cheerful	The Pretenders	Sweeties	The Real Thing
Sekt (Germany)	Cava (Spain)	Asti (Spumante)	champagne
Lambrusco (Italy)	Saumur Brut (Loire)	Moscato d'Asti	
Prosecco (Italy)	Crémant (France)	Prosecco Dolce	
	New World Sparkling Wine		
	(California, New Zealand,		
	Australia, and Canada)		
	Franciacorta (Italy)		

Fortified

Fortified wines can be dry and tangy or sweet and warming. The first category are better served as an apéritif, or with soups or tapas, while the sweet and warming wines are good to plonk down with in front of a roaring fireplace, or maybe with dessert.

Fortified wines don't have to be expensive. It is easy to find good wines for under $25. Better ports—the vintage ones—cost a lot more but they aren't for everyday drinking anyway. Besides, since it's unlikely you will drink these wines at one sitting—remember, they are fortified—you'll get more mileage from one compared to a bottle of still wine. That's our rationalization, anyway, for drinking port and sherry as often as we can.

Dry and Tangy

Sherry is the benchmark wine in this category. This surprises many people because they think sherry is a sweet wine—like Harvey's Bristol Cream or Canadian Sherry, which bears no resemblance whatsoever to the original from Spain. Sherry is one of the world's best-kept secrets and you'll know why once you try it. Try a dry Oloroso; you won't be disappointed.

Sherry is deliciously tangy and the best are made bone dry. Some versions come in small bottles, so you can experiment. Best of all, it's not expensive. Here's what to know when buying sherry:

- *Fino* sherries are the palest, driest, and tangiest. Gonzalez Byass Tio Pepe is a fino sherry but there are many other examples. It will say fino somewhere on the label.
- *Manzanilla* is a type of fino sherry, but from a different area in Spain. It has a subtle, salty tang due to the coastal location of the solera.
- *Amontillado* is essentially an aged fino and has developed a darker color and more toffee flavors. Delicious!
- *Palo Cortado* is richer than an Amontillado but not as concentrated as an *Oloroso*.
- *Olorosos*, when well made, are fabulous. Dark and dry, they have lovely aromas of nuts, figs, and raisins. They are an excellent and unusual apéritif—surprise your friends but have lots of it on hand, as you'll probably be asked for seconds. There are sweet-style Olorosos but we recommend drier versions.

Other dry and tangy fortified wines include Vin Jaune from the Jura region of France, the two Madeiras Sercial and Verdelho (which is a bit off-dry) from Portugal, and Sicily's Marsala Vergine—a dry version of this traditional sweetened wine. Montilla-Moriles, a neighboring region to Jerez, produces wines similar in style to Sherry but just not as popular.

Sweet and Warming

Port from Portugal is the benchmark wine in this category. There are "ports" from Australia and South Africa, but they are much sweeter and more toffee-like than real port. Here's what to consider when buying port:

- *Ruby port* and *vintage character port* are the simplest and cheapest, so don't expect a lot from these wines. They are okay to have on hand, but drink them soon after purchase. They don't improve with age.

- *Tawny port* has more character than ruby port. Better still are the aged tawnies. Ten-year-old tawny is good value, and the extra price for 20- or 30-year-old tawnies doesn't make much sense. Tawnies are meant to be consumed right away and were filtered, so there's no sediment to worry about.
- *Colheita ports* are aged tawnies from a single vintage, and like tawnies they are not meant to age once they are bottled.
- *Late bottled vintage port* (LBV) has some of the characteristics of *vintage port* but no sediment. These are good value, but they don't age. Drink up.
- *Vintage port* is the top rung. These are only produced in the best (declared) years and can be quite expensive. On top of that you may have to wait 20 or more years (after the vintage) before they're ready. Consult vintage charts to know when it's the best time to drink these wines. And don't forget to decant the bottle—these wines have a lot of sediment.

Others sweet and warming fortified wines include:

- *Bual* and *Malmsey* Madeira from Portugal. Bual is nutty and raisiny while Malmsey—the sweetest of all Madeiras—is more toffee-like. Both have the characteristic Madeira tangy acidity that helps them keep a long time—sometimes many, many, decades.
- Marsala from Sicily comes in different styles and colors. Stick with Marsala *Superiore*, which has a richer honey, brown-sugar sweetness.
- *Vins doux naturels* is what the French call fortified wines. The best of these is Banyuls made from Grenache in the Languedoc-Roussillon. Maury, Rivesaltes, and Rasteau are also vins doux naturels.

> ### Attention Chocolate Lovers
> Banyuls is probably the single best match for chocolate in the world. It might be hard to find, but we know you are a persistent bunch.

There are numerous sweet sherries—the most famous is *pale cream sherry*—that fit better in this category than with their tangy cousins. *Pedro Ximénez*, the sweetest style of sherry, is so thick it can be served as a topping for vanilla ice cream.

Màlaga, also from Spain, fits here as well as does *Commanadaria* from Cyprus. It's made sherry style from sun-dried grapes and offers up lovely sweet, honeyed, raisined flavors.

Wine as Dessert?

There was a time when sweet wines were more valued than dry wines. Now they are usually reserved only for special occasions. It's too bad because these rich and luscious dessert wines are a perfect way to end a meal, as a substitute for dessert or simply to savour around a fire on a cool fall evening. Or if you like foie gras, sweet wines are a perfect accompaniment.

Compared to most still wines, sweet wines are not cheap; top wines can easily cost hundreds of dollars. These wines improve and evolve in the bottle—some for decades—if that is any consolation. And fortunately, since serving sizes are small—1 or 2 oz (30–60 ml)—a bottle, even a half bottle, goes a long way.

Dessert Wine Grapes
Riesling, Gewürztraminer, Vidal, Muscat, Chenin Blanc, Sémillon

The body and flavors of a sweet wine have as much to do with how the grapes were treated (left on the vine, air dried, botrytized, or left to freeze), as it does the grape type. Many of these wines are fuller-bodied due to the higher alcohol levels and the extract (sugars.) As a general rule, though, Riesling produces the lightest versions.

Don't be surprised by the high levels of acidity in dessert wines—that is why some of the best German sweet wines seem to keep forever. Acidity is the perfect complement to the rich sweetness, and makes them less cloying.

An easy way to categorize dessert wines is by price. Less expensive wines tend to be lighter (in color and body). More expensive wines, like icewine, tend to be fuller all around. Unfortunately your biggest problem isn't choosing a dessert wine to try but rather finding one. Some wine shops carry only a few selections.

Starter Sweeties
Late Harvest (*Vendage Tardive* in French) are the key words to look for on the labels. Most of these will cost you under $30, will be fairly light-bodied, and won't be too intense. Here's what to look for from around the world:

- From Canada, Ontario and British Columbia make very good late-harvest wines from Riesling or Vidal. Nova Scotia and Quebec also produce late-harvest wines, usually from hybrid grapes.
- Alsace is known for Vendage Tardive.
- From Germany, look for Riesling Auslese.

- Muscat de Beaumes-de-Venise from France (southern Rhône) is probably the best starter dessert wine from the Old World and usually there is a fair bit of it around.
- Chile exports inexpensive late-harvest Sauvignon Blanc (from Errázuriz, for example) that is worth seeking out.
- For something different, and red, look for Recioto della Valpolicella from Veneto (Italy).

Getting Serious

As we move up in price the wines in this category may include some botrytized and icewine versions. What they all have in common is that they are rich and luscious.

In the $30 to $75 range, there's obviously more choice:

- California Orange Muscat
- Alsace Selection de Grains Nobles
- Australian Semillon or Liqueur Muscats
- Canadian icewine.
- German Beerenauslese Riesling.
- Hungarian Tokaji Aszú
- Botrytized Sémillon/Sauvignon Blanc blends from Monbazillac, Loupiac, Ste-Croix-du-Mont, and Cadillac.
- Vin Santo and Recioto di Soave DOCG from Italy.

Serious Sweeties

At over $75—every drop unctuous nectar—some of these wines may be as difficult to find, as they are to budget for. While the demand at this price point may be small, it is more of a supply issue—there's so little juice to work with there's simply very little made. If you can't justify the price for personal consumption, they do make excellent and unique gifts. Here are a few examples:

World's First Dessert Wine

The legendary Tokaji Essencia of Hungary is so rich in sugar that it can take decades just to ferment the must. The resulting wine is intensely aromatic (apricots, marzipan, orange peel, tea, spices...) with almost perfect acidity to balance its syrupy sweetness.

Tokaji was created over 400 years ago—centuries before the sweet wines of France and Germany were developed.

- German Eiswein and Trockenbeerenauslese Riesling.
- Vouvray (*Liquoreux*), Quarts de Chaume or Bonnezeaux from the Loire Valley in France.
- Sauternes and Barsac from Bordeaux, France.
- Tokaji *Essencia*, a rare wine from Hungary.

Chill Out: Temperatures for Wine

Regardless of the style of wine you prefer, it should be warm enough to bring out the flavors, yet cool enough to be refreshing but not chilling.

Temperature has a great effect on the aromas, body, and taste of wine and it's important to your overall enjoyment. Most people drink their white wines too cold and red wines too warm. When a white wine is served too cold, its fruit flavors are muted and its harsher elements—acidity and bitterness—are emphasized. A red wine served too warm will taste unbalanced—the alcohol and tannins overpowering the fruit flavors.

Sparkling wine, if not well-chilled, will shoot out of the bottle like a geyser. So unless you just won a Formula One race, chill those sparklers.

Dessert wines should also be well chilled.

Don't Bet the Spread

The temperature spread between red wines and white wines is actually much narrower than you may think. Light, fruity, low tannin red wines (e.g., Beaujolais) should be served at lower temperatures than full-bodied, complex white wines like grand cru white Burgundy. The list below is a guideline for ideal serving temperatures.

Medium to full-bodied reds	60–65°F/15–18°C
Port or sweet sherries	55–60°F/13–15°C
Full-bodied whites	55–60°F/13–15°C
Light-bodied reds	50–55°F/10–13°C
Rosé	50–55°F/10–13°C
Light- to medium-bodied whites	50–55°F/10–13°C
Dry sherries	45–50°F/8–10°C
Sparkling wines	40–45°F/5–8°C
Dessert wines	40–45°F/5–8°C

If you don't have a thermometer, red wines should feel cool to the touch, white and rosé wines should feel cold, but not ice cold, and sparkling wine should feel quite cold.

White Wines—A Chilling Experience?

Refrigerators are simply too cold for white wines. In fact, as a rule you shouldn't let your wines near the fridge, except to extend the life of an opened bottle. Using the freezer as a quick chiller is risky—unless you like winesicles! A better quick-chill method is to place the bottle in an ice and water mixture for a few minutes.

A temperature that's too low dulls the wine's aromas and neutralizes the taste. This may not be such a bad thing for simple wines, but it's your loss when you're about to open a good bottle you've been saving for a special occasion. If it is a sparkling wine, very low temperatures actually suppress the bubbles. (Fortunately, they come back as the wine warms up.)

In a restaurant, your white wine doesn't need to be kept in an ice bucket throughout the meal. That's as much for show as anything. If wine sits for only 20 minutes in an ice bucket, its temperature can drop about 20°F (10°C). Try drinking a glass of wine once it has reached a temperature of 40°F or 5°C and it will freeze the enamel off your teeth.

If the restaurant is warm, you just need something to keep the wine's temperature constant. Some restaurants have clay or plastic bottle holders. If they don't, drive your server crazy by moving the bottle back and forth between the table and the ice bucket.

Bad Fridge!

If left for a long time—weeks or even months—the low humidity in the fridge can dry out the cork. Your wines will either end up leaking in the fridge (and won't that be fun to clean up) or absorbing some interesting food odors, just like that box of baking soda in the corner of the fridge. Imagine your nice bottle of Riesling coming out smelling like last night's leftover moo goo gai pan!

Whose Room Temperature?

Red wines are supposed to be served at room temperature. Room temperature in a French Château (60°F or 15°C), that is. If you have central heating, your room temperature (70°F or 20°C) is just too warm for red wines.

So if you have a temperature-controlled cellar, leave the wine on the counter for about 30 minutes before serving it. If you don't have a cellar, take your room-temperature wine and chill it in an ice bucket for a few minutes before serving. Some lighter, juicy red wines like Beaujolais might benefit from 5 minutes or so in an ice bucket.

Chilling a Sparkling Wine

Make sure your sparkling wines are well chilled before opening. When sparklers are properly chilled, the bottles are easier to open and the bubbles will last longer.

The one exception to this is vintage champagne, which needs to be treated more like a fine white wine and should be not served overly chilled. At the high end of the sparkling wine range (45°F/8°C) is good.

> **Did you know?**
> The average refrigerator temperature is 36–40°F/3–5°C.

Resist the temptation to cut corners. Don't chill the glasses to make up for a wine that's not chilled enough. The condensation on the glasses will dilute the wine and burst the delicate bubbles.

In a Hurry?

Here are three ways to lower the temperature of a bottle of wine from room temperature to serving temperature (for a white wine), and the amount of time it would take to do so:

- Ice and water—20 minutes
- Freezer—40 minutes (set a timer!)
- Refrigerator—3 hours

If you have overchilled your wine, let the bottle stand on the counter for a few minutes before opening. Wine will warm up about 2°F (1°C) every couple of minutes at room temperature, even faster if it is in a glass.

A Case of Wine for a Desert Island

Often we sit around and think about what wines we liked to have if we were marooned on a desert island. These are our personal favorites and shouldn't influence your own choices. If you're wondering, no money exchanged hands in compiling this list (although if any of the producers would like to send us a supply that would be okay).

1. Sherry Dry Oloroso *Don Nuño* (Lustau)
2. 2004 Sancerre (Henri Bourgeois)
3. 1990 Riesling *Haardter Herrenletten* (Müller Catoir)

4. 2005 O Rosal (Terras Gauda)
5. 1996 Meursault *Les Genevrières* (P. Jobard)
6. 1996 Chambolle-Musigny (Ghislaine Barthod)
7. 2001 Alma de Tobia Rioja (Bodegas Tobía)
8. 2000 Chianti Classico *Riserva* (Poggio Amorelli)
9. 1999 Brunello di Montalcino Riserva (Fattoria La Lecciaia)
10. 1986 Bordeaux (Château Beychevelle)—our wedding anniversary wine
11. NV Prosecco (Masottina)—to maintain our spirits
12. 2000 Champagne *Dom Perignon*—for the rescue of course

Would You Like Wine with That?
The Art of Food and Wine Matching

"Red wine with red meat, white wine with fish." Most of us have heard this one. Follow the rule or risk some raised eyebrows from your server or even your table companions!

Contrast this school of thought with the approach "Drink whatever wine you like with whatever you want to eat—there are no wrong combinations." Which approach is right?

Each one is, to a point. Rules provide guidelines to steer us toward more successful combinations. Spontaneity allows us to test the rules, maybe break them, and find some new ones that work. Here's one rule we hardly ever break, though, wine is meant to go with food.

Food and wine matches are all about finding a balance. Usually, you'll make your wine choices after you've decided on the menu. At other times, the wine will be the showcase of your meal.

Whatever your starting point, the following guidelines will give you options to explore. The old rules of wine and food matching were based on chemistry and logic, but above all, practice and experience. As you practice and gain experience with different wine and food combinations, your own palate will evolve.

As for the rules, you get to write the ones that work for you.

Practical Pairing Principles

Wine should make food taste better; food should make wine taste better. It's as simple as that. You don't need to be an expert to make great food and wine combinations. All you need to do are follow some basic guidelines:

- Match the weight of the wine to the weight of the food
- Adjust for the cooking method and for sauces

- Mirror ingredients but also look for contrasts
- Order makes a difference

Matching Weights

All foods have body and texture, a sense of how they feel in the mouth. Foods that are full of flavor, like steak or Camembert cheese, almost coat your mouth when you eat them. Light-textured foods, like a green salad or poached fish, feel delicate and refreshing in the mouth.

The wines you choose to complement each dish must match the weight and texture of the food, neither overpowering the other. A steak would be no match for a light-bodied wine, especially a light-bodied white wine. A full-bodied, full-flavored, bruiser wine like Shiraz would make a much more even match. However, the same Shiraz would just flatten poached flounder. This dish needs a light-bodied white wine, like Pinot Grigio.

Keeping with the light-, medium- and full-bodied classification, here are some dishes that would go well with each category:

Dry White Wines

Light-Bodied Wines	Medium-Bodied Wines	Full-Bodied Wines
Raw vegetables	Prosciutto with melon	Pâté
Clear soups	Vegetable soups	Cream soups
Green salad with a mild dressing	Green salad with creamy dressing	Warm mushroom salad
Sushi	Broiled shrimp or scallops	Grilled salmon
Poached fish	Panfried fish	Lobster
Roast lemon chicken	Chicken pot pie	Roast turkey
Veal schnitzel	Baked ham	Jerk pork
Steamed asparagus	Stuffed bell peppers	Grilled vegetables
Pasta primavera	Pasta with seafood	Pasta in cream sauce
Omelets	Quiche	Eggs benedict
Goat and other fresh cheeses	Jarlsberg and other firm, mild cheeses	Brie and other semi-soft cheeses

Dry Red Wines

Light-Bodied Wines	Medium-Bodied Wines	Full-Bodied Wines
Pizza with seafood	Grilled sausages with dips	Chicken and pork satays
Lentil soup	Beef barley soup	French onion soup
Grilled vegetable salad	Warm chicken salad	Grilled mushroom salad
Deep-fried calamari	Mixed grilled seafood	Chicken cacciatore
Fish with wine sauce	Grilled tuna	Barbequed chicken
Grilled chicken	Chicken stew	Grilled lamb chops
Hamburgers	Grilled pork chops	Steaks
Pasta with pesto sauce	Cheese or meat tortellini	Beef stew
Quiche	Omelet with smoked salmon	Vegetable lasagna
Swiss and mild firm cheeses	Parmigiano Reggiano	Aged hard cheeses

Making Adjustments

Foods can be prepared many different ways. Fish, for example, can be steamed, poached, baked, fried, broiled, grilled, or even raw, as in sushi. The way food is prepared determines the intensity of its flavor. When it's steamed or poached, the flavor is very mild, even bland. Flavor picks up when the same food is fried or baked, and shifts up another notch when broiled, grilled, or slow-cooked.

As cooking methods differ, the food's intensity changes, and so too does the need to match it with a bolder, fuller-bodied wine. The length of time something is cooked will also influence your choice of wine. Steak cooked rare goes best with a young tannic red wine; steak cooked well-done, or even as a roast, is better suited to more mature, less- tannic red wines. The tannins in the young red wine bond with the proteins in the rare steak, taking the edge off the wine (it will taste softer) and cutting through the richness of the meat.

Here are some basic guidelines:

Wine	Cooking Method				
	Poaching or Steaming	Sautéing or Pan Frying	Deep Frying	Roasting or Broiling	Grilling
Light-bodied whites	√	√	√		
Medium-bodied whites		√	√	√	
Off-dry white wines		√	√	√	
Full-bodied whites		√	√	√	√
Light-bodied reds		√	√		
Medium-bodied reds		√	√	√	√
Full-bodied reds				√	√

Thinking Saucy

A change in sauces can re-balance the entire relationship between a food and wine. Sometimes it's the sauce that dominates the dish. When we think of pasta, for example, we don't think of the shape—farfalle or bucatini—we think of the sauce: Alfredo, Arrabiata, Funghi, Marinara, Puttanesca, and so on. Sauces can be light or rich, smooth or chunky, creamy or zippy.

Different wine styles complement different sauces. With a delicate sauce, choose a delicate wine. With a more robust sauce, pick a heartier wine.

Light-Bodied Wines	Medium-Bodied Wines	Full-Bodied Wines
Pesto sauce	Marinara	Bolognese
Lemon-butter	Velouté	Béarnaise
Chicken stir fry	Chicken stew	BBQ chicken

Mirror, Mirror

Wines can also boost the flavor of a meal by mirroring its complexity: the simpler the meal, the simpler the wine.

Let's say you're planning to serve a simple grilled steak for dinner, with a fresh tomato salad and bread on the side. You need something equally simple to complement the meal, perhaps a light-bodied red wine like Chianti.

Now, if this were a pepper steak, served with red pepper and ginger chutney, the slightly sweet and spicy accompaniment and the peppery coating on the steak now dominate the dish and would overpower the Chianti. You would need something with a flavor profile that would work with the sauce. Full-bodied wines with peppery undertones like Shiraz or a Zinfandel would work well.

The aroma and flavor profiles of the wines we covered earlier will help you identify other wine matches for different styles of sauces. Here are few examples:

Wine	Has undertones of:	Suits
Old World Sauvignon Blanc	Herbs	Herb vinaigrette
Oaked Chardonnay	Creaminess	Garlic mayonnaise
Red Burgundy	Earthiness	Mushroom sauces
Riesling	Fruit	Chutney
Rosé	Fruit	Cranberry
New World Sauvignon Blanc	Tropical fruits	Salsa (e.g., mango)
Syrah/Shiraz	Spice	BBQ, pepper sauces
Cabernet Sauvignon	Mint	Mint sauce
Muscat	Orange	Fruit sauce

Opposites Attract

Sometimes wine works best when it provides a contrast to the food, rather than a complement. Tannins and acidity in a wine can offset fat, its fruit flavor can moderate spiciness, and its sweetness can balance saltiness.

In food terms, think of fish and chips. Some people like to intensify the richness of the fries by dipping them in mayonnaise. Others like the contrast of vinegar on the fried food, cutting through its greasy goodness. Still others slather the whole meal in ketchup, enjoying the contrast between salt and sweet.

Contrasting food and wine works much the same way.

- Creamy-textured, rich, or fatty foods moderate the tannins in wine (for example, a young Chilean Cabernet Sauvignon), allowing the fruit flavors in the wine to show through.
- Acidity, in a German Riesling, for example, cuts the fattiness in fried foods—filo pastry appetizers, pork schnitzel, deep-fried anything—just like a squeeze of lemon would.
- The sweetness in a wine counters the saltiness of food. Likewise, the saltiness of food, makes the wine's flavors stand out even more. Sweetness in wine also cools the heat of spicy foods. An off-dry, lower-alcohol Riesling makes a great match for Thai or Indian curries.

Hooked on Classics

Most of the tried and true food and wine combinations originate from Old World countries like France, Italy, and Spain. There, they've had centuries to develop and perfect their regional cuisines and regional wines to bring out the best in each other.

Here are some of those classic combinations:

- **Champagne and caviar**—The cooling, refreshing acidity and bubbles of the wine contrast with the salty richness of the fish eggs.
- **Dry Oloroso Sherry and consommé**—The rich nutty aromas of the wine complement the intense earthy aromas of the soup.
- **Sancerre and chèvre**—The acidity of the wine complements the tangy acidity in the goat cheese. Matched together, the acidity of each is actually toned down.
- **Barolo and braised beef (osso buco)**—The complex, exotic aromas of the wine complement the flavors in long-roasted meat.
- **Sauternes and foie gras**—The rich, syrupy texture of the wine complements the rich, silken fattiness of the liver; the sweetness of the wine contrasts with the liver's savory flavor.
- **Port and Stilton**—The fullness of the wine complements the fullness of the cheese; the sweetness of the wine contrasts with the saltiness of the cheese; and, the bitter tannins in wine counteract the bitterness in the blue veins.

Cabernet Sauvignon and grilled steak is more of a New World "classic." The heavyweight wine complements the big, smoky meat.

And Now for Something New

The old rules of food and wine matching still make sense. But they were established in the days of regional cuisines, when French foods could only be matched with French wines, Italian foods with Italian wines, and so on.

New rules are being created all the time. Pinot Noir, a red wine, is now accepted as an excellent match for salmon. The acidity in the wine cuts through the fattiness in the fish; the weight of the wine and the food complement each other. A big, fully oaked Chardonnay with a well-done steak? Sure, why not?

For many cuisines—Thai, Japanese, Indian, for example—wine is not part of the mealtime ritual, and there are no time-tested food and wine combinations. So we are free to experiment. How about

Spanish Albariño with Asian spring rolls, Prosecco with sushi, or Beaujolais with curry?

Now that we also have access to quality wines from all points of the globe, we also have the freedom to adapt the classic food and wine combinations. If Sancerre and chèvre work well together, shouldn't New Zealand Sauvignon Blanc work just as well with Salt Spring Island goat's cheese? Why not substitute a dessert wine like icewine for the classic Port and blue cheese combination? Or with foie gras?

Here are some new combinations to try:

Food Style	Wines
Brunch—egg dishes	Sparkling wines, Beaujolais
Chinese	Off-dry Riesling
Indian	Rosé, Beaujolais
Japanese—sushi	Dry Riesling, sparkling wines, fino sherry
Mexican	Sauvignon Blanc, Malbec
Fusion	Unoaked Chardonnay, Pinot Noir, Gamay
Southwestern BBQ	Off-dry Riesling, Zinfandel, Shiraz
Thai	Riesling, Sauvignon Blanc, Albariño
Death by chocolate dessert buffet	Orange Muscat, Banyuls, Tawny port

Order Makes a Difference

There are a few basic principles for serving wine with a meal:

- **Dry before sweet**—Dry wines, especially ones with some acidity, prepare your palate for food. They stimulate the appetite, as do sparkling wines, and enhance the kinds of foods served early in a meal. Sweetness lingers on the palate and makes it difficult to appreciate a dry wine following it. Sweet wines close the palate and end the meal.
- **Light before full**—Think of all of the components that make a wine taste full-bodied: alcohol, sugar, tannins. If you serve a light-bodied wine after a full-bodied one, it will taste weak and watery by contrast.
- **Young before old**—Young, simple wines are the warm-up act for older, more complex wines. Usually when more than one wine is served over the course of a meal, the oldest (and presumably best) one is reserved for the main course.

The "white wine before red wine" debate is more about the color of wines and doesn't take into account body or sweetness or flavor, or even age. For example, we would serve Beaujolais (a light- to medium-bodied red wine) before a full-bodied Chardonnay (a white wine). It's one rule that makes sense to break.

Pudding Wines

A number of wines can be used to end a meal to accompany dessert. We have touched on some of them already. Here are a few more:

- **Apple pie**—Off-dry white wines, like Riesling Auslese or Vouvray, go well together.
- **Cakes**—Moscato d'Asti, Madeira, Orange Muscat or tawny port
- **Cheesecake**—Off-dry Gewürztraminer or any medium-bodied white wine, with some sweetness.
- **Dark chocolate mousse**—Port or vins doux naturel
- **Fruit tarts or fresh fruit**—Demi-sec sparkling wine or icewine.

Wine and Cheese

Cheese is increasingly being offered as a separate course at the end of a meal. In Europe, the cheese tray would be offered before dessert. Wine and cheese parties are also the rage. Here are some things to keep in mind when matching wine and cheese:

- Sauvignon Blanc or Chablis go well with young acidic goat cheeses.
- Dry red wines, particularly complex reds like Amarone or Shiraz, work well with hard cheeses.
- Sweet wines and fortified wines, like port, work best with aged blue cheeses.
- Very sweet or fortified wines pair with extreme cheeses like Époisses or Muenster.
- Avoid higher-acidity wines if you are serving soft (particularly unfermented) or creamy cheeses.

Here are some great matches:

- Chardonnay and Brie;
- Port and Blue;
- Syrah and aged Cheddar;

- Sancerre and Chèvre; and,
- Amarone della Valpolicella and Parmigiano Reggiano

Knowing the Limits

Not everything works with wine. No matter how hard you try, some wines and foods are on a collision course:

- **Salty foods**—Highly salted foods clash with the tannins in wine and make the wine taste bitter, astringent, and sometimes even metallic. Salt also emphasizes the taste of the alcohol in wines. Try lower-alcohol, fruity white wines with a touch of residual sugar instead.
- **Spicy foods**—Hot and spicy foods accentuate the alcohol in most wines, sort of like throwing gasoline on a fire. Try low-alcohol, fruity white wines—Moscato d'Asti or German Riesling—or a low-tannin fruity red wine like Beaujolais. Serve slightly chilled. If all else fails, there's always beer.
- **Acidic and pickled foods**—Extremely acidic foods can make wine taste flat and sweet, even unpleasantly sweet. Artichokes, for example, are so acidic they even make water taste sweet. But when acid in food—even vinegar-based salad dressings—is matched with acidity in wine (for example, Sauvignon Blanc), the overall perception of acidity is lowered and the other flavors in the food and wine show through.
- **Unfermented dairy products**—Medium- to high-acid wines are not recommended for butter- or creamed-based sauces as they will make the food taste rancid. Try warm-climate Chardonnay instead.
- **Fish and red wine**—Some red wines work with seafood, but many more don't, hence that old rule. The tannins in red wine clash with the iodine and other components in seafood, and the result is a nasty metallic taste. With salmon or other fatty fish, lower-tannin, low-alcohol red wines such as Pinot Noir, Barbera, and Beaujolais work well. Grill, broil or blacken the fish to bring out a "meatier" taste and texture. Acidity (like a squeeze of lemon) is a good counter to the fishiness of oysters, sushi, or other shellfish. Stick to unoaked, crisp, light-bodied, white wines like Chablis, Muscadet, and even sparkling wine.
- **Meat and white wine**—If we're talking about a big, juicy steak, grilled to perfection, then most white wines, or even a light-bodied red wine, will taste like little more than lemon juice and water next to it. If you prefer white wine to red,

poultry, veal, and pork (especially when accompanied by sweet or spicy sauces) are better matches. With a big rare steak, stick to red wine. If the steak is well done then it's okay to try an oaky Chardonnay—think Californian.

- **Eggs**—Wine may not be first thing that comes to mind when you think of breakfast. But what about brunch or egg dishes like omelettes? Eggs are delicate but with sufficient fat content—in the yolks or the sauces—to create a problem. Stick with light-bodied, low-acid, neutral white wines, sparkling wines, or very light-bodied red wines. Beaujolais goes well with omelets and Alsace Riesling or Sylvaner is a classic match for quiche.

> **Wine's Worst Enemies**
> Artichokes, Asparagus, Spinach, Vinegars

- **Sweet desserts**—If you're ending the meal with a sweet dessert, always make sure the wine you choose is sweeter. Ice cream and tropical fruits can't be out-sweetened by wines, so avoid matching them up.
- **Chocolate**—A special problem; chocolate's sweet intensity and body make it a tough match—but not impossible. Sweet Muscats, Banyuls, and ruby or tawny port are worth a try. Cabernet Sauvignon is a good match with dark chocolate.

Never Cook with Wine You Wouldn't Drink

If a wine doesn't taste good in the glass, don't cook with it. All flavors in a wine, good or bad, are intensified once the wine is heated. Here are some general guidelines for cooking with wine:

- **Use blends**—Fruity, medium-bodied wines that are made from a blend of grapes (Côtes du Rhône, for example) contribute more complex, well-rounded flavors than single-varietal wines.
- **Avoid oak**—Sauces made with more heavily oaked wines (e.g., Napa Cabernet Sauvignon) may develop astringent, bitter, and sometimes harsh tastes.
- **Use wine as a bridge**—The wine you cook with should be of the same style or grape variety as what you are drinking. This forms a bridge between the wine in the glass and the wine in the sauce.
- **Use wine to flavor the food**—Use wine as you would herbs and spices, to bring out other flavor dimensions in the meal. You can also use wine to tenderize, color, baste, and as a base for sauces.

- **Cook off the alcohol**—When cooking with wine, use low, slow heat to evaporate the alcohol, leaving only the flavor of the wine behind. Rapid heating of a wine will result in a sauce that is tart and murky. "Raw" wine is rarely used in a dish.
- **Don't spend a lot**—You can get good to excellent results using wines that cost under $15 a bottle.

Wine for all Seasons

Wines have a "season" just as foods do. That light-bodied Pinot Grigio you happily enjoyed on the patio last summer won't be as comforting as a glass of Amarone or port in front of the fireplace in the wintertime. Just as salads and sandwiches keep us cool when the weather is hot, and soups and stews warm us up on winter days, your choice of wines will vary over the course of the year.

Here are suggested menus and wine matches geared to the seasons:

Spring

Menu Item	Wine Suggestions
Baked ham Scalloped potatoes Zucchini and red pepper compote Raw fennel and apple salad Pineapple upside-down cake	• If you were going to go with one wine, try a Riesling or a rosé with a hint of residual sugar. • For reds, try a lightly chilled Beaujolais, Barbera, or Ribera del Duero Joven. • Sauvignon Blanc would complement the zucchini and fennel. • Try Moscato d'Asti with dessert.

Summer

Menu Item	Wine Suggestions
Raw veggies with white bean basil dip Grilled herbed chicken with aioli Hamburgers Potato Salad Chocolate chip cookies	• For a single crossover wine, a lightly chilled Dolcetto, Cabernet Franc (Loire), or rosé would go well. • Sauvignon Blanc or a Pinot Grigio would work with the veggies and chicken dishes. • Oloroso sherry with dessert

Fall

Menu Item	Wine Suggestions

Turkey with all the trimmings
Roasted root vegetables
Broccoli and cauliflower in a
  cheese sauce
Pumpkin pie
	• There's an undercurrent of sweetness in this
	  traditional meal. Off-dry Gewürztraminer or Riesling
	  would work well. Even a full-bodied rosé would be
	  okay. Zinfandel or Gamay are good choices for a
	  red wine.
	• Late-harvest Riesling or Gewürztraminer with
	  the pie.

Winter

Menu Item	Wine Suggestions

Beef stew
Ratatouille
Cornbread
Coleslaw
Brownies
	• For a red wine, try Rioja, something from the
	  Côtes du Rhone, or a Syrah/Shiraz to match this
	  hearty meal.
	• Most white wines (except maybe an oaked
	  Chardonnay) will be too light-bodied for this menu.
	• Try a glass of port or Banyuls with dessert.

Buying Wine in a Restaurant

Restaurant wine lists, on the whole, are not exactly user-friendly. Although this is changing, more often than not they are grouped by type of wine: sparkling, white, red and dessert wines, but after that, all bets are off.

Some lists are organized by country, while others group wines by grape variety—Chardonnay, Sauvignon Blanc, Cabernet Sauvignon, and so on. The restaurants that use these formats are expecting that you know what these wines are, where they are from, and whether the vintage is good, in order to select them.

Some wine lists include a section for special and expensive wines, called the "reserve list". This is always fun to look at, like window-shopping at a Porsche dealership.

Consumer-Friendly Wine Lists

Kudos to those restaurants that organize their lists by style—from light and crisp white wines to robust, full-bodied red wines. It makes it so much easier to select a wine that you aren't familiar with or to try something unique. The restaurant might even suggest certain food-wine matches—"*We recommend the German Riesling with the Thai Ginger Carrot Soup dotted with Coconut Cream*", for example—which is great since they should know their own food the best.

Here's a Clue

If the wine list is laminated, and you don't see any vintages listed, don't expect any great "finds."

A wine list organized by price, preferably in ascending order, makes it easier to find a wine that matches what you are planning to spend. We've even seen wine lists that are organized by price point: under $25, $25–$50, and so on. These are great if you want to compare different wine styles within a specific range.

Finally, restaurants that want your business indicate vintages on the menu and actually have the wines available that are on the list, or mark them "temporarily out of stock" when they're not. There is nothing more frustrating than picking a wine to match your meal only to find out after you've made the selection, "Sorry, we no longer have that wine available." A restaurant can redeem itself, however, by offering a suitable alternative, at the same price.

Ordering Wine with Confidence

Here's a quick five-step process for ordering wine in a restaurant with confidence:

Step 1.
Look at the food menu and discuss what you and your fellow diners want to eat. See if there are any strong preferences for certain wines. If more than one of you wants to help choose the wine, ask for another copy of the list.

Step 2.
Agree on what you want to spend. If you are having more than one bottle, keep that in mind, too. A regular 750 ml bottle of wine gives you about five glasses of wine. Scan the wine list to see what's available in your budget range. Look at the kinds of wines you like, what matches the food you want to eat, and the prices. Don't be rushed, take as much time as you need to choose the wine.

Step 3.
Don't worry about remembering vintage years because most restaurants sell the current vintage available. You probably won't have much of a choice. If you want to order a more expensive bottle of

wine you might want to ask for some advice about the vintage. If you have a vintage card in your wallet, it never hurts to sneak a peek, just to make sure the sommelier's recommendation matches what others have said about the year.

Step 4.

Stick with the wines that match the restaurant's food theme. You might love Australian Shiraz, but at Uncle Tony's House of Pasta it's a good bet the Chiantis are *bellissimo*!

Step 5.

If the restaurant has a sommelier (the name may appear on the wine list), ask him or her to recommend a few options and describe them. Let them know your budget, or discreetly point to another wine you were considering that was in your price range. A good sommelier will get the point. Also have an idea of what you and your guests are planning to eat, as the sommelier will likely ask.

Wine Picks by Restaurant Type

In Step 4 we recommended sticking with wines that match the restaurant's food theme Here's a quick reference on what to order in different types of restaurants. It's likely you will find at least one of these suggestions on the wine list. If not, refer back to the guidelines on food and wine matching from the last section.

The Dilemma.

In The Opening we described a scenario to you. What wine to pick with salmon, a vegetarian entrée, and pork? What would you recommend?

We'd go with a crossover wine like Pinot Noir (Oregon, Canada, or New Zealand) or Chianti. Both have sufficient body, flavor and acidity to make a great match. You should find one for under $40 on most restaurant wine lists.

In This Type of Restaurant	Go For Any of These Wines
Italian	Simple Chianti or Valpolicella for pizza and pasta. Splurge on Barolo, Brunello di Montalcino, or Amarone if it's a special occasion.
French	Match regional dishes with regional wines—for example, Muscadet with moules frites; red Burgundy with beef casseroles; aged Bordeaux with simple grilled meats; Provençal wines with Mediterranean-style dishes; and, champagne with most everything.
Bistro	Look for village wines from the southern Rhône, Provence, or Languedoc-Roussillon. These wines are also usually a bargain.
Sushi	Try the traditional—sake, which is actually closer to beer than wine. Otherwise, try Riesling or unoaked Chardonnay like Chablis. Champagne is fine if you're splurging, but other sparkling wines, like Prosecco, will do just as well.
Indian	Low-alcohol, off-dry Riesling or Vidal tempers spicy hot foods.

In This Type of Restaurant	Go For Any of These Wines
Steakhouse	Any warm-climate Cabernet Sauvignon on the list—Californian or Australian, the bigger the better. Northern Rhône Syrahs or Australian Shiraz are good choices with pepper steaks.
Chinese	Stick with whites, preferably Riesling.
Thai	Sauvignon Blanc will enhance the lemongrass and herbal flavors; aromatic Rieslings or soft, fruity Pinot Blanc are also good picks.
Tapas	Dry sherries like fino or Oloroso sherry; rosé wines from Navarra; Rioja or Ribera del Duero reds with anything grilled.
Seafood	Muscadet or Chablis with mussels or oysters; Sauvignon Blanc for light fish dishes; oaked Californian Chardonnay with lobster or salmon.
Fusion	Crossover cuisine calls for crossover wines. Try unoaked Chardonnays, Sauvignon Blancs, New World Pinot Noirs, Chianti, Dolcetto, or Beaujolais/Gamay.

When in doubt, think, "When in Rome, do as the Romans do." You're always wise to stick with the local wines, especially when you're in a restaurant from a country with a strong wine and food culture. Of course, when you are traveling, you may not have any option but to follow this rule—don't expect to see your favorite Australian Shiraz in a Marbella tapas bar.

Am I Paying Too Much?

When you buy a bottle of wine at a restaurant, what you're really paying for is careful cellaring (you hope), clean, well-sized glasses (or at least bigger than the water glass), and the overall experience of being served. How much is that worth? That's up to you to decide. Some restaurants charge a small mark-up and others charge two to three times what the wine costs retail.

If you want to be pampered, you will have to pay for it. If you are on a budget, look for restaurants that charge a small mark-up or offer alternatives. Here are a number of other options available to you:

- **House wines**—We'd like to think that most restaurants carefully chose their house wine to reflect their menu. The reality is that many are chosen for their price point, their availability, and that they are least likely to offend anyone (which isn't always the case). If the restaurant cares about their wine program then they should also care about their choice of house wine.

  Most restaurants have at least two house wines: one white and one red wine. They may have a couple of choices for each so ask what they are. A glass of house wine is usually a 6 oz (180 ml) serving, and a half-liter is about three glasses worth and should cost a little more than half the price of a full bottle. Ask to try a sample of the house wine, and if you like it, order it. Don't settle for bad, or less than fresh house wine.

- **Wines by the glass**—Not all restaurants offer this option—we wish more would—and again we find, the better the wine list, the better the wine-by-the-glass program. Ordering wines by the glass gives you the flexibility to match different wines to each course or the different wine preferences of your guests. You can order something specially selected by the restaurant, and some restaurants have been known to even open a bottle from the regular wine list to give you a glass. The restaurant might have a minimum charge—two glasses, for example—so it's a good idea to check first.

  Inquire if the restaurant has a wine preservation system. If they don't, the bottle may have sat open for a few days, especially on a slow week. Don't accept wine if it hasn't been stored properly—ask for a sample to check that the wine is in good condition. As with a full bottle, it's your right to be served a perfect glass of wine.

  If a few of you are ordering the same wine by the glass, you may be better off splitting a half-liter or going up to a full bottle. An added bonus with ordering a bottle is that you know the wine is going to be fresh.

- **Half bottles**—This is the sign of a restaurant that caters to its customers (especially those who dine alone.) Half bottles are great even if there are two of you and you want to try one wine with your appetizer and another with your main course. Dessert wines often come in half bottles.

  As a rule, half bottles age much faster than large bottles, so try to buy more recent vintages.

- **Odds and ends**—Ask if they have other wines that are not on the list—not the expensive "reserve list" though! They may have changed the wine list recently and have a few odds and ends to clear out. If you are interested in any of the wines, ask for prices and make an offer. If you become a regular customer, the restaurant may bring in special wines for you, from time to time, at good price points.

- **BYO**—If you are lucky enough to live in an area where BYO (bring your own) is allowed, you've got the best of all worlds. BYO allows you to bring in a bottle of your own wine and only be charged a "corkage" fee ($10–30 per bottle) for having someone else serve it—its not SYO (serve your own wine.) Local laws will govern what you can bring to the restaurant (no homemade wine, for example), and if you can take unfinished bottles home.

Use the BYO option to bring in something special to the restaurant—perhaps an anniversary wine—but *never* a wine that already appears on the restaurant's own wine list. It's good form to tip the server on the fair cost of your wine, not just on the corkage fee.

Getting the Right Service

Most servers are trained to open and serve wine ordered by customers. But they don't always have the training, or the experience, to help you *choose* a wine.

Sommeliers go a step beyond. They are wine professionals, there to enhance your dining experience. They help you make a wine selection that will bring out the best in the food and the wine combined. Don't feel intimidated to ask for help, it's the sommelier's job to enhance your dining experience, not ruin it. Sit back and let the sommelier guide you through the meal.

And don't be concerned about being pressured into buying something outside of your price range. When discussing a recommendation, be clear about the kinds of wine you most enjoy (including brand names or styles). A good sommelier should figure it out.

Some restaurants have larger-sized, crystal glasses that they would be happy to provide if you request them. And sometimes they are provided even if you don't ask. But whenever we've had to ask, the sommelier has always been able to provide something bigger and better than the glasses that were on the table when we arrived. Don't forget to show your gratitude for the extra attention.

Even if you don't want—or need—the sommelier to be part of your wine decision, you still benefit from their expertise. The sommelier is the one who selects the wines for the restaurant, organizes and designs the wine list, and helps to train the other servers.

Do I Sniff the Cork?

As if ordering the wine isn't bad enough, the tasting ritual is when the pressure really builds for some people.

Before the cork is even pulled, the sommelier or server should present the bottle to you, if you're the host. This is to make sure the wine is the one you ordered, and the vintage you expected. Don't simply glance at the bottle—it's hard to explain after you receive the bill that you weren't actually pointing to the '61 Château Margaux on the wine list.

Then comes the grand opening. While you may think the whole process is intimidating, for many servers it can be equally nerve-wracking. Imagine what it would feel like to open a bottle of wine in front of a table full of staring people.

The server opens the bottle and places the cork next to you—what do you do? The short answer is, "not much." It doesn't merit the attention it usually is afforded. In fact, in many European restaurants they don't even present the cork to you. The server inspects it then discretely tucks it away into a pocket—frustrating if you like to keep corks as a memento.

That said, if you do get a chance to see the cork, there are some clues you can discover from its condition that will in turn alert you to the condition of the wine:

Cork Condition	Why	Remedy
Completely dry	Wine not stored on its side	• Probably okay if wine is young and simple. • One sniff of the wine will confirm if its oxidized.
Soaked through	Wine stored on its side a long time	• Okay if an old wine. • One sniff of the wine will confirm if its oxidized or is "over the hill."
Broken	Poor corkscrew technique or tightly fitted cork	• The wine will be okay, but you'll probably need a new bottle. A skilled sommelier will handle the problem without you having to ask.

Just glance at the cork to pick up these clues. You don't need to touch or sniff it. The cork is only an indicator; the real proof will come in the tasting (of the wine).

If the wine needs to be decanted for sediment, the server will do so at this stage, before the tasting ritual.

To Taste or Not to Taste?

Once the cork has been pulled, or the wine has been decanted, the server should pour a small sample of wine for the person who ordered the wine to taste. An interesting ritual and one that sends more shivers up the spines of some novice wine drinkers.

In some restaurants, they take the pressure off you. The sommelier pours a splash of wine in a glass and sniffs it to make sure it is of good quality before serving it to you. They have the training to do this and you should trust their judgement.

At many restaurants, however, servers may not be that wine savvy. Your wine knowledge, as limited as it may feel to you, may far exceed that of the person serving you. Besides, you're the one paying for the wine.

So what *do* you do? Remember the Four S's? First look at the wine and make sure it's clean and doesn't have anything floating in it. Next, sniff—this should tell you enough about its condition to make a decision. The tasting step confirms it all but you don't have to taste a wine that you think is off. If you do taste the wine we never recommend spitting in restaurants—its better to swallow.

If you think there's a problem with the wine, indicate what you think it is. Ask one of your tablemates to join in to give you moral support. Defective wines are rare but when you come across one that is musty (corked), flat and flavorless (oxidized), or smells of sulphur, acetone, or vinegar, don't accept it. Send it back. The restaurant should willingly replace the defective bottle with an alternative without question.

Of course, don't expect to return a good wine that you just don't like. How this is handled is up to the discretion of the restaurant. We know a number of restaurants that have the policy, "If you don't like the wine, we'll replace it." This practice should be praised and supported but never abused.

When the Wine Is Poured

If you think the wine is in good condition, ask the server to pour for the rest of the guests. If it's a white wine, check the temperature and ask for an ice bucket if the wine isn't chilled properly—don't let the server pour it right away.

The server should apportion the wine so that everyone who wants wine gets some, plus there should be some left in the bottle. The server should not fill the glasses more than half full.

Now, if you do decide to order another bottle of the same wine, you won't need new glasses for everyone. What you will need to do is make sure the second bottle is as good as the first. Don't let the server simply top up glasses of good wine with one that could be bad. The server should bring a clean glass so that someone can taste the wine from the new bottle. We've forgotten this before and it's any easy step to miss when you are engrossed in table conversation.

That's all you really need to know. Sit back, relax and enjoy your meal.

Buy, Buy Wine
Hello Empties

The day has finally come to buy wine. But where to start? How much to spend? Where can you find what you want? And how many bottles should you stock up on?

Where Can I Buy Wine?

Some of you are luckier than others with respect to what you can buy and where, how, and when you can buy it. Countries have different laws governing the sales of wine and spirits. Since we don't know where you live, we'll leave these details up to you, but here are a few of the options:

- **Retail**—This can include specialty wine shops, government-run stores, supermarkets, and discount warehouses.
- **Wineries**—Although local laws govern this, you may be able to ship directly from a winery. Some wineries have mailing lists, or allocation lists, where they sell their more limited wines.
- **On-line**—If on-line retailers can stay in business (a current problem in the industry) this is a relatively convenient option, if you have access to a computer. Purchases may also be controlled by local shipping laws, and you may not want to risk shipping your wine across the country in July.
- **Auctions**—The best option for finding older wines, but auctions aren't always conveniently located. Many do offer phone-in service.
- **Wine clubs**—Members-only wine clubs, especially those that offer mail order, are perfect for people who live in small rural locations and don't have the selection available in larger cities.

How Much to Spend?

A single bottle of wine can sell for $10 or for $1,000. Both are packaged in similar 750 ml bottles, both have a paper label, and both, of course, contain wine. We know the $1,000 version will taste better—it's probably been well cared for in the vineyard and in the winery—but will it taste 100 times better?

Since not many people regularly buy $1,000 bottles of wine, the question is perhaps moot. But what about the difference between a $10 bottle and one costing $25? That's where it gets tricky. Decide how much money you want to spend, then get the *best* bottle of wine you can for that amount.

Value versus Quality

So what can you expect to pay for a decent bottle of wine?

- **Under $15**—The wine should show something of the character of the grape—a Merlot that tastes like Merlot, for example. Once in awhile you will come across a Rosso Piceno from Italy or a Bulgarian Cabernet Sauvignon in the under-$10 range, and if it's a grape type you already like, go ahead and try it. There are New World wines in this bracket as well as Old World wines. Old World wines will be mainly from the regional and table wine categories, and Vin de Pays d'Oc wines are particularly good bets.

  Wines under $10 are not always well-made, however, and so it's important to get a personal recommendation—ideally from a trusted source. Don't be seduced by cute labels, funny names, or unique packaging, as more often than not these wines don't live up to the marketing efforts behind them.

- **$15 to $40**—As you climb up the price scale, the wine should be even more true to its variety and type. These wines are more concentrated, and they linger longer on your palate after you've swallowed them. They are polished, complex, and have a nice textured finish. A good, long finish is one of the extra benefits you get with a more expensive wine.

  There is a lot available in this range from the New World and the Old World. You can expect to get Old World wines in the quality range but not necessarily at the very top. You could find Reserve (for example, Chianti Classico Riserva) or single-vineyard wines at this price, but not many.

- **Above $40**—Now you are either paying for a wine that's in limited supply, made with no expense spared, or from an excellent vintage. Or you're paying for the name of the winery or winemaker. Sometimes you pay for all four—these wines will have been lovingly cared for from the vine to the finished wine. Some wineries produce only one barrel's worth of a particular wine. That's only 300 bottles, or 25 cases!

  There is little dispute that these are high-quality wines, especially those that are made by a well-respected producer in a very good vintage. Almost every major winemaking region in the world makes wines in this price range. Bordeaux classed growths or California "cult" wines start around $200 when released and can cost thousands later through auction.

When you decide to pay top dollar for a wine, you want to know "Will it be worth it?" Here are some clues to look for:

- **Location, location, location**—Better wines tend to have the region or the vineyard identified on the front label (e.g., Le Montrachet). The more specific the location—a vineyard is better than a region—the better the wine. Words like cru and clos (French), vigna and sori (Italian), and Grosslage and Einzellage (German) indicate the wine is from specified vineyard location.
- **Winemaker**—The best winemakers take what nature gives them in the grapes and express it through their particular style. They make good wines in even difficult vintages. Ask your wine seller for some names of reputable winemakers or check wine magazines.
- **Reserve**—This can be a sign of excellent quality or just a marketing term. These wines—the word "reserve" will appear somewhere on the front label—should be made from grapes grown in the winery's best vineyards and sometimes only in the very best vintages. In Spain, for example, "reserve" indicates the producer has aged the wine longer before its release.

  The meaning of reserve seems to vary from country to country and producer to producer and in some cases it has no meaning, so be careful. Read the back label or ask the salesperson for an explanation before spending the extra money.

Flying Winemakers

Some winemakers travel around the world consulting to different wineries in different countries. It was a name originally given to the Australian winemakers who came to the northern hemisphere to practice their craft during their winter season.

- **Vielles vignes or old vines**—The older the vine, the lower the yield and often the more concentrated the wine. The actual definition of "old" is sometimes suspect so again check the claim. Vines start to produce at about three years old. A 12-year-old vine is not "old"; a 100-year-old vine, on the other hand, is.

Does a Wine Have to Be Expensive to Be Good?

Ah, the million-dollar question. Sometimes we're asked about the greatest wine we've ever had. One of the best was a '61 Château Lascombes the two of us shared about 15 years ago. Out of a dusty bottle with a label we could hardly read came a wine that holds in our memories forever. The wine's finish lingered on and on, and still does.

Another one was a bottle of inexpensive Lambrusca shared over chunks of cheese, Prosciutto di Parma, and plates of pasta when we stopped for lunch at a truck stop in a small town in Italy one year. The food and wine combined perfectly in an atmosphere where everyone took the time to enjoy the experience. It too was memorable.

The difference in the price of these wines was immense but the value was the same. The enjoyment you derive from a wine may have no relationship to its price. It has more to do with a sense of occasion or sense of place than anything else—who you're with, if you're celebrating anything, the mood you're in, where you are, and what you're eating.

Bottom line, you can find great value, and even memorable wines, at every price point.

What's in Store For You?

It seems no matter where you buy your wines at retail, most wine shops look the same: sparkling wine in one section, still wines organized by country, and all the really good stuff in a locked glass case. It's predictable, and it's set up for people who already know what they want. As a wine novice, you race in there, find the wine you know, buy it, and race out.

If you are very lucky, you live in an area with a boutique-style shop with wines organized by style. Looking for an aromatic medium-bodied white wine? Or maybe a concentrated, full-bodied red wine? You walk in and check out the sections that most appeal to you. It's simple, and encourages you to try a wine that's new to you, but in a style you like. Shops (Best Cellars, for example) that organize their wine selections by style, and within specific price ranges, are becoming popular so check your area to see if there's one nearby.

Service

You should expect the staff of a wine shop to have more knowledge than you, and hopefully have some personal experience with the wines they sell. Can they tell you the difference between a Cabernet Sauvignon from California and one from Chile, for example, and have they actually tasted the wine they are suggesting you buy? Listen to how they describe the wine; it will give you clues as to whether they are knowledgeable or in need of this book.

Check the shop's returns policy before you buy from it. Will it take back wines that have faults? What if you bought two bottles of the same wine, tried one and didn't like it—can you bring the other one back for an exchange or a refund?

What "extras" do they provide? Does the shop have a newsletter? Do they offer in-store tastings? Some shops even offer event planning and glass rentals if you buy the wine through them.

Asking for Help

Here are three approaches for getting the wine you want:

- Describe the wine you want in simple terms:
  "I'd like a light-bodied, dry white wine with plenty of acidity for under $15."
  "I prefer red wines that are big and spicy. I usually drink Australian Shiraz and I want to try something different. I want to spend no more than $20."
- Indicate the occasion or the food you plan to serve:
  "We are having pasta with spicy meat sauce tonight. What red wine do you recommend under $10?"
  "I need a special bottle of wine for our anniversary. We usually buy Californian wines but tonight we'd like something unique. It's our twentieth so I'm willing to spend a lot."
- Ask if they have tasting notes. Better still; ask if you can sample the wine. Don't count on this happening with a $50 wine, but they might open a bottle of something that's being promoted or a special purchase, especially if you are a regular customer.

Selection

Wine selection will differ based on where you live and where you buy your wine. Supermarkets and discount warehouses may have better prices, or the convenience of being able to buy wine when you nip in for pastrami, but the staff may be clueless themselves. Plus, you can't be sure if their wines are stored properly.

Specialty shops usually have well-trained and helpful staff, but their selection may only be in a narrow range (for example, primarily Italian.) You may have to frequent more than one store to get what you want.

How the shop organizes its selection is important. It should be obvious by looking at the display to determine if the store has a preference toward one country or another, or wants your business.

Price

Government regulations may prohibit the discounting of wines and spirits. There's never any harm in asking for a case discount or lower prices on discontinued wines. Watch for sales or special promotions.

Storage—Should You Care?

Wine shops can be quite creative in how they merchandise their wines. Some have elaborate racking and bins and others leave the wine in cardboard boxes on skids. Some are temperature controlled and others use the door to regulate the temperature in the store. How they care for the wine is important.

If what you're buying comes from a recently released vintage, the wine won't have been stored long enough to make a difference one way or the other. Just grab a bottle from the shelf or the box on the floor and head to the cash register.

Make sure any older wines you buy have been stored on their side. Avoid older vintage wine that has been stored upright. Older vintage wines should be stored in a temperature-controlled area where they can rest undisturbed.

Even if the wine has been stored on its side, check to see that the space between the top of the wine and bottom of the cork (*ullage*) is not too great, say less than about 1 inch (2 cm) When a wine's been kept upright, or its fill level looks unusually low, there's a risk the cork has shrunk

Ullage

High fill
(good)

Low fill
(bad)

and the wine could be oxidized, or at minimum it has prematurely aged.

Wine Store Do's and Don'ts

Do buy wine from a shop...	Don't buy wine from a shop...
• with knowledgeable and well-trained staff	• whose staff thinks all white wine is Chardonnay
• that stores its wine in bins or racks	• that stores its wine standing up, next to the deli counter
• with good stock turnover and is well organized	• where you have to dust the bottles to read the label
• that is temperature-controlled	• that uses its door as a temperature-control device
• that offers regular tastings, seminars, or a newsletter	• that doubles as a bowling alley

Visiting A Winery

Visiting a winery is not only one of the best ways to buy wine but it is also a great way to learn more about wine. You may be able to see how the winery works and even meet the winemaker. Many wineries schedule on-site events during the summer or holiday months—jazz festivals, food tastings, and balloon rides—and some areas hold local wine festivals.

Preparing for a Visit

Before visiting a wine region, it's a good idea to know where you are going, who you are going to visit, and how you are going to cover all the places on your list. Here are some pre-planning suggestions:

- Get a map of the region. Contact the region's tourism office, wine council or association, or Chamber of Commerce.
- Are there organized tours of the area? If you'd like to take your bike with you, are there trails or is the region bike-friendly? If there are special events taking place when you are visiting, do the events take time (a balloon ride) or need a reservation (a jazz festival)?

- Do you need to make an appointment? Book ahead and give the winery ample notice of your visit. If you are visiting a wine region on vacation, the place where you are staying may make appointments for you—especially for wineries that rarely see visitors.

  With the exception of certain, larger, wineries in France (like the Alsace, Burgundy, and Champagne) most European producers aren't set up for wine tourism and prefer an appointment. Write a letter, fax, or e-mail, in advance of your visit and indicate that you are interested in a tour. We find they are more accommodating if you are expected.

- Which wineries have a tasting room and what hours do they keep? Hours may vary according to the season, and the work that is required in the vineyards or the winery.

  In Europe, fewer wineries have tasting rooms—you're more than likely to be welcomed in the cellar room itself. The larger producers do offer tours and some are offered in English.

- Which wineries offer tours? Not all do. Don't expect smaller wineries to offer tours during the harvest, but if they do it is the best time to take a tour. Tours in the middle of winter can be boring—wine sitting in barrels is less exciting than grapes being crushed and pressed. In our experience, very few wineries charge for tours, and when they do it is usually something unique.

- Does the winery have picnic facilities or a restaurant on the premises? If you are planning a picnic, bring a corkscrew and glasses. Some wineries will oblige you by opening the wine (after you buy it of course) and providing glasses, however, others have gift shops where they prefer sell such items.

Planning the Day

While you may think you can visit 20 wineries in a day—and we have seen people try—plan to visit four or five. Two in the morning and three in the afternoon is realistic and allows you to focus on the wine styles you like and to make comparisons among the different styles you try.

Tasting-room people are friendlier if you appear attentive and not in a rush to set the world record for most winery visits in day. If they see you appreciate their wines, they may let you taste something special.

If a winery offers picnic facilities or has a restaurant, plan to visit it during your trip. There is nothing better than sampling wines with local foods. Don't forget to make reservations as lots of other people may have the same idea.

Don't just go to the famous wineries. They tend to be over-crowded. You may get a better reception at the smaller wineries and in any case we find they usually make more interesting wine. Tasting Daniel Lenko's wine (in Beamsville, Ontario) and eating his mother Helen's pie in the family kitchen/tasting room is an expe-rience that the big wineries simply can't match!

Allow enough time to drive between wineries. Most are on coun-try roads, and not superhighways, so it could take more time to travel in the region than you'd expect. It's nice to visit wineries while there are grapes on the vines but be aware that this is also the busiest time to be traveling in wine country.

Assign a designated driver as you will be consuming wine. Better still, hire a driver so everyone can enjoy the event.

At the Winery

One of our best experiences was in Burgundy, tasting wines out of the barrel in an ancient cellar with Ghislaine Barthod, the wine-maker. Another was with Vincent Arroyo in Calistoga, California, comparing barrel samples of his Petite Sirah from different types of oak. We've toured old châteaux, but also some state-of-the-art facil-ities, and in all cases we learned so much more about the wine and the people behind it.

Wineries that accept visitors usually have a tasting bar. At the smaller wineries, or in Europe, don't be surprised if you end up tast-ing in the cellar. And if you do end up in the cellar with the winemaker, don't worry if you don't know the local language. You'll be surprised how you can still communicate with gestures and few simple wine words.

Newer ones may offer all their wines for tasting, to introduce more people to their products. The more established wineries might only have certain wines available for tasting. Of course, depending on the time of year, some wineries, particularly smaller ones, may not have any wine left to taste—they've sold out! Late spring, early summer, or during local wine festivals are the safest times to visit if you want to make sure they have wine. Or call ahead if you are concerned about availability.

Sometimes the winery charges for samples. Or they charge for the tasting glass, which usually has their logo etched on it. If you buy wine, this charge is often deducted from the purchase price.

Tasting Etiquette

Here are some suggestions for tasting at a winery:

- Limit your group to four to six people. You will be treated better by the tasting-room staff and be able to focus more on the wine. If you are traveling in a large group, call ahead. The winery, if it can handle a large group, may arrange a special tasting just for you.
- Avoid overpowering colognes or perfumes. They will affect your tasting abilities, as well as those of others around you.
- Wineries are providing you with free samples: don't abuse the privilege. Bring bottles of water with you. Don't use wine to quench your thirst.
- Dress appropriately: wine tasting isn't a fashion show. In the New World think casual dress; in the Old World dressy casual. Bring a sweater as some wineries get quite cool.
- Pace yourself. The novelty of free wine may have you drinking everything put in front of you. It is okay to spit and you don't need to finish the sample. The people serving at wineries won't be offended if you pour it out, and they will usually have a bucket or spittoon on top of the tasting bar for this purpose. In Europe, follow the lead of the winemaker and spit in the cellar floor drain.
- Don't hog the bar. If there is a crowd, and you want to take your time, take your sample and move back to a quieter spot. Let the tasting-room staff serve everyone equally. Your questions may be important to you, but other people may just want to taste the wine and move on.
- Thank the staff for their time and for the samples of their wine. If you found something you like, buy a couple bottles to take home.
- Due to the concerns about vine diseases, wineries prefer you not walk in the vineyards without permission. Definitely don't touch the grapes.

Tasting Wine

Use the Four S's and write tasting notes. Wineries sometimes give you their own literature about the wines, but it is always worthwhile to record what you think of the wines. It will help you remember what you tasted when you get home. Besides, it's good practice.

Ask lots of questions—especially if you meet the winemaker. Ask why he or she thinks their wines are unique, what got them into winemaking in the first place, or what awards the wines have won. If you want to give feedback on the wine, remember most winemakers pour their hearts and souls into their wines.

Getting to know a winery and the winemaker adds to the overall appreciation of the wines. A personal connection to the winery always adds to the enjoyment of the wine.

Buying Wine

The real benefit of visiting wineries is having a chance to try the wine before you buy. Also, many wines are available for sale only at the winery. These are usually specialty wines, in short supply, and are the best bets for buying. Otherwise, why carry around something you can get back home at your local store, unless it is less expensive at the winery? And it often isn't.

You may come across a producer you really like whose wines sell out every year. Get on their mailing list if you want to buy their wines before they sell out. California cult wineries started this trend, and they now allocate who gets their wines, putting them even further out of reach for most people. It's all part of the cachet.

If you're buying a lot of wine, ask for a discount, or a bonus bottle (buy twelve get one free). They may be unable to do this due to local laws, but it costs you nothing to ask.

Getting It Home

Do you want to carry your wine home with you or have it shipped? Depending on local laws, shipping can be your best bet. Most wineries are set up to handle mail order or courier shipments. Check this out before you make the trip. However, make sure your wine doesn't arrive home before you do.

- At times when shipping isn't practical, or necessary, carry a cooler to protect your wine purchases, especially during the summer months. Extreme prolonged heat will shorten the lifespan of some wines, but even after a few hours in a locked car the cork could be forced out of the bottle.
- Shipping wine home from overseas is very costly. On top of the shipping costs, expect to pay duties, taxes, markups, brokerage, and handling fees. Your $15 wine could end up costing another $30 a bottle just to get it into the country. Check local availability and pricing before you buy abroad, so you won't be upset when you return home to find you could have bought the same wine at a cheaper price.

- To save shipping, brokerage and handling fees, be selective about what you buy and carry it home if at all possible. A 750 ml wine bottle weighs about 2 lbs (1kg) and is sturdy enough to travel well in your carry-on luggage. (We've tested it out—in the interest of wine travelers everywhere.) We have seen other people check their wine on planes in unprotected cartons—not a good idea! Some airlines don't allow wine as checked baggage—again check the policy before you leave.
- If you are planning to bring wine back with you, check your duty-free allowance and be prepared to pay tax and duty for anything above those limits. It may be possible to declare wine that isn't accompanying you on the trip as part of your allowance. You may be able to save some extra duties this way.

Buying over the Internet

Did You Know?
Even if you can't or don't want to order wines through a Web site, many of on-line retailers are great resources or gateways to other wine-related sites.

In the event that you don't have enough places to buy wine locally, or if you live in a remote area where the only wine on store shelves has the word "hearty" somewhere on the label, then the Internet may be the place for you. Like any purchase over the Internet, the choices may be great but there are many cautionary tales to consider. It is one thing to have a book shipped to you in Moose Jaw in January, another thing to have a case of wine rattling around in the back of a delivery truck all day.

There Are Rules

Assuming your area has no restrictions on buying wine from a Web site and, more importantly, having it shipped to you, how do you go about it? The first step is to set up an account. You will be required to provide personal information such as date of birth and credit-card information to pre-qualify you as a buyer. Web site retailers must ensure that they're not selling alcohol to a minor, so some request a fax copy of your driver's license, passport or official ID before anything is sold or shipped to you.

Buyer Beware

There are certain extra precautions to take when buying wine on-line:

- Wine, has a shelf life, and if subjected to extremes of heat or cold, or poor storage conditions, it can spoil. You need to know at least two things about the Internet retailer: how do they *store* and how do they *ship* their wine?
- Before you place an order, do a little research into how the Internet wine retailer operates. Explore their sites, look into their buying, storage, and shipping policies, and ask questions of the staff by e-mail.
- When you're satisfied with what you've seen and heard, place a small order first as a trial run.

Shipping the Wine

The responsibilities for arranging, and paying for shipping, generally rest with the buyer.

- Before ordering, check local laws regarding shipping. Can the wine you're buying be shipped to you?
- What arrangements might have to be made before you get the wine? Are there any extra fees or charges?
- When making shipping arrangements, consider the time in transit (is it days or weeks?) and the prevailing weather conditions. One Internet retailer has a link to the Weather Channel so that buyers can decide on the best time to place an order for shipment.

Buying at an Auction

Auctions can be dangerous to your bank account. Often the excitement of the auction relieves you of all logic; on the other hand it allows you to acquire wine you otherwise wouldn't be able to get at a local shop.

Auctions give you access to wines that have long since sold out at the retail level—special vintages, unique bottles, or hard-to-find producers. You may want these to celebrate a special birth year, an anniversary, or some other milestone event. The wines you'll see featured at an auction tend to be rarities and keepers—wines that are special in some way because they are of limited availability and have demonstrated longevity. Don't expect to find bargains or a $10 everyday wine for your next party.

Types of Auctions

Depending on local laws, wine auctions tend to be either be commercial (live and via the Internet), estate, or for a charitable cause. Commercial and charity auctions can be large scale, with hundreds of lots (the bottles or cases of wine for sale) to bid on. We've seen lots as small as one bottle, and as large as a 55-year *vertical* (a successive series of vintages of one wine) of Château Mouton-Rothschild.

Different types of auctions have different fees or *premiums* attached to them. Check in advance to see if there are any hidden costs.

Preparing for an Auction

Do your homework. Auction wines are usually sold "as is". You assume all risk once your bid has been accepted.

- Request an auction catalogue, which will be free or at a nominal charge. In it you will find descriptions of the wines up for bid, with quotes from internationally recognized wine experts who have tasted these wines before.
- Auction wines are appraised. There is usually an estimated per bottle price provided, and sometimes a reserve price, a minimum below which the lot won't be sold.
- Use the catalogue to do some research on local availability and price. That way you won't find out later that the two bottles you just bought for $300 were also available at Joe's Wine Mart for $100!
- The catalogue description also gives you clues to a wine's condition before you bid—in particular the level of wine in the bottle. As wine ages, the fill level gradually decreases. A low fill level means some of the wine has leaked out or evaporated, or both, and may mean the wine has oxidized. Low fill levels are to be expected with very old bottles of wine.

To participate in an auction, you'll have to register for the auction, either the day of the event, or in advance. You'll get a numbered paddle or card, and the right to bid on any lot.

Ullage Levels

High fill	Normal fill	Mid-shoulder	Low-shoulder
Excellent	*Good*	*Start to worry*	*Bad news!*

At the Auction

Like most auctions, the bidding tends to go very quickly. Charity auctions less so, especially if there's a celebrity auctioneer. Professional auctioneers typically sets the level of the first bid, and bidders jump in from there.

When price levels exceed your limit, it's best to let the lot go. You'll hopefully have other opportunities to find wines you're looking for at other auctions.

Wine-Buying Clubs

Wine clubs offer members a chance to buy wines not otherwise available through regular channels. They might also organize private wine tasting events, where you'll get a chance to taste, and possibly buy, unique wines and to meet fellow wine enthusiasts.

Most clubs require a one-time enrolment fee and annual dues. You should weigh this against the selection of wines offered and the convenience of the club. Does the club require you to buy a certain amount of wine each year to remain an active member? Does it offer adequate descriptions of the wine it is selling? It's a good idea to check out how the club delivers its wines to you and how long it will take.

One limitation of many wine clubs is the requirement to buy wine in case quantities: either six or 12 bottles. You either have to really like what you're buying, or find someone else in the group who's willing to trade some of what they bought for some of what you bought.

Wine-of-the-month clubs run by a winery or a wine retailer— every month you may receive a package of wines chosen by them—may seem like a good idea but you often have little or no say in the selection. It's one way to try new wines but not the best. On the other hand, if you live in an isolated area it may be the only option you have. Getting a surprise package every month from a winery you like, however, will be something of a treat.

Giving It Away!

Wine and wine-related items make excellent gifts. They can be given to acknowledge someone, or to mark a special occasion, as long as you're sure there are no health, cultural, or religious reasons to avoid them. Even if you don't know the recipient very well, think back to whether you've ever seen the person drink wine, or express an interest in it.

Wine doesn't have to be expensive to be a successful gift. Here are some reasons for giving the gift of wine, along with suggestions:

Acknowledging Someone

You may want to use wine as a reward or to acknowledge a special contribution someone has made. Choose something that is less well-known, or has personal meaning or a story to tell. Consider giving wine: from a winery you visited, specially selected to go along with a person's favorite food, or made by an up-and-coming winemaker.

> **Trockenbeerenauslese?**
> If you can track down a bottle of this highly prized dessert wine, it will make a special gift for anyone on your list. If your dear Aunt Mabel has great taste, she'll love it!

Beyond what's in the bottle, think about packaging and presentation. A special gift box or wrapping can make a difference. Non-standard bottles—small and large—are often attractively packaged for gift giving. Make sure the wine inside is good too.

If you are considering a large-volume wine purchase and you live near a wine region, you may be able to get personalized labels printed up. Many wineries don't label their wines until they're ready to sell, and would be willing to customize a label for you.

Moving up the price scale, you can always count on name recognition with wine from a well-known producer—Château Mouton-Rothschild in Bordeaux, or the Super-Tuscan Sassicaia from Italy, for example—to make a particular statement. Now you might think these are safer bets, but if too expensive they may be inappropriate for the occasion.

For Special Occasions

Birthdays and anniversaries are easy when it comes to wine. For starters, you have the birth year or anniversary year to match with a vintage. Of course, this assumes the birthday person isn't sensitive about sharing his or her exact age.

Finding the right vintage for someone who is going to be 40 years old next week is going to be difficult, and expensive, so you could make it very easy for yourself by planning ahead and buying well in advance. But how many wines age successfully for 10 or 20 years, let alone 40?

You'll have to consider both the wine itself and its vintage. Bordeaux red wines, for example, are renowned for longevity, but whether they peak at 10 or 35 years will depend on the vintage. Usually only the better, more expensive wines will last 20 or more years, and few New World wines have established the track record of Old World wines.

Sweet wines, especially those with good acidity, are safe bets. As are fortified wines like port and Madeira. They age very well, and aren't as expensive when released. Port—in particular the recent 2000 vintage—is the safest bet as even the best versions aren't nearly as expensive as top Bordeaux, yet will appreciate in value as they age. You can buy the 2000 port now when your niece is in kindergarten, and give it to her on her twenty-first birthday.

Here are a few options for wines that should be able to find and will likely age well for up to 25 years:

White Wines	Red Wines	Fortified
Sauternes	Bordeaux Cru	Vintage ports
German Rieslings—Beerenauslese,	Barolo	Madeira
Eiswein, or Trockenbeerenauslese	Northern Rhône (Syrah)	

Now that you know which ones to look for, there's still the vintage to consider. Actually this is relatively easy to find out. Wines from bad vintages will have been consumed long ago, and ones from good vintages may still be kicking around in auctions. You're in luck if you're looking for a gift for someone born in 1945. That was a fabulous vintage for both Bordeaux and Sauternes wines, and they're still available for sale—if money is no object.

What about other occasions? Here are some ideas:

Occasion	Gift Idea
Valentine's Day	St. Amour Beaujolais
Wedding shower	Rosé
Wedding gift	Vintage champagne
Baby's birth	Vintage port
First job	Cava
Promotion	Non-vintage champagne
Best friend makes partner	Vintage champagne
New boat	California Sparkling Wine
New canoe	Asti (Spumante)
Thanksgiving	Zinfandel
Housewarming	Chianti Classico
New wine cellar	Barolo
First snowfall	Amarone

The most immediately gratifying special-occasion wine gift is sparkling wine. A perfect wine to celebrate anything!

Bringing Wine to a Dinner Party

When bringing wine to a dinner party, keep in mind the following:

Did You Know?

The general rule of thumb is one-half bottle (three glasses—one white and two red) of wine per person for dinner. If the guests are staying over you may want to increase this slightly. Take into account the designated drivers, and scale back the quantities if the guest list includes pregnant women or teetotalers.

- Don't expect that the wine you bring will be consumed that evening. Your host may have other plans. Likewise, don't expect that it won't be consumed either.
- It's a good idea to contact the host in advance if you would like to bring along something appropriate to that evening's menu. If he or she is open to the idea, see whether the wine you had in mind works with the planned menu. Or if the menu is a surprise and the host wants you to bring a surprise wine, consider these food-friendly wines:

White wines	Red Wines
Riesling, Sauvignon Blanc, or Pinot Grigio	Pinot Noir, Chianti, or Rioja

- Even if your host has selected wines to accompany the meal, ask about bringing something for before or after—an apéritif wine to stimulate the appetite, or a dessert wine for afterwards. Here are some great ideas to try:

To Start	To Finish
Sparkling wine (Prosecco or Cava)	Late-harvest Riesling
Dry sherry (Amontillado, dry Oloroso style)	Tokaji from Hungary
Muscadet, Vino Verde	Port (ruby or tawny)

Wine-Related Gifts

Wine is a great gift; ideally, it will leave the recipient with an experience to remember. But when it's gone, it's gone. For those times when you want to give something more durable, wine-related accessories may fit the bill.

- **Books**—The choice of wine-related books is wide-ranging, and there are new books being published every year. For someone with an interest in a particular region or a particular type of wine, there are many books to choose from. There's even great books devoted only to icewine that would be a great gift for your sweet-toothed friends.

   Some of our favorite authors include: Hugh Johnson, Jancis Robinson, Oz Clarke, and Andrew Sharpe. The pinnacle of wine books is Jancis Robinson's *Oxford Companion to Wine*, which any wine enthusiast would love to have. There is a version specific to North America as well as a shorter *Companion* version.
- **Videos**—There aren't many new serious, educationally-oriented video series around, but the two by Jancis Robinson and Hugh Johnson are classics. The movie *Sideways* is hilarious and a great gift for wine lovers, while *Mondovino* is perfect for those who are concerned with globalization in the wine world.
- **Magazine subscriptions**—For those who like to stay current on what's happening in the wine world, a magazine subscription can be a great gift. Besides the news and the articles, most wine magazines contain reviews of recently released wines. If the recipient likes to buy wine, choose the magazine that best represents what's available in their home market. *Wine Spectator*, *Wine & Spirits* and *Wine Enthusiast* have a distinctly US perspective; *Vines*, *Tidings* and *Wine Access* present the Canadian viewpoint; and, *Decanter* and *Wine* publish out of the UK.

- **Newsletters**—A number of wine writers publish regular monthly newsletters that can be given as a gift subscription. For example, Robert Parker Jr. publishes *The Wine Advocate*—probably the most influential, if not most controversial, newsletter in North America. Many write only for their local wine market and are more appropriate for people who want to know what's available closer to home.
- **Tools and toys**—Earlier we talked about three corkscrews that work very well. Either the Screwpull®-style model or the waiter's style would make good gifts. They are available in different colors and finishes, and the waiter's style can be engraved as well. If you want to give someone something really special, the Laguiole® handmade corkscrew is the waiter's *real* friend.
- **Wine preserver**—An even more practical gift is a wine preserver system like Vacu-Vin or Epivac or the inert gas Private Preserve. This assumes that your friend has bottles of wine left over to preserve.
- **Glassware and decanters**—From the all-purpose tulip shape to extreme customized glass shapes, there's glassware for everyone. What's their favorite wine and would they appreciate a glass specifically designed to enhance its taste?

Decanters are another option; especially if the receipient enjoys young red wines that need aeration, or older wines or port that have sediment.

Thinking Outside the Box

Think chillers (in marble, terra cotta, freezable ones), pewter bottle stoppers, decanting funnels and coasters, glass aerating funnels, wine racks, wine tags to identify bottles in the cellar, and even red wine stain remover.

For the real wine fanatic, there are a few aroma kits on the market including *Nez de Vin*. These kit to help the taster learn to identify the hundreds of aromas contained in wine.

And if money is no object, try a wine cellar. They hold from 50 to 1,000-plus bottles in a temperature and humidity controlled environment.

For accessories, cellars, and more ideas, the Internet is a great place to source items.

Mine, All Mine
Why Keep Wine?

It's been said that most wines are consumed within 36 hours of purchase, so why have your own collection? For convenience, variety, because some wines taste better with time, and because you'll save money.

Once you have a few bottles of your favorite wines on hand, all you need to do is walk over to your closet or down to your basement and grab something out of your "cellar."

It's also been said that most of the world's wines are produced to be consumed within a few years of the vintage, so only a small proportion are worthy of cellaring. It's one thing to have a few wines ageing nicely in your basement, but it is another thing to know *when* to drink them. We'll try to help you out with that too.

We're not going to talk about collecting for investment purposes. While wine is considered by some to be a good financial investment, it is our opinion that wine is to be enjoyed—either soon after purchase or following some much needed rest in cellarland.

What Should We Have Tonight?

One of the simplest reasons for having a cellar is convenience. Just like a restaurant with a chalkboard wine list, you too can have a supply of ready-to-drink wines available by the bottle, or even by the glass. You can try out different wines with what you're serving, and see which ones work best. Any partial bottles can be sealed up for another time using your vacuum hand pump or inert gas.

If you haven't developed any personal favorites yet, it's a good idea, and a lot of fun, to experiment with different varieties, regions and producers. This way you'll be able to try wines within a range of styles and flavors. Just don't buy a lot of one wine.

If you are lucky enough to have a good wine shop a few blocks away, don't worry about keeping more than a few everyday wines

Time Sensitive

Buy three bottles of the same wine; drink one right away and save the others to drink in six months, and then in a year or so. Keep notes of when you tasted the first wine and discover how the wine evolved with time in the bottle.

P.S. Not recommended for Beaujolais Nouveau.

on hand. Let the shop be your wine storage location and save your money for longer-term keepers.

If you don't have a good shop nearby, or would prefer to do your wine shopping less frequently, then you need to do some planning. Based on the style of wine you like, your eating habits, the space you have and of course your wine-drinking habits, there should be something for everyone. The key is to buy versatile, food-friendly wines that will appeal to a variety of tastes.

Wine Staples

Variety Pack

Keep a case on hand of the following wines. One bottle of each should do it:

- Reds: Chianti, Barbera, Rioja, Beaujolais (or Gamay), Merlot, Côtes du Rhône-Villages, Pinot Noir
- Whites: Unoaked Chardonnay, Riesling, Sauvignon Blanc
- Other: Prosecco, dry rosé

Basics Pack

Another option is to double up on some of the more versatile varietals. Here's what a case could look like:

- Reds: Chianti (2), Pinot Noir (2), Shiraz
- Whites: Riesling (2), Sauvignon Blanc (2), Oaked Chardonnay, Unoaked Chardonnay
- Other: Prosecco

Remember, most of the wines you will be buying are for short-term storing—we call them your wine staples—and the vintages are whatever the store has available to sell. We'll leave prices up to you, but versions of these wines usually cost under $20. You can go for a variety of wines or some real basics—your choice.

Top Seven

If you want to buy the wines that are made from the Top Seven grapes, here are some options ranging from the classics to regions where you'll likely get a good deal:

Grape	Classic Regions	Regions to Explore	Value Regions
Chardonnay	Burgundy (France) United States	Spain Canada	Chile
Sauvignon Blanc	Loire (France) Bordeaux (France) New Zealand	South Africa	Entre-Deux-Mers (France)
Riesling	Germany Alsace (France)	Niagara (Canada) Clare Valley (Australia)	Niagara
Cabernet Sauvignon	Bordeaux (France) United States	Chile	Australia Eastern Europe
Merlot	Bordeaux (France) Washington State	Chile Italy (Piave)	Chile
Pinot Noir	Burgundy (France) Oregon New Zealand	Canada California	New Zealand
Syrah/Shiraz	Rhône (France) Australia	Languedoc (France) California	Fitou or Minervois (France) South Africa

Quick Picks

Here are 20 or so wines to keep in the back of your mind. Consider them stress relievers when you are in a rush to buy something on the way home from work.

These wines made our list because of their versatility—they go pretty well with anything. They are all either light- or medium-bodied and have ample acidity. They will never overpower the food and they still have enough fruit and flavor to stand on their own. Best of all, good examples of these wines can be found for well under $20.

Twenty Wines Under Twenty Dollars

Country	Sparkling Wines	White Wines	Red Wines
France		Entre-Deux-Mers	Beaujolais-Villages
		Mâcon-Villages	Côtes du Rhône
			Chinon
Italy	Prosecco	Soave	Chianti
			Valpolicella
			Dolcetto
Germany		Riesling Kabinett	
United States			Pinot Noir
Canada		Riesling	Gamay
Australia			Shiraz
New Zealand		Sauvignon Blanc	
Spain	Cava		Ribera del Duero Joven
Chile		Sauvignon Blanc	Merlot

And for those of you with even more hectic lifestyles, here's only five things to remember:

- Riesling is versatile enough for even fusion foods.
- Sauvignon Blanc, with its good acidity and flavors, shows you are in the know.
- Pinot Noir is a great crossover wine—the wine to serve even if you are having fish, meat, *and* something vegetarian.
- Shiraz is a crowd pleaser. Who doesn't like it?
- Italian wines in general. Chianti is another good crossover wine. It and Soave will be easy to find in most wine stores.

Buying for the Future

So you got yourself a subscription to *The Wine Spectator* or *Decanter* and now you want to buy some of those big, tannic wines you've been reading about. You've read they need a few years cellaring time before they are drinkable. When you checked to see if any of the 1990 Barolos that are "drink now" are in your wine shop, you were surprised to see them selling for more than double the price of the current vintage. It's time to start buying now and holding for the future. What to do?

Did You Know?

Not all wines benefit from aging. In fact, less than 10% of all wines produced benefit from aging of more than two years.

The three things you need to consider are: the kind of wines you like, what you're willing to spend on something you can't drink for a few years, and how many wines you can store under the proper conditions.

Which Wines Age?

If you only drink light-bodied white wines or rosé wines, this section isn't for you. These wines don't improve with age and in fact will start to lose their fresh fruit aromas and flavors with cellaring. The same applies for most light-bodied red wines; however, a year in a cellar won't hurt them as much.

If you prefer full-bodied wines, sweet or fortified wines, then longer-term cellaring of these wines is a good option. Good fruit flavor supported by sufficient acid and/or tannins are the essential components that allow wines to age. If a wine has the potential to age, you can buy what you can afford now, while prices are low, and keep it until the tannins in the wine have softened when it's at its prime. Only very good wines have any flavor left when this happens.

The following grape varieties tend to age well. Some other grapes varieties (for example, Sémillon, Sauvignon Blanc, Chardonnay, and Sangiovese) are candidates for long cellaring but usually only when associated with certain regions and producers.

White Grape Varieties	Red Grape Varieties
Riesling	Cabernet Sauvignon
Chenin Blanc	Syrah
Furmint	Nebbiolo

Good wines have more of the components that allow them to age properly than average wines. If you are looking for specific wines, here are some regional candidates for medium-term cellaring of about five years:

White Wines	Red Wines
Burgundy—premier cru	Bordeaux—cru bourgeois and lesser cru classé
Chablis	Burgundy—premier cru
California Chardonnay	Châteauneuf-du-Pape
German Riesling—Auslese	Chianti Classico
Alsace Riesling and Gerwürztraminer	Vino Nobile di Montepulciano
Graves	Rioja—Reserva
Hunter Valley Semillon	Ribera del Duero—Reserva
Canadian Icewine	New World Cabernet Sauvignon
Monbazillac	New World Pinot Noir
	Australian Shiraz
	Zinfandel

If you have the space, and the budget, these regional candidates are ideal for even longer-term cellaring:

White Wines	Red Wines
Burgundy—grand cru	Bordeaux—top grand cru classé and equivalent
German Riesling—Auslese and up	Burgundy—grand cru
Alsace—vendage tardive	Northern Rhône
Pessac-Léognan	Barolo
Vouvray—moelleux	Brunello di Montalcino
Sauternes & Barsac	Chianti Classico Riserva
Tokaji	Super-Tuscans
	California Cabernet (top wines)
	Australian Shiraz (top wines)
	Vintage champagne—prestige cuvées
	Vintage port
	Madeira

Here's what you may be able to expect out of certain wines if you wait long enough:

- Burgundies in exceptional years are at their best in 15-plus years.
- Bordeaux in exceptional years can last over 20 years.
- Top Barolos and Brunello di Montalcinos in exceptional years can last 20 to 25 years.

- Vintage port can last 40 or more years.
- Malmsey Madeira has been known to last over 100 years.
- And a few Tokaji Essencia have even made it to 200 years.

Sometimes a great winemaker can perform miracles in a bad vintage, but the only way to know this is to read wine magazines. Almost everyone else relies on vintage charts.

Vintages

Certain vintages, in certain regions, are better than others for cellaring.

For red wines, tannins help wines age. In dry years, the grape skins are thicker and therefore contribute more tannins. In vintages where there is more rain, there is more pulp and the skins are thinner—the wines are more dilute and won't age as well.

For white wines, acidity is important. In cooler years, acidity levels are higher and the grapes will age better.

Whether red or white, the grapes must still be sufficiently ripe so that there is enough flavor (extract) in the wine for it to age properly.

Bottle Sizes

Oxygen speeds up the aging process of wine. Once a wine gets into the bottle it is only exposed to the small amount of oxygen at the top of the bottle, called the *headspace*. Once the wine has used that up, the process of aging becomes reductive—which is much slower and better than oxidative. The amount of headspace is more or less the same for all sizes of bottles. It would stand to reason then that larger format bottles—like magnums—have less oxygen relative to its volume of wine than a much smaller half bottles. Small bottles, therefore, age faster than large bottles. How much faster is anyone's guess, but most collectors bet on the large-format bottles for serious aging.

Do You Have to Spend Much?

Wines for longer-term cellaring don't have to be expensive. We started to put wines away about 20 years ago after reading an article by Canadian wine writer Tony Aspler entitled "Ten Wines Under $10 That Will Taste Like $20 Wines in Five Years." We bought two bottles each of the recommended wines and stored them, lying on their sides, in a couple of old shelving units in a cool place in our basement.

We started enjoying the wines over time and finished the last one in our starter pack after about seven years cellaring (okay, we lost track of a few of them!). This proved to us early on the benefit of buying ageworthy wines we liked, because they did improve in the bottle.

Although we saved a bit of money (because the current vintage of the wines had increased in price), these aged wines, based on how they had evolved, were actually more like wines that cost double the price (as Tony had promised). So your cellar does not have to be full of Super-Tuscan wines. Just buy wines that you like and can afford, in good vintages that will improve over time.

What about a cellar, does it have to cost a lot of money to build? Not at all, in fact you may not even have to build anything. A wine cellar can be as simple as a few wooden boxes in the back corner of a dark closet, or an old bookcase, or some inexpensive shelves. At the other extreme, your cellar can be a temperature-controlled room with redwood racking and track lighting in the basement of your house.

It all depends, do you want to spend your money on wine or on storage? As long as you keep your wine away from its true enemies—heat, light and vibration—a wine cellar can cost you next to nothing.

The Right Conditions

Here are all the things your wine needs when you store it for any length of time: constant temperature, darkness, humidity, clean with good ventilation, and lastly, peace and quiet.

Constant Temperature

The most important factor in wine storage is maintaining a constant temperature. Temperature fluctuations—even 5°F (2–3°C) over the course of the day—are detrimental to wines.

Find an area where the temperature is within the range of 50–60°F (10–15°C), and where temperatures don't vary on a daily basis. A variation of about 10°F (4–5°C) between summer and winter is fine as long as the shift is gradual. The ideal temperature is 55°F (13°C).

If you don't live in a château in France, it may be difficult to achieve this temperature range. If your wine rack catches the evening sun, or the broom closet where you store your wines has the water heater in it, try to move your wines to where the temperature is at least constant. See if you can insulate the area in some way—not with fibreglass insulation as it absorbs moisture. And if there is nothing you can do, don't worry, even a constant 70°F (20°C) isn't going to ruin your wines—maybe just knock a year or so off their development.

But if the temperature where you store your wines fluctuates dramatically, or you are getting serious about collecting wine, you may have to break down and buy a temperature-controlled unit.

Darkness

Wine likes to be kept in the dark. Direct sunlight not only increases the temperature of the wine, UV rays also penetrate the bottle and harm the wine. The dark green glass used for most wines doesn't completely protect the contents.

Don't store wines near a fluorescent light source either. Whether you use the corner of a dark closet, or something bigger, don't have any more light than you need to move around and retrieve wines. Even a bare incandescent light bulb left on will give off heat.

Humidity

A high, constant level of humidity will save corks and protect your wine. Anything within the range of 60%–80% humidity is fine, with the ideal level being 70%–75%. Humidity is most important when you plan to store bottles for more than five years.

Below the 50% mark, corks will dry out, start to leak, and the wine will oxidize. Above the 80% level, mold will form and labels will get damaged and may fall off. Given the choice between low- and high-humidity environments, think, is it better to ruin my wine or my wine labels?

A quick fix is to keep an opened jug of water on the floor where you store your wines. If this doesn't work, the need for controlled humidity is in order. Temperature-controlled units also take care of humidity.

Did You Know?
If you don't know the level of humidity is in your house, you can buy an inexpensive hygrometer with a digital readout at your local hardware store. They are fairly accurate and will give you a sense of what you may need to adjust.

Clean and Well-ventilated

Clean means odor free. Don't keep your wines near laundry detergents, paints, fertilizers, or other chemicals. That goes for anything smelly, including cooking odors or gym equipment.

Remember, wine breathes. Slowly, over time, minute amounts of air pass through the cork, making contact with the wine. You don't want your wine to remind you of the garlic you stored in the cellar three years ago, do you?

The same goes for cardboard boxes. If the storage area is humid, the cardboard will start to rot and may contaminate your wine. Ask your local wine shop if they will give or sell you any of the wooden wine crates the more expensive wines are shipped in.

As for ventilation, does the air circulate where your wine is being kept? Or is it too drafty? A racking system helps the air circulate and is better for long-term storage than sealed boxes.

Peace and Quiet

Think of your wines as "sleeping" in the cellar. If they don't get their sleep, they won't develop properly and will age prematurely.

Make sure you keep them in an area that is free from vibration. Keep them well away from the washing machine and the fridge. Resist the temptation of picking up your bottles every two to three months and looking at them. Nothing has changed, trust us.

Try to dedicate one area for wine storage. Having to move your wines frequently isn't good for them, or your back.

Keep Away From the Fridge!

There's only one place worse than storing your wines in the fridge, and that's in a wine rack on top the fridge. It might look pretty and you're not using the space anyway, but vibrations, temperature, and light fluctuations will harm your wines.

And while it's dark inside the fridge, the temperature is too cold and the humidity is too low for long-term storage. The vibrations from the motor cycling on and off will also harm the wine eventually.

Show and Tell

If you have accumulated a few hundred wines and want to control temperature and humidity, you can purchase a self-contained, temperature-controlled unit that you can plug into any electrical outlet. These are usually wood veneered and feature a glass window so you can see your prized collection. Prices start at about $800 for a 200-bottle capacity and go up to a few thousand for walk-in units.

What about Shelving?

The key thing about shelving or racking, isn't what its made of, but that it allows the bottles to lie horizontal—not standing up. Otherwise the corks will dry out.

Crates may be fine in the short-term, but eventually, you'll get tired of finding the wine you want is always at the bottom of the crate. When you are ready to set up some shelving to organize your collection, here are some options:

- Use an old bookcase.
- Put a few simple shelves together. Make sure they're solid. Square clay chimney pipes work well if you have the space.
- Inexpensive pine shelves designed for wine bottles are relatively easy to find.
- Wine supply stores sell pre-made wine racks in various styles and sizes. Racks that have a space for each bottle are more expensive than ones that hold six to eight bottles per section. You can usually mix and match these systems for look and convenience.
- Hire professionals to custom build racking for your storage space. Use redwood if its available. It's strong, resistant to moisture, and doesn't give off odors that could taint the wine.

The key points to remember when planning your wine storage space are:

- **Circulation**—Can air circulate around the bottles?
- **Flexibility**—Can bottles with larger bases (e.g., champagne), half bottles, and large bottle formats (e.g., magnums) fit in the racking? How easy is it to add on to the shelving if you want to expand your collection?
- **Space**—Always plan for more space than you think you'll need!

When planning a storage space, think ahead. If you are planning on moving in the foreseeable future, limit the size of your collection. Wine is heavy—a case ways about 24 lbs (16.8 kg)—and cumbersome. You might not think 240 wines is a lot, but that's 20 cases.

It's All about Balance

The kinds of wines and number of bottles you decide to keep in your cellar will depend on your budget and your motivation for having a cellar. Ultimately, it's about balance. What's inside your cellar should strike a balance between immediate enjoyment and future appreciation.

In the beginning, your wine budget may only cover less expensive wines, most of which will be suited for immediate consumption, plus a few that are capable of improving with time.

The balance will start to shift as the wines you originally put aside for long-term cellaring start to mature, and become your "drink now" wines. These get replaced with more wines to lay down for the future. Over time, you'll need to buy fewer and fewer wines for your current needs.

Organizing Your Wines

A dozen of so bottles isn't too hard to keep track of, but as you add to your collection, you'll need a system. It's never a pleasant surprise to discover a couple of bottles of five-year-old Beaujolais Nouveau tucked away in a crate somewhere. You don't want to lose track of the wines that are for early drinking. You need to know their whereabouts at all times.

The simplest system you can set up is based on a logbook. In it, list your wines, their prices, short notes from wine write-ups, and whether they are "drink now" or "keepers." For "keepers," indicate in bold letters the "drink by" year you were given when you bought the wine.

As you drink each wine, add your tasting notes, including who you shared the wine with and what was on the menu. If you have multiple bottles of the same wine, highlight whether the wine tasted was great (at its peak), needed time (too young), or was starting to fade (overmature). Plan a party if you have a few bottles in that last category!

If you want to put your wine list on the computer, you can do it yourself or buy cellar management software. We took the DIY route and have our wine list on a spreadsheet. A database program would work fine too, but they weren't very user-friendly when we first set up our system 15 years ago. The different fields we use are: year, wine type, producer, tasting notes, and last known price. This system is good if you like poring over your wine list, sometimes exclaiming, "Hey, forgot we had that one!"

The beauty of cellar management software is it allows you to look at your wines from many perspectives. You can see whether you have different years of the same wine (a vertical), which wines are ready to drink now, and which wine and food matches would work best. If you're already using a spreadsheet or database, you can easily import the information. Most software also allows you to download cellaring guidelines and tasting notes for your wines from the Internet. Some also have search capabilities so that you can find certain wine styles quickly.

Buy a Couple or a Case?

Start by buying your wines in one-, two-, or three-bottle increments. Don't even think about purchasing a case of one wine when you first start your cellar unless you are very sure you like the wine. You'll have great deal of money tied up in one type of wine, and as your tastes evolve, you might not like it as much as when you first bought it.

Even if you do like the wine, why narrow your options? One summer, one of us fell in love with a nice Moscato d'Asti, and got carried away and bought a case. It's a great little wine, but it doesn't keep and our friends didn't like it as much as we did. The prospect of having to drink the same wine every week for the rest of the summer wasn't too appealing. Luckily, we were able to exchange half the case for something else.

As a general rule, only buy a case if you have tried it before, you like it and the wine has aging potential.

Sample Cellars

Below is a menu of wine choices based on wine styles. Wines in the "near future" column are wines for mid-term storage. Wines in the "hold" column are for longer-term storage. Wines you purchase for long-term storage should be from good to excellent vintages and from good, reliable producers.

	Drink Now	Near Future	Hold
Under $15	Light-bodied whites Light-bodied reds Sparkling wines	Medium-bodied reds	
$15–$40	Rosé Sherry Medium-bodied whites Sparkling wines	Late-harvest Dessert Full-bodied whites Full-bodied reds	Select Late-harvest Dessert Full-bodied reds
Over $40	NV champagne	Vintage champagne	Full-bodied whites Full-bodied reds Dessert (e.g., icewine) Vintage port Madeira

Building for the Future

How much wine do you need? And how much space do you need to allow for your cellar? Here are some calculations that might be useful:

If You Drink:	Include Extras for Gifts, etc.	Annual Consumption	Need for Short-term (2 Years)	Need for Long-term Consumption (10 Years)
1 bottle/wk	1 bottle/mth	64 bottles	128 bottles (11 cases)	640 bottles (53 cases)
2 bottles/wk	1 bottle/mth	116 bottles	232 bottles (19 cases)	1,160 bottles (97 cases)
5 bottles/wk	4 bottle/mth	308 bottles	616 bottles (51 cases)	3,080 bottles (257 cases)

Having a cellar doesn't mean you need to rush out and buy 10 years worth of wine today. You can build towards the goal of a perpetual cellar over time, with wines that are going to be consumed in the short-term, as well as long-term keepers. Always buy wine to replace what you drink plus a few for longer-term storage.

Does Wine Improve Indefinitely?

In a word, no. The life cycle of wine can be short and sweet, or can be long and fruitful. Wines have to have that rare balance of fruit,

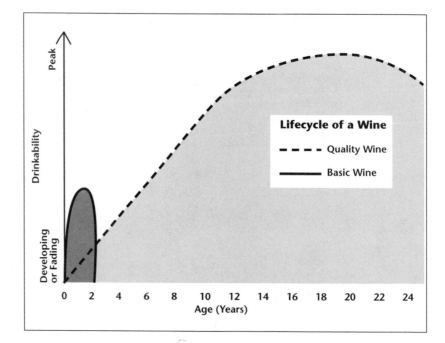

acidity and tannins to make it over the long haul. But even wines with that rare balance will eventually decline.

As you taste more and more wine, you will begin to notice the difference between young and mature wines. With more practice, you will notice that some wines seem to need more time, others will have reached their peak or a plateau, or at some point declined. When to drink a wine is a matter of personal taste and only you can decide what you prefer.

It helps to have some idea of when your wine will be ready to drink. Ask the sales person or do some research on your own. There are many books and Web sites that provide this information. Contact the winery directly if you are really interested, although we generally find that wineries seem to think their wines will last twice as long as they actually do. Keep track of the "drink by" date in your logbook, or if you have cellar management software, this information should be part of the regular updates.

> **Did You Know?**
> Up to the 1980s, wines were made for aging—10–15 years or more—but nowadays the trend is toward making softer, fruitier wines that can be consumed right away or with maybe 3–5 years aging.

Fortunately, the window for drinking wine at its best is wide, usually months or even years. You won't need to be home on May 9, 2010 to drink that nice bottle of Brunello you just bought.

As a general rule, it's better to drink a wine early, when it still has life in it, than to hang on too long and drink it past its prime.

Is My Bottle of '56 Barolo Ready Yet?

We are often asked question just like this and unfortunately we don't always have a simple answer. It depends on the wines vintage, the producer, how it was made, and how and where it was stored.

It's been said, "There are no great wines, only great bottles of wine." Although a single bottle of wine has as much in common with others of the same vintage, once it leaves the winery it is subject to the care and handling of many different people until it reaches you.

May the wine you drink have been cared for in every stage of its journey from the vineyard to your glass.

Index

Numerals in italic indicate sidebars, illustrations, charts.

ABC (Anything-but-Chardonnay) campaign, *14*
Abruzzo (Italy), 82
acetone, 137
acidic foods, 162, 166
acidity, 11, 12, 120
acids, 12
Aconcagua (Chile), 104
adaptation, 117
aeration, 128–129
age, 34, 39, 46, *46*, 56, 82, 116, 119, *200*, 201–202, *211*
Ahr (Germany), 87
Ah-So (corkscrew), 126–127, *126*
Albariño, 19
alcohol consumption, 49, 50, 51
alcohol levels, 10, 30, 119
allergies, 50–51
Alsace (France), 68–70
altitude, *26*
amines, 50
Amarone, 78, 119
amphorae, 29, 34, 82
antioxidants, 49
AOC system, 54
appearance, 114–115
appellation, 57
Apulia (Italy), 83
Argentina, 104–105
aroma, 10–11, 117, *118*, 132–133
aroma kits, 196
aromatized wine, 49
assemblage, 41
Asti, 43, 74, 75, 76
astringency, 119
auctions, 177, 189–191
Australia, 105–109
Austria, 93
AVAs (American Viticultural Areas), 54, 56, 95

Baco Noir, 21
Baden (Germany), 87
Bairrada (Portugal), 92
balance
    taste, 121, 122
    wine collection, 207–208
Barbaresco, 75, 76
Barbera, 21, 75, 76
Barolo, 13, 74, 75, 211
Barosa Valley (South Australia), 107
barrels, *34, 39*, 45, 49 (*See also* oak barrels)
Basilicata (Italy), 84
Bay Area (California), 98
Beaujolais (Burgundy), 65
Beaujolais Nouveau, 22, 65, *65*
Beerenauslee, 86
Bierzo (Spain), 92
biodynamic winemaking, *33*
bitterness, 121, *121*
blind taste, *122*
blush wines, 23, 40
bocksbeutel, 35
body, 119, 140–141
books, 195
Bordeaux (France), 58–61
Bordeaux-style bottles, 35
Botrytis cinerea, 47
bottles
    Bordeaux wines, 59
    Burgundy wines, 62
    Chianti, 80
    color, 34–35, 37
    fatigue, 119
    German wines, 86
    history, 30
    opening, 123–127, 129–130
    shapes, 35–36
    sizes, 36, 203
    Verdicchio, 82
bottling information, labels, 56
bouquet, 118–119
breastfeeding, 50
British Columbia, 102

Brix, *33*
Brunello, 81
bubbles, 41, 42, 68, 120, 156
bulk method, 43
Bureau of Alcohol, Tobacco and Firearms (BATF), *95*
Burgundy (France), 61–65
Butler's Friend, 126–127, *126*
buying wine
    auctions, 189–191
    Internet, 188–189
    in restaurants, 169–176
    tips, *57*, 60–61, 88
    wine clubs, 191
    wineries, 187–188

Cabernet Franc, 22, 40, 71
Cabernet Sauvignon, 13, 16, 32, 39, 56, 59, 96, 106–107
Calabria (Italy), 84
California, 95–96
calories, 50
Campania (Italy), 84
Canada, 100–102
carbonation, 43
cardiovascular disease, and wine, 49–50
Casablanca (Chile), 104
Casella Yellow Tail, *106*
Cataluña (Spain), 91
Cava, 41, 42
cellars (*See also* storage)
    amount of wine, 207–208, 209
    basics, 199–200
    bottle sizes, 203
    drink-by date, *198*, 210–211
    the future, 200–1, 210, *210*
    multiple bottles, 210
    organization, 208–209
    price, 203–204
    sample, 209, *209*
    top seven, 13–18, 199, *199*
    variety, 198
    vintages, 203
    wine staples, 198

Central Coast (California), 98
Central Otaga (New Zealand), 110
Chablis (Burgundy), 27, 64
Champagne (France), 27, 42,
   67–69
champagne, 30, 38, 41, *41, 42,* 56,
   67–68, *68,* 148–149, *149*
chaptalization, 10
Chardonnay, 14
Charmat method, 43
Châteauneuf-du-Pape, 22, 35, 68,
   68
Châteaux, 60, *60*
cheese, and wine, 163, 165–166
Chenin Blanc, 19, 71
Chianti (Italy), 80–81
Chianti Classico, 55, 80
Chile, 103–104, *103*
China, 112–113
chocolate, *151,* 165, 167
cholesterol, 49
Clare Valley (South Australia), 107
clarity, 115
classification systems
   Alsace, 70
   Australia, 54, 106
   Bordeaux wines, 59–60, *60*
   Burgundy wines, 62–63, *62*
   Canada, 54, 100–101
   Champagne, 68–69
   elite designation, 54
   France, 57
   Germany, 53, 85–86
   history, 30
   and labels, 56
   levels of classification, 53
   Loire, the, 71–72
   Portugal, 53
   Rhône, the, 65–66
   South Africa, 54, 111–112
   Spain, 89–90
   United States, 54, 56, 95
climate, 24–25
color
   bottles, 37
   wine, 33, 38, *44,* 115–116,
      115
Columbia Valley (Washington
   State), 99
communes, 58–59, *59,* 61, *63*
consorzio, 74
cooked wine, *45*
cooking methods, 160, *160*
cooking wine, 167
Coonawarra (South Australia), 107
Cooperative Wine Growers
   Association of South Africa
   (KMV), *112*

cork, 30, 42, 69, 114–115, 123,
   124–127, *124,* 129–130, 174–175,
   175
cork pieces, 137
cork sniffing, 174–175
corked, 11, *124,* 137
corkscrews, 30, 123, 125–127, *125,*
   196
Côte Chalonnaise (Burgundy),
   64–65
Côte de Beaune (Burgundy), 64
Côte de Nuits (Burgundy), 64
Côte d'Or (Burgundy) 64
country wines, 54
crown caps, 124
cryo-extraction, 48
Curicó (Chile), 104
crystals, *115*

Dão (Portugal), 92
darkness, 205
decanters, 196
decanting, 127–128
dégorgement, 42
desert island wine, 156–157
dessert wine, 46–48, 152–154, *152,*
   153
desserts, 165, 167
depth, 116
dinner parties, 194–195
DOCA (classification), 89
DOCG (classification), 73
Dolcetto, 22, 75, 76
Dom Perignon (monk), 30
Dom Perignon (*préstige cuvée*), 69
drink-by date, 19, 189, 210–211,
   211
driving, and drinking, 51, *51*
dry, 10, 38, *69,* 85, 141–142,
   142–143
   red, 145–146
   white, 143–144
Duoro (Portugal), 44, 92
DVAs (Designated Viticultural
   Areas), 100–101

Eastern Europe, 94
eastern Mediterranean, 94
Edelzwicker, *70*
Eden Valley (South Australia), 107
Edna Valley (California), 98
eggs, 167
Einzellegan, 87
Eiswein, 48, 86
Emilia-Romagna (Italy), 79
England, 94
Entre-Deux-Mers, 58
Essencia. See Tokaji Essencia

fatty foods, 162
fermentation, 9, 10, 12, 33–34, 39
fetal alcohol syndrome, 50
Finger Lakes (NY), 100
finish, 122
fish, 166
flavor, 11
flawed wine. *See* wine, defective
flor, 46
flûte, 35
food and wine
   cheese, 163, 165–166
   classic combinations, 162–163
   cooking methods, 160, *160*
   end of meal, 165
   matching complexity, 159, *159,*
      160, 161, *162*
   new rules, 163–164, *164*
   opposites, 162
   order of service, 154–165
   poor combinations, 166–167,
      167
   principles, 158–168
   sauces, 161, *161*
   seasons, 168–169
   weights, 159
fortified wine, 43–46, 149–151
foulage, 39
Four-Step Program (wine tasting),
   131–135
France
   Alsace, 69–70
   Bordeaux, 58–61
   Burgundy, 51–65
   Champagne, 67–69
   Jura region, 48, 72
   Languedoc-Roussillon, 72–73
   Loire, the, 79–72
   producers, 57
   regn'l identification, labels, 57
   Rhône, the, 65–67
   Savoie, 72
   vintages, 57
   wine classification, 53, 57
Franken (Germany), 87
Fraser Valley (BC), 101
free-run juice, 33
French Paradox, 49
Friuli-Venezia Giula (Italy), 78
frizzante, 77
frost, 26
fruit words, 136

Gallo brothers, 95–96
Gamay, 22, 65
Garganega, 19
Gentil, 55, *70*
Germany, 84–88

Gewürztraminer, 19–20, 69, 70, 79, *136*
GI (Geographic Indications System), 54, 106
gifts, wine/wine-related, 191–196
Gisborne (New Zealand), 110
glassware, 130, *130*, 174, 196
grape juice, 9, 10, *34*, 49
grapes
    altitude, *26*
    Bordeaux, *59*
    Burgundy, 61–62
    Chile, 104
    climate, 24–25
    components, 12–13
    dried, 48
    growing conditions, 25–27
    harvesting, *25*, 32
    medicinal qualities, 29, 30
    Piedmont, 75, *75*
    red wine, 16–18, 21–23
    smell, lack of, 10–12
    top seven varieties, 13–18, 56, 199, *199*
    other varieties, 19–24
    treading, 33, *44*
    Veneto, *77*
    white wine, 14–16, 19–21
    wine-growing regions, 24–25, *24, 25*
Greece, 93
green harvesting, 32
Grenache, 22, 40
growing conditions, 25–27
Grüner Veltliner, 20, 93

halbtrocken (off-dry), 85
harvesting, 32, *32*
Hawkes' Bay (New Zealand), 110
health and wine, 49–51
histamines, 50
house wines, 172–173
Hudson River Valley (NY), 100
humidity, 205, *205*
Hungary, 93
Hunter Valley (New South Wales), 108

icewine, 48–49, 86
India, 113
intensity, 116
Internet, buying wine on, 177, 188–189, *188*
Italy
    classification, 53, 73–74
    northeast, 78–79
    northwest, 76–77
    Piedmont, 74–75

regional style, 74
south, 83–84
Tuscany, 79–82
Veneto, 43, 77–78

Jura (France), 48, 72

Kabinett wines, 86
Kir (aperitif), 62
Kremstal (Austria), 93

labels, 13, 29, 31, 34, 36, 41, 43, 57, 72, 75, 78, 84, 85–86, 106
    components, 55–56, *55, 69*
    German, 87–88, *87*
    health warnings, 56, *95*
    history, 29
    Spanish, 89
Lake Erie North Shore (Ontario), 101
Languedoc-Roussillon (France), 72–73
late-harvest wines, 47, 48, 86
Lazio (Italy), 82
Left Bank wines, 58
legs, *132*
Lett, David, *99*
lever-type openers, 127
Liebfraumilch, 15, 85
Liguria (Italy), 77
lifecycle, wine, 210–211, *210*
Livermore (California), 98
Loire (France), 70–72
Lombardy (Italy), 76
Long Island (NY), 100
lychee, *136*

maceration, 33
McLaren Vale (South Australia), 107
Mâconnair (Burgundy), 65
Madeira, 45
madeirized, 137
magazines, 195
Maipo (Chile), 104
Malbec, 22–23
Marches (Italy), 82
Margaret River (Australia), 109
Marlborough (New Zealand), 110
Marques, 69
Martinborough (New Zealand), 110
Maximus (biggest bottle wine), *37*
meat, 163, 166–167
Mendoza (Argentina), 105
Merlot, 16–17, 39, 56
méthode traditionelle, 41–42
Mexico, 102–103

Molise (Italy), 82
Monterey County (California), 98
Mosel-Saar-Ruwer (Germany), 87
mouthfeel, 120
Müller-Thurgau grapes, 15, 85
Muscadet, 20, 59, *71*
Muscat, 20, 68, 76
must, 33

Nahe, the (Germany), 87
Naoussa (Greece), 93
Napa Valley (California), 96–97
Navarra (Spain), 90–91
Nebbiolo, 23, 75
négociants, 57, 64
Nemea (Greece), 93
New South Wales (Australia), 108
New World wines, 52–53, 54, 55, 55, 56, 72
New York State, 99–100
New Zealand, 109–111
newsletters, 196
Niagara Peninsula (Ontario), 26, 101
Niederösterreich (Austria), 93
noble rot, 47
Northern Rhône, 66–67
nose, 116–117, *117*
Nova Scotia, 102

oak barrels, 34, *34*, 82, 118
odorous compounds, 10, 117
off-dry, 38, 85
Okanagan Valley (BC), 101
Old World wines, 52–53, 55, *55*, 56, 72
oloroso, 46
Ontario, 101
opened bottles, 138–139
opening the bottle, 123–127, 129–130
Oregon, 98–99, *99*
origin, 121
oxidation, 39, 45, 51, *116*, 137
Overberg (South Africa), 112
Oxford Companion to Wine (Robinson), 195

Paarl (South Africa), 112
Paso Robles (California), 98
passito wines, 48
Patras (Greece), 93
Pelee Island (Ontario), 101
Penedès (Spain), 91
Pfalz (Germany), 87
phenolics, 49
Phylloxera vastatrix, 31, *103*

pickled foods, 166
pieage, 39
Piedmont (Italy), 74–75
Pinot Bianco, 20
Pinot Blanc, 20, 69–70
Pinot Grigio, 20
Pinot Gris, 20, 40, 70
Pinot Meunier, 41
Pinot Noir, 13, 17, 32, 38, 39, *41,* 56, 61, 96, *99*
Pinotage, 23
pipe (wooden barrel), 45
Pliny the Elder, 29, 95
polymerize, *116*
polyphenols, 50
port, 44–45, 150–151
Portugal, 92
pouring wine, 176
preciptation, 26, 33
pregnancy, 50
price, 172–174, 178–180, 182, 203–204
Priorat (Spain), 91
production methods. *See* winemaking, techniques
Prohibition, 31, 95
Prosecco, 20, 43, 77
Provence (France), 72
Puglia (Apulia [Italy]), 83
punt, *129*

QbA (category), 86
QMP (category), 86
Qualitätswein, 85–86
quality, wine tasting, 122
quality wines, 54
Quebec, 102

racking, 34
raisining, 47, 49
Rapel (Chile), 104
red wine
    aging, 39, 116, *116*
    allergies, 50–51
    attitude, 147
    caloric content, 50
    colour, 39, *115*
    dry, 145–146
    fermentation, 33,
    food for, *160, 166*
    fruity/mouth-watering, 146–147
    grape varieties, 16–18, 21–23
    maceration, 39
    medicinal properties, 49–50
    packaging, 35
    smooth & silky, 147
    styles, 39

tannins, 39, *113*
    temperatures, 154–155
refrigerators, 155, *155, 156,* 206
regional wines, 54
remontage, 39
remuage, 42, *42*
reserve 179
residual sugar, 10
restaurants
    BYO (bring your own), 173–174
    half bottles, 173
    house wines, 172–173
    opening the bottle, 125–126
    ordering, 170–172, *171–172*
    pouring, 176
    price, 172–174
    service, 174
    tasting, 174–175, *175*
    type of food. *See* food and wine
    wine lists, 169–170, *170*
    wines by the glass, 173
resveratrol, 49–50
retail purchases. *See* buying wine; gifts, wine/wine-related; wine stores
retronasal passage, 121
retsina, 49
Rheinhessen (Germany), 87
Rhône, the, 65–67
Rías Baixas (Spain), 92
Ribera del Duero (Spain), 23, 55, 90
riddler, 42
Riesling, 15
Right Bank red wines, 58
Rio Negro (Argentina), 105
Rioja (Spain), 23, 54, 90
riservas, 80, 81
Robertson (South Africa), 112
room temperature, 155
rosé, 37, 40, 91, 147–148
Rueda (Spain), 92
Rutherglen (Victoria, Australia), 108

Salta (Argentina), 105
salty foods, *121,*162, 166
Sangiovese, 23, 39, 80, 81
Santa Cruz (California), 98
Santa Maria Valley (California), 98
Santa Ynez Valley (California), 98
Sardinia (Italy), 84
sauces, 161, *161*
Sauternes, 47, 58
Sauvignon Blanc, 14–15
Savoie (France), 72
screwcaps, *110,* 124

Screwpull® Corkscrew, 126, *126,* 196
seasons, 168–169
second label wines, 60–61
sediment, 34, 127–128, 136
Sekt, 43, 85
selection, 182
Sémillon, 20, 55, 59
service, wine shops, 181
shelving, 206–207
sherry, 45–46, 90, 92, 150, 151
shipping wine, 187–188, 189
Shiraz, 18, 106
Sicily (Italy), 83–84, *83*
Similkameen Valley (BC), 101
smell, 116–119, 141–142
Soave, 77, 77
soil, 26–27
solera system, 46, 46
sommeliers, 174
Sonoma County (California), 97
South Africa, 111–112
South America, 103–105
South Australia, 107
Spain, 88–92
sparkling wine, 9, 30, 40–43, 48, 76, 77, 148–149, *149*
    chilling, 156
    opening, 129–130
    tasting, 120
spicy foods, 162, 166
spitting, 133–134
Stellenbosch (South Africa), 112
"stickies," 46, *107*
still wine, 38–40
storage, 182–183, *183*
    clean, 205–206
    darkness, 205
    humidity, 205, *205, 206*
    shelving, 206–207
    refrigerators, 206
    temperature, 204–205, *206*
    ventilation, 206
    vibration, 206
style
    body, 140–141
    dessert wine, 152–154, *152, 153*
    dry, 38, 144–145, *143–44*
    flavor, 141–142
    fortified wines, 149–151
    preference, finding, 142–154
    rosé, 147–148
    sparkling wine, 148–149, *149*
    sweet, 141–142
    white wines, 143–144
sugar, 9, 10, 12 (*See also* Brix)
sulphur dioxide, 51, 138
sulphur, smell, 137

sunshine, 25, 37, 205
super-Tuscans, 80, 81–82, *81*
sweet, 10, *121*, 141–142, 167
Switzerland, 94
Syrah, 18, 56, 65, 66

table wine, 38–40, 53, 54
tank method, 33, 34, 39, 43
tannins, 12, 39, 119
tartrates, 136–137
Tasmania (Australia), 108
taste, 10–11, 116–119
tears, *132*
temperature
growing conditions, 26, 33
wine, 33, 39, 97, 120, 154–156,
204–205
Tempranillo, 22, 23, 88, 91
terroir, 11, 16, 18, 53, *53*, 55
texture, 118–121
Tokaji Essencia, 47, 93, *153*
tongue, 120–121, *120*
top seven grape varieties, 13–18,
56, 199, *199*
transfer method, *42*
Trebbiano, 21
Trentino-Alto Adige (Italy), 79
trocken (dry), 85
Trockenbeerenauslese, 86, *192*
Turkey, 94
Tuscany (Italy), 79–82
tyramines, 50

ullage, 182, *182*, 190, *190*
umami, *121*
Umbria (Italy), 82
unfermented dairy products, 166
United States, 95–100

Val D'Aosta (Italy), 77
Valpolicella, 77, 78, *78*
Vancouver Island (BC), 101
Veneto (Italy), 43, 77–78
ventilation, 206
Verdelho, 21, 45
Verdicchio, 21
vermouth, 9, *76*
Victoria (Australia), 108
Vidal, 21, 48
videos, 195
vin de paille, 48
vin de pays, 72
vin gris, 40
Vin Santo, 48, *81*
vinegar, 137

vineyard, 32–33
Vinho Verde, 92
Vino Nobile di Montelpulciano, 81
vintages, 56, 57, 68–69, 203
Viognier, 21, 40, 66
vocabulary, 11, 134–136
VQA (Vintner's Quality Alliance),
54

Wachau (Austria), 93
waiter's corkscrew, 125
Walle Walle Valley (Washington
State), 99
Washington State, 99
water (impure) vs. wine, 30, *50*
Western Australia, 109
white wine
aging, 39
allergies, 50–51
attitude, 144–145
caloric content, 50
color, *115*
dry, 144–145, 143–144
fermentation, 33
foods for, *159*
fresh & crisp, 144
grape varieties, 14–16, 19–21
maceration, 39
neutral, *144*
smooth & creamy, 144
styles, 39–40
tannins, *13*
temperatures, 155
White Zin, 23, 40, 46
Willamette Valley (Oregon), 99
wine
buying tips, 60–61, 88
cooking with, 167
defective, 137–138, 176
defined, 9
lifecycle, 210–211, *210*
open, saving, 138–139
special following, *96*
where to buy, 177
Wine Advocate (newsletter), 196
wine brokers, 57
wine cellars, gift, 196
wine clubs, 177, 191
wine travelers, 188
wine coolers, 49
wine consumption, 194, *194*
wine glasses. *See* glassware
wine-growing regions, 2425, *24*,
25
wine-in-a-box, 36

wine labels. *See* labels
wine preserver system, 196
wine production figures, 31
wine tasting
appearance, 114–115
blind, *122*
breathing, 128–129
clarity, 115
color, 115–116, *115*
decanting, 127–128
etiquette, 186
filling the glass, 131
flaws/defects in wine, 136–138
Four-Step Program, 131–135
intensity, 116
opening the bottle, 123–127,
129–130
preparation, 122–123
rating, 134
the senses, 114–122
sipping, 133
smell, 116–119
sniffing, 132–133
spitting, 133–134
swirl, 132–133, *132*
taste, 116–119
texture, 119–121
visual inspection, 132
vocabulary, 134–136
at wineries, 184–187
wine stores, 177, 180–183, *183*
wine terms, 11, 134–136
wine writers, 29, 134
winemaking
biodynamic, *33*
bottling, 34–37
at home, 32
history, 28–31
techniques, 32–37
vineyard, 32–33
winery, 33–34
wineries, 33–34, 177, 183–188
wines with distinction, 54
WO (Wines of Origin), 54, 111–112
Würtemmberg (Germany), 87

Yakima Valley (Washington State),
99
Yarra Valley (Victoria, Australia),
108
yeast, 9, 10
yield, 32

Zinfandel, 23–24, *23*, 39, 40, 96
Zitsa (Greece), 93